LETHAL LEGACY

CURRENT NATIVE CONTROVERSIES IN CANADA

J.R. MILLER

M&S

National Library of Canada Cataloguing in Publication

Miller, J. R. (James Rodger), 1943-
Lethal legacy : current native controversies in Canada / J.R. Miller.

Includes bibliographical references and index.
ISBN 0-7710-5902-7 (bound). – ISBN 0-7710-5903-5 (pbk.)

1. Indians of North America – Canada – History.   2. Indians of North America – Canada – Government relations.   I. Title.

E78.C2M537 2004   971.004'97   C2004-900141-8

We acknowledge the financial support of the Government of Canada through the Book Publishing Industry Development Program and that of the Government of Ontario through the Ontario Media Development Corporation's Ontario Book Initiative. We further acknowledge the support of the Canada Council for the Arts and the Ontario Arts Council for our publishing program.

Map on page 145 is by VisuTronx, based on the original from J.R. Miller's *Skyscrapers Hide the Heavens*, courtesy of UTP and J.R. Miller.

Typeset in Bembo by M&S, Toronto
Printed and bound in Canada

This book is printed on 50% post-consumer waste recycled paper.

McClelland & Stewart Ltd.
The Canadian Publishers
481 University Avenue
Toronto, Ontario
M5G 2E9
www.mcclelland.com

1 2 3 4 5   08 07 06 05 04

Contents

To Mary

Preface

This book originated in my concern about developments in Canada, especially in Aboriginal affairs, in recent decades. For some time I have observed with growing anxiety the increasingly vexed nature of discussions over public policy affecting Aboriginal peoples. For at least the past quarter-century the place of indigenous peoples in Canada and the nature of their relationship with the non-Native majority have been prominent topics in Canadian life. Beginning as a subsidiary issue in the debates over constitutional renewal that consumed political elites from 1977 until 1982, and again from 1987 until 1992, Native peoples and issues have at times assumed central importance in the national debate. Thanks in part to a series of political and military confrontations in the 1990s, Aboriginal matters have often gripped the attention of politicians and the general public. First, the role of Oji-Cree Member of the Legislative Assembly of Manitoba Elijah Harper in 1990 in killing the Meech Lake Accord for constitutional renewal confronted political Canada with the widespread and intense disgruntlement among First Nations leaders about the way in which their concerns had been sidelined in the negotiations for which Meech Lake was supposed to be the culmination. Next, the clash between Mohawk Warriors and Quebec Provincial Police that consumed public attention during the summer of 1990 broadened awareness of Aboriginal anger from the political classes to the Canadian general population. During the remainder of the 1990s a series of major land disputes and Supreme Court of Canada rulings helped to maintain the high profile of Aboriginal concerns. Finally, early in the present century, the Liberal government of Jean Chrétien moved to amend legislation regulating the political and financial affairs of Indian bands, resulting in an eruption of First Nations anger that fuelled a militant stand by the Assembly of First Nations in opposition to passage of the legislation in 2002–03.

For a historian, observing these events was engaging, but assessing the Canadian public's reaction to them unsettling. Canadians greeted the disruptions in Native-newcomer relations that occasionally erupted during the 1990s with incomprehension. Politicians, journalists, and ordinary citizens understood neither how nor why the crisis of the moment had arisen, much less how its deep historical roots made it resistant to solutions. The upshot of the situation all too often has been a willingness of voters to latch on to simplistic "solutions" proposed by one group or another, and then, when these nostrums turn out not to be viable, to lapse into apathy, cynicism, or hostility. The syndrome of uncomprehending surprise, flirtation with responses that have little chance of working, and gloomy disenchantment does not bode well for effective public debate or sensible policy-making. It has proved impossible to observe these developments in Native-newcomer relations in recent decades without being alarmed about the state of Aboriginal policy.

I have also been concerned that the contribution that history can make to understanding issues of public policy seems largely overlooked in Canada. It is not that history, properly probed, yields pat formulas that can be applied to the emergence of new problems that bear some resemblance to difficulties that the country faced in the past. History does not repeat itself exactly, and no one, professional historians included, can pluck answers from the past for application to the questions of the present. However, an examination of the development of indigenous-immigrant relations can shed light on the conditions in which good relations thrive or turn sour. It can also provide insight into why different groups react in particular ways to certain issues or problems, and can furnish cautionary lessons as to what sorts of solutions are unlikely to be well received. There are no easy solutions to public policy affecting Native Canadians, but study of the past can help Canadians to understand how issues evolved to where they are today. In such understanding lies at least the beginning of working out solutions to difficult issues.

The problems that can arise from ignoring the history of issues were particularly glaring in the aftermath of the failed Meech Lake Constitutional Accord of 1987. Federal, provincial, and territorial political leaders in 1987 were oblivious to the increasing militancy and skill in negotiations and public relations that had characterized Inuit, First Nation, and Metis leaders for decades, not to mention the Native leaders' steady insistence that their constitutional concerns be addressed as Quebec's were. Consequently, the non-Aboriginal leadership was stunned in the spring of 1990 when Indian leaders rallied behind MLA Elijah Harper, who withheld his consent. The Manitoba legislature needed unanimous consent to ratify the Meech agreement and save the constitutional package. With rare exceptions, journalistic commentators were as blissfully ignorant and as stunned by these developments as the politicians whose antics they recorded and analyzed. Another example of the difficulties that ensue when historical background is not understood was the aftermath of the Supreme Court of Canada's *Marshall* decision on Mi'kmaq treaty rights to fish in the Maritimes in 1999. Not appreciating the importance of the eighteenth-century treaties on which the case turned or the long and painful history of dispossession and marginalization to which First Nations in the region had been subjected, non-Native fishers reacted violently to assertions of Mi'kmaq rights after the ruling.

For the same reason, Canadians in general were not prepared for the angry insistence with which some Mi'kmaq communities stood up to the attempts of non-Native fishers to deny them harvesting rights that the highest court in the land had just upheld.

The chapters that follow are predicated on the assumption that it is worth examining the historical forces and processes that helped to shape a particular public policy issue into what it is today in order to understand it properly. Such an approach, which involves trying to understand the factors that produced a specific issue, does not allow one to predict, much less control, the future. If historians know anything about the limits of their discipline and the forces it studies, they know that human affairs are contingent, the interplay of interests too complex and unpredictable, to permit them to believe that their analyses are society's key to managing the future. I wrote this volume because I believe that better historical understanding of public policy affecting Native Canadians can help us to more fully comprehend the issues and their ramifications. Operating on that belief, I selected five topics concerning Native people for historical analysis. From the large, complex field of Native-newcomer history this volume deals with the ill-understood area of Aboriginal identity (Who is an Indian? an Inuit? a Metis? What determines Aboriginal identity?), self-government among Aboriginal peoples, treaties, claims that often ensued either from the failure to make treaties or from treaties themselves, and Canada's long and largely unavailing attempt to assimilate Aboriginal peoples to the ways, attitudes, and outlook of non-Natives.

Why these particular topics? For one thing, there is considerable confusion about Aboriginal identity and how it has been shaped in part by the efforts of non-Natives to change that identity. Critics of some programs that are designed to assist Native peoples or deal with their grievances level the allegation that "race-based" policies are wrong and unacceptable, not knowing that if race defines aboriginality, it is because non-Native governments imposed it on Aboriginal groups. The historical roots of

Aboriginal self-government, and how governments often tried to confine and control it, need to be understood because of the centrality of Native self-government in an age when political leaders are struggling to interpret the Constitution's protection of Aboriginal rights for twenty-first-century Canada. Treaties, as some fifty ongoing sets of negotiations in British Columbia alone illustrate, are also a lively matter of discussion that affects Canadians everywhere. Even someone living in a part of the country where negotiating treaties is no longer necessary because of the creation of earlier agreements in their region, has a stake in treaty making in other provinces or territories. All Canadians, including non-Native Canadians across the country, help to finance treaty settlements. Similarly, claims involve all Canadians, not just those living in the claim region or in the province or territory where a claim is settled, because the federal role in resolving claims involves all taxpayers. Finally, the history of attempted assimilation of Aboriginal peoples to Euro-Canadian norms is widely relevant both because its legacy in part is resentment among Native peoples and because Canadian governments have not given up on the failed panacea.

Operating on the assumption that the historical background of the issues matters, the chapters that follow deal with the genesis and evolution of each of the five topics. For example, a chapter picks up the story of Aboriginal identity and self-government at or soon after Europeans made contact and established enduring relations with indigenous societies along the St. Lawrence and in what are now the Maritimes and southern Quebec and Ontario. The chapters trace the role of treaties in the evolution of Native-newcomer relations through the successive phases of that relationship. For most parts of the country, Native-newcomer dealings were in commercial relations, usually in the fur trade, in which the interactions between indigenous and immigrant were generally co-operative, and frequently mutually beneficial as well. In the Eastern Woodlands, this initial commercial partnership was supplemented in the eighteenth century by a heightened emphasis on the role of diplomatic ties and military alliance within the relationship. Although the increase in military action from about 1700 until 1814 inevitably entailed loss of life as First Nations fought in alliance with one European power or another, the diplomatic-military relationship still fostered a co-operative spirit between newcomers and Natives. As in the fur trade, so, too, in diplomacy and warfare, the former were dependent on the latter to fulfill their objectives. The co-operative relationship broke down in the era following the dominance of commercial and military links, as a settler society intent on building farms and towns, rather than harvesting beaver and manoeuvring to overawe other European powers, now found alliances with Aboriginal peoples less beneficial and, hence, less desirable. This was the era that gave birth to the conditions that produced many a new form of treaty making, led to a series of coercive policies that targeted Aboriginal people, and resulted in unhappy decades of claims disputes and assimilative policy aimed at changing Aboriginal peoples culturally, economically, and politically.

With all five of the topics under historical examination in this book, coverage of both the nineteenth and twentieth centuries concerns the sorry tale of non-Natives' attempts to impose their will on Native societies. Governments in which Natives had little or no representation attempted to interfere with Aboriginal autonomy in defining their own identity. They tried to control and reshape Aboriginal self-government. They sought to impose their own interpretation of what treaties, some of them venerable even by the late 1800s, meant. Governments of non-Natives worked to thwart Aboriginal groups' efforts to assert and vindicate their claims, and, perhaps most corrosive of all to the relationship between Native and newcomers, to change the nature of Aboriginal societies. It is this coercive phase that has so embittered relations between Aboriginal people and non-Natives, contributing thereby to the intractability of many of the issues with which this volume deals. This coercive and interfering phase of relations also stimulated indigenous peoples' political drive, leading to increased Native political organization, greater militancy and stridency in

Native-newcomer relations, and increased confrontation between Native and non-Native governments. The coercive dynamics of relations that sought over a century and a half to control, confine, and reshape Aboriginal peoples are a vital part of the history of these issues, as is the political reaction that they produced. Much of the heat of public debate and the anger in political relations between Aboriginal communities and non-Native governments over the last quarter-century, and the last decade or so in particular, have been generated by the length and intensity of the coercive phase of relations. It is the story of the origins, evolution, and, most recently, reaction against these processes that this volume probes in its five main chapters.

Finally, this book is not a set of answers to "the Aboriginal question" or a body of policy proposals, much less a political platform. A significant part of the motivation for this effort is the belief that there have been far too many answers and not enough explanations of how the challenges in Native policy were formed. Consequently, many of the chapters that follow conclude with no more than general suggestions of how Canadians, Aboriginal and non-Aboriginal, might begin to approach the task of finding solutions to the problems together. One reason why non-Native Canadians should study the history of Native-newcomer relations is that doing so is an effective antidote to hubris: one cannot delve into the history of these complex and deep-rooted issues and surface with a facile approach to solutions. This volume is intended to be a historical exploration of a quintet of related Native policy issues, not a set of glib answers to the question of the future of relations between Aboriginal and non-Aboriginal Canadians.

CHAPTER 1

Designer Labels:

Shaping Aboriginal Identity

ouis Riel, a Métis man who profoundly influenced Canadian history, was born in 1844 in St. Vital, one of the French Roman Catholic parishes in the Red River Settlement in what is now Manitoba. He was the son of Louis Riel, Sr., a prominent Métis, and Julie Lagimodière. On his father's side he was descended from French-Canadian traders such as his grandfather Jean-Baptiste and his wife, Marguerite Boucher. Young Louis was educated in the Catholic school that the missionary priests operated in Red River, where his mental quickness and ability to learn were noticed by the priests. The missionaries sponsored him and other promising young boys from the colony for higher studies in Montreal, but Louis eventually departed from his mentors' chosen path for him, the priesthood, and first studied law, then dabbled in journalism, and fell in love. Cupid proved cruel as well as tyrannical so far as young Riel was concerned. Although the young Québécoise he fancied returned his affection, her parents forbade further courtship, apparently because of Riel's background. His romantic hopes crushed and feeling himself a disappointment to those who had sponsored his studies in Montreal, Louis Riel returned to Red River in 1869. At the age of twenty-five, his best years seemed to lie behind him.

Even more influential than Louis Riel in the Canadian West of his own time, Peter Lougheed was born eighty-four years after Riel, in 1928, in Calgary. He was the son of Edgar Lougheed and Edna Bauld, and the paternal grandson of Sir James Lougheed and Isabel (Belle) Hardisty. Edgar Lougheed was a lawyer, like his father before him and his son afterwards, but success did not attend his career as it did theirs. Edgar managed to drink the considerable fortune that his father had left behind, leaving his son Peter with a troubled legacy he had to overcome growing up and going to school in Calgary. At Calgary's Central High School, he proposed that a students' union be created, and subsequently served as its first president. Peter went on from Central to the provincial university, the University of Alberta, in Edmonton, earning a B.A. in 1950 and an LL.B. in 1952. While attending university Peter played at various times for the University of Alberta Golden Bears football team and the Edmonton Eskimos of the Canadian Football League. His sports career added to the lustre of his social and educational success; he served as president of the university students' union and editor of the sports page of the campus newspaper. In 1952 he married well and went with his bride to Harvard University, where he earned an M.B.A. in 1954. Back in Calgary after graduation from Harvard, he articled and was admitted to the Alberta Bar in 1955. In spite of the inauspicious beginnings his father had left him in, Peter Lougheed had succeeded brilliantly as a young man.

The remainder of his adult life continued just as successfully, now on a wider stage to even greater applause. He worked for the powerful Mannix Corporation from 1956 until 1961, when he re-entered private legal practice. And then it was politics that beckoned. In 1965 he became leader of the provincial Conservative Party, then in the wilderness in a legislature that had been dominated since 1935 by the Social Credit party. Elected for Calgary West to the legislature in 1967, he led the Conservatives to a majority and the premiership in 1971. He served effectively as premier until 1985, emerging as the principal spokesman for the western provinces in a showdown with the federal government over taxation of natural resources in the 1970s and again after the Trudeau government introduced the National Energy Program in 1981. He was a powerful proponent of provincial interests in the constitutional talks that culminated in 1982 in a new constitution with a Charter of Rights and Freedoms. Lougheed retired from active politics in 1985 and was recognized by appointment as a Companion of the Order of Canada in 1986. He has been the recipient of many awards and distinctions, including honorary chief designation by the Cree in 1971, the Blood or Kainai nation in 1974, as well as a number of honorary doctorates in law from universities. During the 1988 federal election he re-emerged in public life as one of the champions of the free trade agreement that the Mulroney government negotiated with the United States. After the triumphal re-election of the Mulroney Conservatives, Lougheed returned to private life. He continued to live in Calgary, serving on a number of corporate boards and occasionally speaking out on national issues from time to time.

Louis Riel, Jr., in contrast, had little but trouble and woe after he returned to Red River. He led a resistance to the assertion of Canadian rule over the West in 1869–70, and although triumphant, and lauded by the people of Red River for his efforts, Riel had to flee for his life to the United States with a price on his head in 1870 as Canadian troops closed in on Red River. Although elected to the House of Commons by grateful followers back in Red River in 1873, he dared not take his seat for fear of arrest. During a period of exile in Quebec in the 1870s, he suffered serious mental illness and was incarcerated in asylums on two occasions. In the early 1880s he turned his back on a Canada that had shown him nothing but scorn and hatred, and made his home in Montana teaching at a Roman Catholic mission school. When a group of Métis arrived from settlements along the South Saskatchewan River in the summer of 1884, he accepted their invitation to return to the Saskatchewan country and lead their efforts to get the Canadian government to recognize their land rights. The movement of peaceful protest that Riel inherited became an armed insurrection in March 1885, and when Canada crushed the Métis revolt that spring and summer, Riel surrendered and found himself facing trial for high treason, of which he was convicted. He was executed in Regina in November 1885 and buried in the grounds of the basilica in St. Boniface, back in the Red River region where he had been born, grew up, and enjoyed his brief success.

Though apparently so different, Riel and Lougheed, in fact, had a shared heritage. One might be a poor young man, a failed student in some ways, who emerged unexpectedly as the leader of the Red River Resistance, and the other the product of a prominent family of the Calgary elite, but each of them had a grandmother who was indubitably a Native woman. Riel's paternal grandmother, Marguerite Boucher, was the daughter of a French-Canadian father and Dene mother, making Riel, biologically speaking, one-eighth Indian. Peter Lougheed's grandmother, Isabel (Belle) Hardisty, was the mixed-blood daughter of a non-Native father whose family were part of western fur-trade aristocracy and a Métis mother, making him, also, of one-eighth Indian descent. And yet, while Riel is always identified as a Métis, Lougheed never is. As perceived by Canadians, one is Native or Aboriginal, the other white or non-Native. Why is this? Why are two people of a similar background – partially First Nation, but mostly Euro-Canadian – viewed so differently? Why is one westerner with a mixed-blood Indian grandmother Métis and another not? Who determines who is a Métis or an Indian, and how is it decided that one person is "Native" but not another?

The question of Native identity in Canada is not complicated only by apparently mysterious and arbitrary separation of people of similar backgrounds into sharply different social categories. Answering the question "Who is Aboriginal?" also requires Canadians to appreciate that the Canadian state, operating through both its political and judicial components, has the power simply to declare a person an "Indian." In 1939 the Supreme Court of Canada defied the social science of anthropology and declared that Inuit (then referred to as Eskimos) were in fact Indians, at least for the purpose of deciding where they fit in the sometimes bizarre assignment of legislative jurisdiction in the written portion of Canada's constitution. More recently, courts in Alberta and Saskatchewan have differed over whether Métis are, or are not, "Indians" in Canadian law.[1] Politicians have been more prone to play bureaucratic god and categorize people than have the courts. In 1920 the Department of Indian Affairs granted the request of a young man of mixed Cree, Santee Sioux, Blood, and Scottish background in southern Alberta, declaring him an "Indian" and eligible to reside on the Blood reserve and avail himself of the then dubious benefits of Indian status. The young man, James Gladstone, would go on to be appointed to the Canadian Senate in 1958 by Prime Minister John Diefenbaker.

Nor is Gladstone's experience unique, or even all that rare. There are cases of individuals, demonstrably "white," who were categorized by the government of Canada as Indian. One year, in a class I was teaching, a middle-aged white woman with a charming southern U.S. accent, informed her classmates that she had Indian status. More recently, a young man with fair skin told his fellow students in one of my classes that he was Native. Private conversations with these individuals revealed that the southern woman was "Indian" because she had married an Iroquois man (since deceased) and obtained his status, while the young man had been recruited to play for a hockey team sponsored by a Saskatchewan reserve that promised to secure documentation of his new-found Indian status.[2]

These personal stories, like the parallelism in the backgrounds of Louis Riel and Peter Lougheed, raise a blunt question. How have Canadians – and how has their government – historically regarded Native identity? Why is one westerner with a mixed-blood Indian grandmother Métis, but another with similar genealogy is regarded as non-Native? How does a man like James Gladstone, of mixed Blood and Scottish ancestry, come to be an "Indian" whose status is recognized by the government? How does a Caucasian woman from the southern United States become an Indian in Canada? How can the government simply declare a young non-Native man who is a talented goalie an instant Aboriginal person when a Cree community needs a good player? How do Canadians decide who is a Métis or an Indian? Quixotically and arbitrarily. Like the Inuit who, thanks to the Supreme Court of Canada, became "Indian" in 1939, the Canadian state in one guise or another has simply issued a fiat that gave these people Indian status, or imposed it on them. This is too simplistic an answer, however, for underlying the question of *how* these labels came to be applied so arbitrarily, lurk the more important questions of *why* and *with what results* these powers are exercised by the state. Why has Canada evolved so that its government has the power to make such decisions, and does the state's application of these labels influence the public's perception of who is an Aboriginal person?

These questions about the fashioning of Aboriginal identity are important, and the social categories that are at issue in labelling are the subject of this volume. Who are Indians, Métis, and Inuit in Canada? Why are some Indians called "status Indians," while others are described as "non-status"? Where do these labels come from? What do they mean, both historically and at present? Have Indian, Métis, and Inuit always been racial categories, or have non-Natives turned them into that?

As is notorious, of course, Indians never had anything to do with the Indies, the Columbian inspiration for the label they have worn since 1492. At the time Christopher Columbus was exploring westward on behalf of Spain, he, like other navigators of his era, was in search of Asia. Thanks to recently developed theories of geography and navigation, these explorers believed that if they sailed west far enough they would reach the East and its spices and other riches. Accordingly, when Columbus landed in the Caribbean in 1492 and encountered indigenous people, he mistakenly thought he had reached the subcontinent, or South Asia. The label he applied to the people he encountered, Indians, stuck for a long time in spite of its inappropriateness.

The names that the French, who were the first to establish permanent settlement in eastern Canada, came up with for the people they encountered were equally inaccurate and, unfortunately, as long-lasting. Some of the first Native people that French fishers and explorers encountered were the Beothuk of Newfoundland, a people who were noteworthy for decorating their bodies with ochre, a reddish clay. French observers called them *peaux-rouges*, literally "red skins" in English, and the label persisted for a long time in some quarters, thanks in large part to the influence of Hollywood and its "cowboys and Indians" adventure films of the early twentieth century. The other common French term for Aboriginal people, *sauvages*, was an even more unfortunate choice. The problem with this label was largely that it had a variety of meanings and connotations. *Sauvage* could have a benign meaning such as someone or something found in natural surroundings or in a state of nature, or something that had not been controlled and trained by humans. So, for example, the term *riz sauvage* meant "wild rice." In this respect, one connotation of the French term *sauvage* is close to the now archaic Dutch word for "Indian": *wilden*. However, *sauvage* could also have the same connotation as its most common English translation, "savage," in cases where the French meant to refer to Indians in a context that involved violence, bloodshed, or anti-social behaviour.

If a French commentator used the term *sauvage* for Indian in describing how captives from other Indian nations were treated when taken back to the victors' village and tortured, then "savage" was reasonably close to what the commentator meant to express. However, describing a Native who had converted to Christianity and was living a life in accordance with the precepts of the Roman Catholic faith as *un bon sauvage vraiment chrétien* certainly did not mean to convey the idea that the convert was "a good, truly

Christian savage." Crude translation of *sauvage* into "savage" in such a context made no sense at all. However, the problem has been that most Anglophone translators of French sources rendered every *sauvage* in seventeenth- or eighteenth-century records as a savage, whether the individual was a good, truly Christian Huron or a vengeful Mohawk with torture on the mind. It has, in short, been the misfortune of First Nations people to be misunderstood and misrepresented in such a basic matter as their identity. They have come down through history written by non-Natives as Indians, *peaux-rouges, sauvages*, or worse.

First Nations had a simpler and more accurate way of identifying themselves. They referred to their own groups by a variety of names that sometimes indicated salient features of their lives, or other times simply marked them as "the people." In the former category, for example, were the Wendat and the Haudenausanee. The Wendat, whom the French labelled Huron (*hure* or boar's head, brute, ruffian) in reference to a hairstyle affected by Huron men, which the French considered unflattering, referred in their name to the region of southwestern Ontario that was almost surrounded by water in which they lived. *Wendat* in their own language literally meant "dwellers on an island." The Coast Salish of the Lower Fraser Valley in B.C. refer to themselves as *Sto:lo*, meaning "river people." Haudenausanee, the Mohawk name for the Iroquois League or Confederacy, the five nations (later six) who lived south of Lake Ontario when the Europeans arrived, meant "people of the longhouse." The term denoted one of the striking features of this people: the palisaded villages composed of large, bark-covered dwellings in which a number of families resided. They were, indeed, the people of the longhouse. Many other First Nations, then and now, simply referred to themselves by terms that indicated they were human beings. The name the subarctic Dene gave themselves, for example, translated as "the people." One group of them, Desuline, had a name that translated as "the people," or the "real people." Old Lodge Skins, memorably portrayed by Chief Dan George of British Columbia in the 1971 movie *Little Big Man*, always referred to his Cheyenne people, not as Indians or Natives, but as the "human beings." Other groups did, too, including the Inuit of the Arctic. These were societies that European explorers, and later Euro-American administrators, would designate by a variety of names, such as Maliseet, Cree, Iroquois, Chipewyan, Nootka (now Nuu-chah-nulth), and Haida.

The premier non-Native namers of Aboriginal people, though, have been anthropologists and linguists. These social scientists have classified all the First Nations of North America according to linguistic families. Within Canada the peoples thus classified by anthropology fall into Algonkians, Athapaskans, Iroquoians, Siouans, Wakashans, Salishans, Tsimshians, and several small families in British Columbia (for example, Haida and Kootenay). Each of these linguistic families in turn is made up of many different peoples. Among Algonkians, for example, a listing of nations, moving from the Atlantic in the east to the Rocky Mountains in the west, would include Beothuk, Mi'kmaq, Maliseet, Abenaki, Innu (formerly known as Naskapi), Cree, Anicinabe (also known as Ojibwa in eastern Canada, Chippewa in the United States, and Saulteaux in the prairie region), Siksika (Blackfoot), Kainai (Blood), and Piikuni (Piegan). The diversity and complexity does not end there. For example, the Cree were an especially diverse grouping within the Algonkian linguistic family, with distinguishable groups in the north of the central provinces, and subgroups known as Woods Cree, Swampy Cree, and Plains Cree in the Prairie provinces. Most of the other linguistic families were characterized by the same diversity, although none could boast that its members stretched from the Atlantic to the Rockies.

In many cases, the boundary lines of linguistic families and the patterns of First Nations' socio-economic organization were congruent. Algonkians were hunters, fishers, gatherers, and traders who moved in small hunting bands in a seasonal migration that enabled them to harvest different resources in separate locations at various times of the year. Iroquoians were sedentary agriculturalists – corn (maize), beans, and squash were known as the "Three Sisters" in these societies, although some grew tobacco, too – as well as traders. Possession of foodstuffs and tobacco, both of which were in great demand in Aboriginal society, made the Iroquois obvious merchants. Siouans were hunter-gatherers who, with the contribution of horses and firearms from Europeans, would develop a Plains culture that relied on buffalo hunting, trade, and warfare from the early 1700s until the collapse of the buffalo economy and creation of the treaty-reserve system in the 1870s. West Coast groups, of which there were a bewildering number and array, not surprisingly founded their economy and society on marine resources. As corn was to the Iroquois, and the buffalo was to the Plains nations, so was the salmon to groups such as the Nuu-chah-nulth, Tsimshian, Coast Salish, and Haida. The West Coast nations, like all the First Nations both before and following contact with the Europeans, were also traders. One way or another they were all engaged in trade networks that exchanged resources, manufactured products, and, on the west coast, sometimes even exchanged human slaves, over vast distances. Copper, for example, was found near Lake Superior, but was traded as far as the Atlantic in the east and south into the United States. The Haida exchanged massive dugout canoes with other coastal peoples on the Pacific, while the Tsimshian "exported" eulachon oil, a fish product, over the mountains to Athapaskans in the northern interior of British Columbia and Yukon.

Classifying First Nations into linguistic families and their constituent groups imparts a misleading impression of precise boundaries between the various social collectivities. The reality was much more complicated, and more interesting. First, the labels are arbitrary and shifting. A group of Cree bands in the Lesser Slave Lake region of Alberta was classified by a cultural anthropologist as "Western Woods Cree" in the *Subarctic* (1981) volume of the Smithsonian Institution's Handbook of North American Indians series, while a linguistic anthropologist labelled the same bands "Plains Cree" in the later volume in the same series on *Plains Indians* (2001). Second, as noted, groups were sometimes found far from where most other nations of the same linguistic family were located, as were the Athapaskan Tsuu T'ina in Blackfoot country. A First Nation, moreover, might relocate and join another alliance of nations, as the embattled Tuscarora did in the second decade of the eighteenth century. The Tuscarora, under heavy pressure from rival groups in the southern American colonies, moved north and, with the permission of the League of the Five Nations, joined the Iroquois Confederacy, making it a league of Six Nations. First Nations in both the pre-contact period and after the Europeans established themselves frequently incorporated members of other nations into their body, particularly to replace individuals lost to disease or in warfare. This became a pressing necessity in the seventeenth century for the Iroquois, who suffered through both war and illness. According to the most recent interpretation of the Iroquois wars, the Five Nations' primary objective in repeated raids on allies of the French located to the north of them was the desire to replenish population losses.[3] The Iroquois case is simply one of the best-documented, thanks to the extensive European records that were created about them, owing to their importance to the newcomers both in warfare and religious evangelization.

Both the fuzziness of First Nations' ethnic boundaries and the willingness of First Nations to accept outsiders into their ranks are demonstrated well in the treatment they accorded to prisoners of war. Some were tortured to death, but others were adopted into families to replace fallen warriors. Adoptees soon found themselves accepted completely as members of their adoptive nation. The eighteenth-century Jesuit missionary Joseph-François Lafitau was impressed by the treatment of a male prisoner adopted by Mohawk at Kahnawake near Montreal:

> The moment that he enters the lodge to which he is given and where he is to be kept, his bonds are untied. The gloomy attire which makes him appear a victim destined for sacrifice is removed. He is washed with warm water to

efface the colours with which his face was painted and he is dressed properly. Then he receives visits of relatives and friends of the family into which he is entering. A short time afterwards a feast is made for all the village to give him the name of the person whom he is resurrecting. The friends and allies of the dead man also give a feast to do him honour: and, from that moment, he enters upon all his rights.[4]

The adopted were given the identities of deceased family members whom they were replacing, and after a surprisingly short time they enjoyed complete freedom to bear weapons and to move about as they pleased.

James Smith, a New Englander taken captive by the Mohawk of Kahnawake, was amazed at the way he was received. He recounted how an interpreter expressed the Mohawk welcome to their midst:

My son, you are now flesh of our flesh and bone of our bone. By the ceremony that was performed this day, every drop of white blood was washed out of your veins. You are taken into the Caughnawaga [Kahnawake] nation and initiated into a war-like tribe. You are adopted into a great family and now received with great seriousness and solemnity in the room and place of a great man. After what has passed this day you are now one of us by an old strong law and custom. My son, you have now nothing to fear. We are now under the same obligations to love, support and defend you that we are to love and to defend one another. Therefore you are to consider yourself as one of our people.[5]

Although Smith was initially skeptical about these assurances, he soon discovered that "from that day I never knew them to make any distinction between me and themselves in any respect whatever until I left them . . . we all shared the same fate."

The degree to which adoptees were integrated successfully into the new national family of their captors is indicated by two phenomena: captives who eventually became leaders of their adoptive nation; and captives who refused to return to "white" society if the opportunity arose. Prisoner Oliver Spencer became a leader among the Shawnee; Timothy Rice of the Massachusetts colony eventually became "the eldest chief and chief speaker" of the Kahnawake Mohawk.[6] Equally impressive and revealing was the fact that in situations where peace treaties concluding wars between First Nations and Europeans included provision for the return of those prisoners taken during hostilities, to the dismay of the Euro-American colonists, most captives would not forsake their new families. Following a peace made at Albany in 1699 between the French and the Iroquois, for example, the Anglo-American colonists were surprised to discover that most of their fellow colonists who had earlier become prisoners of the First Nations allied with the French had no desire to leave their new communities. Armistices at other points in colonial history yielded the same reluctance of "white" prisoners to return to their native communities. Captives who had been taken at a young age, who had been with their adoptive families a lengthy period of time, or who had married into the nation, were almost impossible to extract. For example, Eunice Williams, aged seven, was captured in a 1704 raid on Deerfield, Massachusetts, and adopted into a Kahnawake family. As a mature adult she visited her relatives in New England with her Indian husband and their children several times, but constantly refused entreaties to return to her home community.[7] The experiences of American colonials adopted into Mohawk society at Kahnawake teach two important lessons about early Canadian history: First Nations defined who was a member of their society; and they exercised that power of definition in a highly inclusive manner.

The power of First Nations to define their own membership came under attack in the nineteenth century, although First Nations continued to believe that the right to decide who belonged to their community was theirs. The inclusiveness of their approach survived, too. In the early 1880s the Muscowequan band in Saskatchewan contained, in the words of its Indian agent, "many French half-breeds," indicating the willingness of First Nations to accept mixed-blood families into their communities.[8] In the 1890s the leadership of the John Smith reserve, also in Saskatchewan, objected to the government's transferring members of the community to other reserves.[9] Also revealing was how the Blood nation in southern Alberta treated Henry Mills, an African-American who ended up in the Canadian West working for fur traders, and his descendants. Both Henry and his son, David, married into the Blood nation; and David's children, Henry's grandchildren, were so completely integrated into Blood society that they were, historian Hugh Dempsey explains, "legally and culturally Indians." Among the Blood, Henry Mills had been known as a "Black White man."[10] Like the decisions to welcome Caucasian prisoners of war in the seventeenth and eighteenth centuries, the Blood community's acceptance and integration of the Mills family indicated that First Nations' definition of "Indian" was inclusive and had little to do with notions of race or ethnicity.

The same, unfortunately, could not be said of Euro-Canadian society from the nineteenth century onward. Non-Natives' attitudes towards Aboriginal people underwent change for the worse in the 1800s. So long as First Nations had been numerically dominant or vital to newcomers for their contributions to warfare and the fur trade, there had never been any suggestion that Europeans would decide who was or was not a Mohawk or Algonkin or any other First Nation member. However, by the nineteenth century relations between Natives and newcomers were changing, first and most noticeably in eastern Canada, but eventually in the West as well. First Nations were no longer desirable to Europeans as diplomats and allies, because after the War of 1812 there were no more major wars in Canada. Nor were Indians valued in the East for their skills in locating, taking, skinning, and trading valuable beaver pelts and other furs because the fur trade declined drastically in the East. As the strategic and economic utility of First Nations to European colonists withered, their proportions in the total population also shrank, thanks both to heavy British immigration from the 1820s on and First Nation population losses to disease and poverty.

The consequence of these changes was that the attitude of both settlers and their governments towards First Nations began to alter. Rather than valuing them as allies and trade partners, Euro-Canadians now saw Indians as obstacles to their own economic development and as people who were becoming dependent economically as a result of the collapse of their traditional hunting-gathering way of life. As a result the state placed new emphasis from the 1830s onward on relieving First Nations of their traditional lands by treaties, establishing them on relatively small reserves, and subjecting them to a barrage of efforts through evangelization, education, and agriculture to change their way of life so that it would resemble that of Euro-Canadians. First Nations, in short, were becoming administered peoples; increasingly, the objective of state administration of First Nations in the eastern colonies of British North America was their assimilation to a Christian Euro-Canadian norm. A young Ojibwa chief in Upper Canada put it well when he said early in the nineteenth century, "You came as a wind blown across the Great Lake. The wind wafted you to our shores. We rcd. you – we planted you – we nursed you. We protected you till you became a mighty tree that spread thro our Hunting Land. With its branches you now lash us."[11]

As this shift in attitude and policy evolved, the non-Native majority began to see the First Nations as an undifferentiated "Indian" population whose Indianness ought to be eliminated. The first step in a process that would dominate Canadian Indian policy until at least the 1980s was legislation in the colony that would become the province of Quebec, legislation that was, ironically, motivated by the desire to protect Native lands. The need to protect Indian property on reserves from claims by non-Natives who resided among the Indians led government to define who was an "Indian." In an 1850 statute titled "An Act for the better protection of the Lands and Property of Indians in Lower Canada [Quebec]" the colonial state defined "Indians" as:

> persons of Indian blood, reputed to belong to the particular Body or Tribe of Indians interested in such lands and their descendents [sic] . . . persons intermarried with any such Indians and residing among them, and the descendents of all such persons . . . persons residing among such Indians, whose parents on either side were or are Indians of such Body or Tribe, or entitled to be considered as such: And . . . persons adopted in infancy by any such Indians, and residing in the village or upon the lands of such Tribe or Body of Indians and their Descendents.[12]

Although this statutory definition was relatively broad, and though it was revised in an 1851 statute to accommodate some First Nations' objections to the 1850 text,[13] it was still ominous. This was the first time in Canadian history that anyone in a position of authority had presumed to define for First Nations who was an Indian.

The implications of defining membership of an administered people became clear six years later in the Gradual Civilization Act of 1857. This measure continued the relatively inclusive definition found in the 1851 statute, but went on to spell out how an "Indian" could cease to be an "Indian" – or, in legal language, become enfranchised – in colonial law. As historian John Tobias has observed, "the legislation to remove all legal distinctions between Indians and Euro-Canadians actually established them."[14] Any adult male Indian who was literate, debt-free, and of good moral character could apply to a board of examiners for consideration. If his examiners were satisfied that he met the criteria, he was subjected to one year's probation, presumably to ensure that he was indeed "civilized," at the end of which he was declared a citizen, allowed to vote, and given twenty hectares of the land on the reserve to hold and use in individual freehold tenure. Enfranchisement meant acquiring all the rights of a male citizen and losing Indian status. The man's spouse, their children, and all their descendants also lost their status as "Indians," their claim to belong to a particular band and reserve, and their ties to a way of life. The supposed genius of the Gradual Civilization Act was that it would be a total solution to the "Indian problem," as many settlers in the future central Canada termed it. As missionaries and school-teachers worked their magic on Natives on reserves, Indians would be educated and assimilated, qualified and encouraged to jettison their Indian status. As they enfranchised one by one, the number of Indians would dwindle, and with that number the extent of land held as reserves would shrink. Eventually, according to the ideology of the Gradual Civilization Act, there would be no more Indians and no more reserves. Enfranchisement portended the extinction of First Nations.

Although enfranchisement never worked as it was intended, the creation of this policy still was significant and alarming. First Nations in Ontario, where the legislation was passed, rejected enfranchisement and fought it by passive resistance, seeing it for what it was – an attack on their identity and lands. The chief of the Mohawk at Kahnawake went to the heart of this legislation when he noted "there is nothing in it to be for their [the Indians'] benefit, only to break them to pieces."[15] Between passage of the Act in 1857 and codification of all legislation dealing with Indians in the Indian Act in 1876, precisely one adult male applied for enfranchisement. Elias Hill of the Six Nations reserve near Brantford satisfied his examiners that he was literate, debt-free, and of good moral character. He was officially enfranchised, but he never received his twenty hectares of reserve land as a freehold tenure because the Council of the Six Nations refused to surrender the tract. However, even if enfranchisement was a failure in its first twenty years of operation, it remained an affront and a menace. Legislatures now presumed to define who was an Indian (and to specify how an Indian might cease to be one), and Euro-Canadian society had the numbers and the strength to make at least part of that offensive regime stick. By the 1860s Canadian society was a long way from the conditions in which a non-Native captive was welcomed by a First Nations group and amicably incorporated into the Indian community. It is equally significant that it was settler society and its colonial government that forced First Nations into these changed and uncongenial conditions.

If what happened to Indians in the nineteenth century showed the negative effects of government intervention, the experience of the Métis, people of mixed Aboriginal and European descent, illustrated the results of wilful neglect. While many other British colonies of settlement have vibrant indigenous communities who are now a significant minority of the population, only Canada has Métis. Australia is noteworthy for the Aborigines, New Zealand for the Maori, and the United States for Native Americans. In every case the indigenous minority, like First Nations in Canada, have been reduced from a dominant position numerically and economically by the forces of epidemic disease, immigration, and, not infrequently, settler violence. However, Canada is unique among these societies for another Aboriginal group known as Métis. In Australia one is *blackfella* or *whitefella*, in New Zealand *pakeha* or Maori; and the United States recognizes Native Americans but not those of part-Indian descent. In Canada Métis people are descended from mixed-blood children born of unions of European newcomers and Native women, usually in the fur trade. They emerged first as a distinctive social type in the nineteenth-century Prairies. To understand why there are Métis in Canada and why they emerged first in the western interior, it is important to appreciate the economic reasons for contact between Natives and newcomers in the territory that became Canada.

Of the four reasons that European newcomers came to the northern part of North America – fish, fur, evangelization, and exploration – the fur trade was the most important. Fishers came to the eastern shores of Canada from the earliest times, but they were soon supplanted in economic significance by those who came in search of animal furs, especially beaver pelts. Much of the demand for beaver fur arose from the seventeenth-century style in men's hats, of which the wide-brimmed hat made of felted (flattened and pressed) beaver fur was the ideal. To obtain furs from the North American wilderness required the co-operation of the indigenous population, for Europeans were few and unskilled in the ways of the forests and waterways, while First Nations knew the land, the animals, and how to engage in trade. Consequently, the dominance in early Canadian history of the fur trade generally forced economic co-operation between the two groups. Whether the trade occurred in the lands of northern Quebec, the forests of the western interior, the maritime-rich Pacific coast, or the Far North, this was true. There was occasional strife, of course, but on the whole commerce led to co-operation. That is a large part of the reason that two of the earliest historians of the Métis wrote, only half-jokingly, that the Métis nation was created nine months after the landing of the first European.[16]

But miscegenation alone does not make a people. Undoubtedly, relations between immigrants and indigenous people in the other colonies of British settlement produced racial intermixing, too. However, in Canada, and more particularly in its western interior, other factors were at work. The western fur trade was controlled by the Hudson's Bay Company (HBC) from the 1670s until the closing decades of the eighteenth century, when HBC dominance was challenged by Montreal-based fur traders who organized themselves into the North West Company, or Nor'Westers. The Montreal-based trade that defied the Bay's monopoly in the West from the 1780s on was the continuation of earlier trade forays from Quebec that for a long time had focused on the upper Great Lakes basin. The emergence of mixed-blood communities of traders in what are now northern Michigan and Wisconsin was part of what an American historian has described as the creation of a "middle ground," a geographical space where European and Indian met, exchanged goods, sometimes fought, and frequently produced cross-cultural family units. Similar communities developed to the west in lands dominated by the HBC and invaded by the Nor'Westers. Here, too, European or Euro-Canadian men formed relationships with Native women in part for companionship and in part because women of the country had skills essential to the strangers' survival and economic success in an often inhospitable land. They could pack, locate and hunt game, prepare food, and craft essentials such as moccasins, parkas, and snowshoes. Because they were part of the Native community, their partners would find themselves more easily accepted, and the women would facilitate communications thanks to their mastery of Native languages. A relationship with an Indian woman was not just a comfort during a cold winter; it was important for living well and trading successfully. A Native partner could be the difference between failure and economic success, and even between life and death. Such imperatives created families like those that produced Louis Riel and Peter Lougheed.

Over time two subgroups developed in the mixed-blood population of the western fur trade. The vast majority of HBC employees were Scots, many of them impoverished Orkneymen who signed on for lengthy periods in difficult climes for modest pay. In the late eighteenth century the Bay's Scottish employees were joined by Scottish Canadians, often the bourgeois or bosses, among the ranks of the Nor'Westers who began coming into the country. In the early nineteenth century some of the more senior officers of the HBC were Scots, too. The remainder of the fur-trading population were either First Nations men from the reserves in southern Quebec, the *domiciliés* as they were known, and *Canadiens* or French Canadians. The mixed-blood offspring of the Scottish and Cree, Dene, or other First Nations women in time would come to be known as half-breeds, country born, or, as some critics of the British preferred to put it, "improved Scotchmen." The *Canadiens* who united with Indian women produced a community whose members became known as Métis, or, occasionally *les bois brûlés* (literally, burnt-wood people). Country born were Anglophone and Protestant in religion, or at least not Roman Catholic. Métis were Roman Catholic and Francophone, although they also developed a distinctive language known as *michif.* Too much should not be made of these ethnic and religious differences, however. Thanks in no small part to events in the first half of the nineteenth century in western Canada, the mixed-blood community was forged into a united community with a strongly developed sense of its uniqueness and how it differed from non-Natives who were beginning to invade the country. By the 1820s in the Red River district of what is now Manitoba there was a mixed-blood community, usually referred to as Métis, which was composed of an Anglophone and Protestant group called country born, and a larger Francophone Catholic population known as Métis. From this point on I will use the term Métis only to refer to the Francophone group, and reserve the unaccented term Metis for the entire population of both country born and Métis.

The Metis of Red River were forged into a group with a strong sense of identity by forces and events in their region of the country that were at work during the first half of the 1800s. Briefly, these forces were the impact of European agricultural settlement and conflict with the Hudson's Bay Company. Red River Metis pursued a mixed economy of some gardening, casual employment, and seasonal buffalo hunting for the large market that was created by the two fur-trading companies, the HBC and the North West Company. When the Scottish Lord Selkirk began to promote settlement near the junction of the Red and Assiniboine rivers beginning in 1812, many of them became uneasy. While they were not opposed to agricultural settlement in and of itself – after all they were becoming increasingly a settled population – they worried that the arrival of a large population of farmers would harm the buffalo hunt and disrupt the transportation networks they used to carry pemmican (the buffalo food product they sold to the traders). This provisioning trade had emerged by the early decades of the nineteenth century as a mainstay of the Metis economy. The Metis' concerns were exacerbated by ill-advised steps taken by the governor of the Selkirk Settlement, in particular his Pemmican Proclamation banning export of the foodstuff from the colony. The governor took this measure to conserve the food supply at a time when the Settlement was having difficulty feeding itself, but it offended the Metis and sharpened their fear that settlement and their way of life were incompatible.

Metis fears of the implications of agricultural settlement in their midst were aggravated by the propaganda preached by the Nor'Westers. The Montreal-based fur company saw the Metis as their natural allies in an increasingly intense competition with the Hudson's Bay Company, and saw the Selkirk Settlement as a threat to its provisioning routes. The Nor'Westers encouraged growing Metis hostility to the settlers, telling their mixed-blood associates that they were the true masters of the country and that the Selkirk Settlement was an affront to them. The combination of Metis irritation and Nor'Wester incitement came to a head in 1816 in what became known as the Battle of Seven Oaks. In this clash west of the settlement, Metis under the leadership of a country-born man, Cuthbert Grant, battled a force led by Governor Robert Semple. When the fight was over, sixteen of the governor's men lay dead, and the Métis sense of national pride had been strengthened and sharpened.

The clash of the Metis with agricultural settlement was soon replaced by economic strife with the Hudson's Bay Company. The rivalry between the HBC and the Nor'Westers was eliminated in 1821, when the two companies united, and the Hudson's Bay Company later sought to mollify Metis leadership by appointing Cuthbert Grant "warden of the Plains" and paying him a large salary. However, in the 1830s and 1840s Metis ire was increasingly directed towards the Bay because of the company's attempt to maintain its trade monopoly at a time when new markets, more especially an American market to the south, were developing for buffalo hides. The Metis resented the HBC's attempts to discourage this trade because more and more they regarded themselves free to pursue economic opportunities where they would, and to some extent also because they believed they were the authentic occupiers and proprietors of the territory. These contending forces came to a head in a judicial confrontation in the Sayer Trial of 1849, when the HBC prosecuted Guillaume Sayer, a Métis man, for trading with an American buyer. The monopolist, the Bay, prosecuted this alleged breach of their trading rights in a court it had established under the authority provided to it by its 1670 Charter from the British Crown. The Metis, Louis Riel, Sr., prominent among them, reacted to the trial by surrounding the courthouse with a force of mounted and armed men in an attempt to intimidate the presiding court officer. The outcome was that, while Sayer was convicted, he was not penalized, and other charges against him were dropped. The Metis not surprisingly interpreted the result as a victory for them, greeting the trial's conclusion with a shout of "Le commerce est libre." ("Trade is free.")

Conflict was not the only factor in the developing cohesiveness of the Red River Metis. The buffalo hunt was also a unifying force, especially in its best years down to the 1850s. The annual spring hunt required the organization of large numbers of hunters, their families, their carts, and, sometimes in the case of the Catholic Métis, their missionary priests. These expeditions travelled far out onto the plains in search of the buffalo that moved south from the parkland as the warm weather approached each year. The buffalo hunt brought both organization and cohesion to the Metis forces, requiring them to develop a quasi-military structure of captains of the hunt to enforce the rules in the interests of maximizing their chances of success in the buffalo hunt and in confrontations with First Nation opponents. The Dakota, a Siouan people, resented and resisted the Metis incursions into what they considered their hunting territories, leading to some titanic battles between the two peoples. Out of this clash, in particular the 1852 Battle of the Grand Coteau between Dakota and Red River Metis, came a renewed sense of military pride, similar to the feelings evoked by Seven Oaks and the Sayer Trial. Metis exploits on the hunt and elsewhere were celebrated by their own historian, bard Pierre Falcon, who recorded them in musical sagas that gloried in Metis achievements. By the 1860s the Red River Metis had developed into a cohesive community with a sense of itself, a perception that it had enemies, a political structure evolved from the hunt that could be used to respond to an emergency, and a history full of daring exploits, courageous actions, and glorious achievements.

Against this background, the Red River Resistance of 1869−70, probably the greatest political-military triumph the Metis ever achieved, is hardly surprising. The newly created Dominion of Canada had moved urgently to fulfill one of the commitments of Confederation by obtaining the Hudson's Bay Company lands with the help of Great Britain and the payment of £300,000 to the HBC. The Metis community of Red River, not having been consulted in any of this, was offended, and the Francophone Catholic Métis among them in particular feared that the coming of Canadian rule might threaten the security of their lands, as well as important cultural institutions such as their religion and denominational education. Under the leadership of Louis Riel, Jr., recently educated in Montreal, the Metis resisted the assertion of Canadian authority in the form of a lieutenant-governor appointed by Ottawa to govern the newly acquired territory with an appointed council. The Resistance, which apparently aimed to force Canada to negotiate the terms of entry into Confederation with the inhabitants of Rupert's Land, succeeded brilliantly in the short run. In the spring of 1870 delegates from Red River negotiated the terms of what would become the Manitoba Act with the federal government. Among other striking features, the Act created a land base of 1.4 million acres (566,560 hectares), which were to be given out to "the children of the half-breed heads of families residing in the Province at the time of the said transfer to Canada." Prime Minister John A. Macdonald explained in the House of Commons that this provision was a recognition that Métis shared in Aboriginal title to western lands. Riel's other objectives were also achieved, and Manitoba entered Confederation in 1870 as a province with two official languages, as well as state recognition and support of Roman Catholic and Protestant denominational schools. Once again, apparently, Metis assertiveness had triumphed.

However, the Red River Resistance merely delayed rather than prevented the dispossession of the Metis. An influx of Ontario settlers, most with intolerant attitudes towards Native people and Roman Catholics, prompted both vigilante actions against some Métis who had been involved in the Resistance and slurs on their language and religion. More serious, settler hostility and government connivance caused a perversion of the rules governing the allotment of tracts under the Manitoba Act's guaranteed land base that resulted in few Metis getting the land that the legislation had promised them. Among the measures used was scrip, a promissory note issued by government either for land or money, which was given to Metis claimants. In many cases, Metis took land scrip and sold it quickly to land speculators. By the early 1880s the combination of settler intolerance and government maladministration of Metis entitlement to lands in Manitoba resulted in a flood of Métis to a new settlement in the Saskatchewan River valley in south-central Saskatchewan. Here, again under the leadership of Louis Riel, the Métis made another armed stand against the government of Canada in 1885, with tragic results. The Métis forces were quickly defeated, and Riel was tried for high treason and hanged. Now the cause of the Red River Metis had pathos and the legacy of defeat, as well as a martyr.

Although the Red River Metis emerged as a distinct people by the 1860s, boundaries between Metis and First Nations in the West remained variable, shifting, and easily penetrated for a long time thereafter. Relations between Indians and mixed-blood people historically had been close, as would be expected given the origin of the Metis and the fact that most mixed-blood populations were found in close proximity to First Nations in the West. In the fur trade era, if a Native woman was abandoned by her European partner, who might, for example, choose to return to Britain or eastern Canada without her or their offspring, she would be absorbed into her home community without fuss or difficulty. As well, when the buffalo were plentiful, relations between Metis and First Nations, with the notable exception of the Dakota, generally remained harmonious. However, as the buffalo resource began to shrink noticeably by the 1860s owing to over-hunting by First Nations and Metis in the provisioning trade and Euro-American sport hunters, tensions began to emerge. Examples included Cree resistance in the Saskatchewan country in the early 1870s to attempts by the newly established Métis in the St. Laurent settlement to regulate buffalo hunting in the interests of conserving the diminishing resource. In 1875 the Blackfoot Confederacy in southern Alberta sent a message to the government of Canada complaining of the incursions on their territory by outside buffalo hunters, including Metis; and in the early 1880s near Batoche, in the St. Laurent Metis community in the Saskatchewan country, relations between Métis and the Indians on adjacent One Arrow reserve suffered over competing interest in land. These frictions were essentially caused by the scarcity of resources, whether of buffalo or land, for which First Nations and Metis contended.

In general, however, relations between the two Native groups remained amicable, as is demonstrated by the suggestions by Saulteaux negotiators during talks in 1874 leading to Treaty 4 at Fort Qu'Appelle in Saskatchewan that they did not want the interests of their Metis cousins to be ignored. Treaty 4 signatory Kamooses, for example, reported to Commissioner Alexander Morris that "we ask that the Half-breeds may have the right of hunting."[17] In the Prairie treaties made in the 1870s individual Metis were permitted to enter or remain outside of treaty, as they wished. If they took treaty, they effectively became members of a First Nation band and were treated thereafter as "Indians" by the government. However, if they preferred, they could instead take scrip as Metis, meaning that they received the government's promissory paper and were not regarded by Ottawa as Indians in treaty.

The borderlines between "Indian" and "Metis" identity were sufficiently indistinct that either choice was possible. As noted earlier, an example could be found on Muscowequan reserve, where in the 1880s a number of "French half-breeds" formed part of the band.

Soon, however, Canadian government policy shifted in favour of pushing Metis to take scrip when Ottawa made treaties with First Nations. By the 1880s, when the buffalo economy had collapsed completely and prairie reserve Indians had not yet adjusted successfully to agriculture, the government realized that the more Indians there were in treaty, the greater its financial liability for assistance with farming, emergency food rations, and other forms of aid. Accordingly, the government instructed its representatives to persuade as many Metis as possible to apply for scrip rather than inclusion in treaty, and it organized several commissions to carry out the distribution of scrip to Metis. In other words, in the interests of economy the government persisted in and promoted a method of dealing with the Metis share of Aboriginal title that its experience in Manitoba in the 1870s and 1880s had shown to be unmistakably flawed. Distributions of scrip in the West in the 1880s and later continued the pattern of promissory paper for land quickly being negotiated, often under circumstances of dubious legality, by the recipient to a land speculator or bank representative. At a time when Metis prospects of maintaining themselves by hunting and casual employment were still reasonably good, and when they could avail themselves of federal land-settlement policies if they wished to acquire a homestead and try farming, perhaps Metis saw negotiating scrip as an advantageous step with no downside. Later, however, when the West had filled up with non-Native agricultural settlers and the resources of the hunt were inadequate for subsistence, the scrip system proved to be a recipe for Metis economic disaster.

In other parts of Canada boundaries between mixed-blood people, First Nations, and non-Natives remained minimal for a long time. The primary reason for this difference between the

Prairies and other regions was that the peculiar conditions that had encouraged the emergence of the Metis as a distinctive and cohesive community in the West in the first half of the nineteenth century did not exist elsewhere. The non-Native majority dominated too quickly, or there was not the same competition for resources that encouraged a people to develop a sense of unity and difference from others around them. Accordingly, in most regions of the country Metis were not recognized as a distinct part of the population. Instead, they blended into the First Nations or gravitated towards inclusion in what was deemed non-Native society. Even in the West, for example, Peter Lougheed, scion of a prominent Calgary family, would emerge by the 1950s as a favoured son of the local establishment. No one would link him to the Native community when he played football for the Edmonton Eskimos in the early 1950s, but in the same years the quarterback for the Winnipeg Blue Bombers, an Aboriginal man, was always known as "Indian Jack" Jacobs.

Two groups in widely separated parts of the country – the Metis in Grande Cache, Alberta, and the "settlers" of Labrador – reveal the indistinct and shifting nature of boundaries between Metis and others in Canada. The Grand Cache group in the foothills of the Rockies some one hundred kilometres northwest of Jasper are descended from Iroquois from Quebec who came west during the fur trade early in the nineteenth century and established themselves as autonomous trappers and traders dealing with the Hudson's Bay Company. Over the decades they intermarried with outsiders to form a sizeable community that was best described as "Native" rather than either First Nation or Metis. The uncertainty of the Metis-Indian boundary was shown by the behaviour of different families in the group as Canada began to extend its influence westward in the 1870s and 1880s. One family that was attracted to Christianity moved closer to a Roman Catholic mission and adhered to Treaty 6 in 1878, while others applied for and were given scrip by the North West Half-Breed Scrip Commission in

1885—86. Ironically, the group that had adhered to Treaty 6, the Michel band, collectively surrendered their Indian status and became regular citizens in 1958. Given the mixed and shifting nature of Aboriginal identities among the Grande Cache community, it is not surprising that in the 1970s, when Alberta's lieutenant-governor, Ralph Steinhauer, himself a First Nations man, visited Grande Cache and asked some of them whether they were Indian, non-status Indian, or Metis, the viceregal representative "found the local people without a ready answer."[18] Grande Cache illustrates clearly the imprecision of borders between Indian, Metis, and even non-Natives.

The case of Labrador "settlers" is equally ironic and reveals much about the fluidity of Aboriginal racial categories in Canada. In contrast to almost everywhere else in former British colonies of settlement, along the Labrador coast "settler" means Native. Labrador settlers were the descendants of the offspring of European newcomers and indigenous Innu. For a long time relations between settlers and Indians remained harmonious and the boundaries separating them highly permeable mainly because of economic co-operation. Innu were principally hunters, and many settlers were trappers; both shared a way of harvesting the resources of the land. Over time, however, economic complementarity declined as sedentary occupations replaced much of the trapping for the settlers and as anti-Indian attitudes arrived with renewed European in-migration. By the 1980s settlers and Innu coexisted without friction, but also without meaningful ties. Settler leaders in effect fashioned a distinctive identity for their community, "retaining sufficient distinctiveness to maintain individual and communal identity but also expressing enough affiliation with Indians to qualify for some kind of native status in the eyes of the outside world."[19] Settlers see and portray themselves as Native for the benefits that can accrue in the form of land claims and government programs, but also maintain their distinctiveness from local Indians because racism has attached a stigma to First Nations identity. Like the Grande Cache Metis they have constructed a label and image of themselves that makes a mockery of government systems for classifying "Indian," "Metis," and non-Natives.

Over time, led at first by the Metis of the prairie West, the mixed-blood groups began to emerge onto the political stage as separate organizations, if not always as distinctive social communities. In Alberta and Saskatchewan in the interwar period some remarkable Metis leaders, particularly Malcolm Norris, Joe Dion, and Jim Brady, worked hard to raise the political consciousness of Metis people, with the result that by the Second World War both of these provinces had well-organized Metis political organizations. In fact, the Metis Association of Alberta managed in 1934 to persuade the provincial government to establish a Royal Commission to investigate the conditions in which mixed-blood people lived in Alberta. The result of the 1938 report by the Ewing Commission, named for its chair, A.F. Ewing, was the Metis Betterment Act, which created eight Metis "colonies" in the northern part of Alberta in which the Metis were meant to adjust to the complexities of modern society – an approach that was warmly supported by Alberta Metis leaders and envied by their colleagues in the neighbouring province. Saskatchewan, too, experimented with Metis farms in the middle of the twentieth century.

Organization proceeded elsewhere, in the 1960s in particular. Metis in northwestern Ontario formed the Ontario Metis Aboriginal Association in 1965, two Saskatchewan Metis organizations united in 1967, and the Manitoba Metis Federation brought mixed-blood peoples together there in the same year. The Manitoba case was unique, because the Manitoba Metis Federation insisted that an ability to trace one's family roots to the Red River Metis of the nineteenth century was a criterion for membership. British Columbian and Northwest Territories organizations were created in the 1970s, and by the 1980s an effective national Metis body was formed that persists into the twenty-first century as the Metis Nation of Canada. Since the 1980s these Metis political organizations have joined with other Aboriginal groups in pursuit of constitutional entrenchment of Aboriginal self-government and land claims. Like First Nations, Metis now are once again a visible and audible part of Canadian public life.

Through the various shifts in Aboriginal labelling during the last century and a half, the one consistent pattern has been the effort of the Canadian government to minimize the number of "Indians" that existed. This thinking was part of the reason for encouraging Metis to take scrip rather than enter into treaty from the 1880s on. The federal government tried to avoid making treaty in any part of Canada in which non-Natives were not interested economically because Native people who took treaty became eligible for various government programs. Better to have people declared Metis and paid off in scrip once and for all. Treaties meant having to recognize and deal with "Indians" officially; it meant, in effect, creating "Indians" as a category of people with whom the government had to deal.

As noted earlier in reference to the 1857 Gradual Civilization Act, from the 1850s onward the preferred policy was not to "make" any more Indians than necessary and, where possible, to "unmake" Indians. Having Metis take scrip was one example, but there were several others, most of which began decades before the first scrip commission was set up in the 1870s. Canada's inglorious tradition of making and unmaking "Indians" began in 1850, with a statute that defined who was an Indian. It was continued in 1857 in the Gradual Civilization Act that defined who was an Indian in order to know who was to be transformed from Indian to citizen status. The voluntary enfranchisement mechanism that was established in the 1857 statute became one of the foundation stones of Canadian Indian policy. It would persist as a prominent part of legislated policy until 1985.

The enfranchisement program – a mechanism to unmake Indians with their agreement – evolved steadily after 1857, with an implacable logic. First, in the British statute that united several of Britain's colonies into the Dominion of Canada, the British

North America Act of 1867 (now referred to as the Constitution Act 1867), jurisdiction over "Indians and lands reserved for the Indians" was assigned to the national level of government in Canada's newly fashioned federal state. After Confederation the Indian policy that the Dominion of Canada pursued was mainly that which had been worked out in Ontario and Quebec from 1830 to Confederation, principally because it was politicians from these two provinces who dominated the federal government for the first thirty years of national political life. Enfranchisement is a conspicuous example of the continuity of Indian policy from the late colonial period in the central colonies to the national period.

From the earliest post-Confederation measures, the intention underlying enfranchisement was clear and ominous. The Gradual Enfranchisement Act of 1869 is a good example. The 1869 statute repeated the definition of "Indian" that had been pioneered in the earlier statute, but added what is usually referred to as a "blood quantum" to the definition. Specifically, the Enfranchisement Act said that "no person of less than one-fourth Indian blood born after the passing of this Act, shall be deemed entitled to share in any annuity, interest or rents" of the band to which the person belonged.[20] This blood quantum, a notion or approach usually associated with American Indian policy, remained on the books up to and including 1927 legislation, although its application appears not to have been systematic or effective.

Much more serious than the blood quantum of the Enfranchisement Act, however, was the gender discrimination that was introduced into Canadian Indian policy in 1869. For the first time, Canadian legislation stated that if an Indian woman married a non-Indian, she and her children – and her children's children forever – would not be "Indians" as the term was used officially. What this meant in practice was that any Indian woman who married a Native, perhaps a Metis, who was not recognized as an Indian by the government, lost her Indian status. The provision discriminated against Indian women because the limitation did not apply to Indian men who married non-Indians. In fact, a non-Indian woman who married a man recognized by the government as an Indian would gain Indian status; her children and her children's children would retain that status so long as no female among them married a non-Indian. It was this discriminatory provision of Canadian Indian legislation that accounted for the white-looking woman with the southern American accent in one of my classes who turned out to be an "Indian," much to the surprise of her fellow students and their instructor. The purpose of the provision was clear: to unmake Indians and reduce the total number of Indians over time. As the senior bureaucrat in charge of Indian policy explained in 1871, the purpose of Canada's legislation "relating to Indian affairs" was "to lead the Indian people by degrees to mingle with the white race in the ordinary avocations of life."[21] The result of that mingling would be fewer Indians. Astonishingly, this discrimination remained central in Canadian Indian policy until 1985.

The implementation and enforcement of laws aimed at First Nations in Canada were institutionalized in 1876 and 1880. In 1876 the first Indian Act was passed. The Act codified existing legislation involving First Nation peoples and brought various scattered legislative provisions of pre-Confederation Quebec and Ontario together in a single, comprehensive statute. This consolidated approach to Indian policy was one of the hallmarks of Canadian policy, distinguishing it, for example, from the diverse body of legislation to which the Bureau of Indian Affairs in the United States looked for its authority. Equally important to the construction of a permanent apparatus for administering "Indians" was the creation of the Department of Indian Affairs in 1880. In fact, something known as an Indian Department had existed since 1755, when Great Britain created a body to handle its diplomatic relations with First Nations in eastern North America. Through the period of colonial British government from 1760 to 1867 this Indian Department had persisted, although over time Britain's direction of it and its policy had declined as the colonies matured. In 1860, for example, Britain transferred jurisdiction over Indian affairs to the colonies, ignoring the protests of First Nations who treasured their special relationship with the Crown in Britain as a shield against the worst of local settlers' assaults on them and their lands. As Canada's involvement with Indian peoples expanded in the early post-Confederation years, it became clear to the politicians that Indian affairs were becoming so complex and wide-ranging that they required their own department, minister, and civil service.

The creation of the Department of Indian Affairs completed the institutionalization of an approach to First Nations that treated them as an administered people. Over the decades the agency's title and bureaucratic location would vary – Department of Indian Affairs, Bureau of Indian Affairs in the Department of Mines and Resources or in the Department of Citizenship, Department of Indian Affairs and Northern Development, and Indian and Northern Affairs Canada – but, whatever the label, the central goal of controlling and unmaking Indians has remained its mandate until very recently.

The Indian Act added an element to enfranchisement that was pregnant with meaning for First Nations. The 1876 statute defined "Indian" more strictly than earlier acts. An Indian was, "First. Any male person of Indian blood reputed to belong to a particular band; Secondly. Any child of such person; Thirdly, Any woman who is or was lawfully married to such person." Now a number of exclusions were listed, and the gender discrimination that had been introduced in the 1869 Gradual Enfranchisement Act was continued and refined. Finally, any male Indian who obtained a university degree or entered one of the liberal professions (law, medicine, religion) was automatically, and without his consent, enfranchised. This provision extended the notion of involuntary – coerced – enfranchisement from women who married non-Indians to a limited class of men, the highly educated or trained. The involuntary portion of this draconian provision was removed in the 1880 amendment of the Indian Act, the educated Indian man or one who became a minister or doctor thereafter qualifying automatically for enfranchisement upon application rather than having to serve a probationary period. However, the temporary broadening of the compulsory approach to unmaking Indians was significant. Women were targeted, too, in the more coercive mood that had seized the Department of Indian Affairs (DIA) by the Great War. An 1918 amendment to the Indian Act permitted unmarried Indian women or widows to enfranchise, and at the same time enfranchisement of males was made easier by removing a requirement that males had to hold land on the reserve to be entitled to enfranchise.[22]

Application of the involuntary approach to enfranchising male "Indians" would return in later versions of the Indian Act. What lay behind the Department's move towards coercion was frustration: status Indians, educated or not, did not voluntarily enfranchise. Beyond the fact that most Indians did not find the idea of losing their identity congenial was the additional barrier that bands had discouraged enfranchisement by opposing any transfer of reserve lands to freehold status for the newly enfranchised man. Impatience glared through the comments of the deputy minister of Indian Affairs, poet Duncan Campbell Scott, to a parliamentary committee in 1920:

> I want to get rid of the Indian problem. I do not think as a matter of fact, that this country ought to continuously protect a class of people who are able to stand alone. That is my whole point . . . That has been the whole purpose of Indian education and advancement since the earliest times. One of the very earliest enactments was to provide for the enfranchisement of the Indian. So it is written in our law that the Indian was eventually to become enfranchised.
>
> . . . Our object is to continue until there is not a single Indian in Canada that has not been absorbed into the body politic and there is no Indian question, and no Indian Department, that is the whole object of this Bill.[23]

The "Bill" to which Scott referred was an amendment to the Indian Act that empowered the Indian Affairs minister to enfranchise any Indian male over twenty-one years of age that the Department considered "fit" for enfranchisement.

The 1920 involuntary enfranchisement provision had a brief and stormy life. A number of bands protested vociferously against the measure, although one western Indian, ironically from the Michel band in Alberta that would voluntarily enfranchise en masse in 1958, supported coerced enfranchisement with the argument that "The day is now here that we Indians have to paddle our canoe."[24] There was also editorial protest from elements of the press against the involuntary provision. This journalistic criticism grew louder when it became apparent that the DIA was considering using involuntary enfranchisement to rid itself of a thorn in its side. The department had been irritated by the efforts of Six Nations man Frederick Loft, a Great War veteran, to organize a League of Indians of Canada. Loft was having enough success, in spite of DIA opposition and mounted police surveillance, that Deputy Minister Scott seriously contemplated using the Act to enfranchise him. Scott apparently believed that Loft would lose credibility with his followers should he cease to be an "Indian," if only in the eyes of government. Beyond Loft were a large faction on the Six Nations reserve in southern Ontario who were pressing for recognition by government as a sovereign people. Their argument was that they were not citizens or subjects; they and their ancestors had always been allies of the British Crown, rather than subjects. Irritants of this kind underlay the move to involuntary enfranchisement in 1920.

In 1921, when a Liberal government with a progressive image replaced the Conservative regime that had enacted involuntary enfranchisement, the tone of Indian policy changed. Led by the reputed social reformer William Lyon Mackenzie King, and eager to distance themselves from the authoritarian habits of their predecessor in government, the Liberals were inclined in some areas of social policy at least towards a more conciliatory and generous approach. The new Liberal minister favoured a policy of dialogue in pursuit of co-operation from the Indians, and the King government had Parliament amend the Indian Act in 1922 to remove the coercion from enfranchisement. Involuntary enfranchisement returned to the Act in 1933 under the Conservative government of R.B. Bennett, but this time the legislation included a safeguard that specified that it could not be used to enfranchise any Indian who had treaty protection from such action.

As is the case with many aspects of Canadian Indian policy, what the impact of this legislation was is not known. While the intention – "to get rid of the Indian problem" by enfranchising status Indians – was crystal clear, the outcome was not. The administration of this and other Indian Affairs policies was often a hit-and-miss affair; the Department was consistent only in its inconsistency. While Scott and Indian Affairs were advocating involuntary enfranchisement in 1920, its officials were also approving the application of mixed-blood James Gladstone to be recognized as an Indian and a member of the Blood nation. It is not clear whether anyone lost their Indian status under involuntary enfranchisement amendments between 1920 and 1922, or from the reintroduction of compulsion in 1933 until its repeal in 1951. What is obvious, however, is that the government of Canada was serious about unmaking Indians wherever they could, all the better, as Deputy Minister Scott put it, to solve what it perceived as a problem. Throughout this period, of course, the gender discrimination aimed at Indian women who "married out" (as marrying a man without Indian status was termed) remained in force.

Another sign of government's seriousness about the business of identifying who was and who was not a status Indian was the creation of the Indian Register in 1951. Mandated by the 1951 overhaul of the Indian Act, the Register consolidated everything the Department had on people with status, thereby replacing the ad hoc lists that officials had been keeping since the Quebec statute of 1850–51 defined an "Indian" for the first time. Anyone on the Register had status; Indians who were not on the Register were non–status Indians. The modern Canadian state was becoming more systematic in enforcing the boundaries between those with status and those who lacked it.

If the government of Canada was especially keen to unmake Indians through enfranchisement in the first half of the twentieth century, it is not surprising that government steadfastly opposed any attempt to have it acquire responsibility for Native groups that were not well established in law as "Indians" within the meaning of the British North America Act. The issue arose in pointed form with the Quebec Inuit in the 1930s. The Inuit, often referred to as Eskimos by non-Inuit prior to the 1990s, were Arctic dwellers who had had only peripheral involvement with Canadian society historically. Apart from interactions with whalers who visited their waters seasonally, they had little to do with Canada until almost the middle of the twentieth century. For their part, Canadians (Christian missionaries, fur traders, and miners excepted) showed little or no interest in the Inuit. Temporarily they had been brought under the supervision of the Superintendent General of Indian Affairs for administrative purposes as a result of an Indian Act amendment in 1924, but that was reversed in 1930. In the 1930s they became a major public issue, with curious results.

A dispute arose between the province of Quebec and the government of Canada over responsibility for Inuit residing within the province's borders. The issue, which soon ended up in the courts, was which level of government had constitutional jurisdiction over and responsibility for these Inuit, who, like many Aboriginal groups, found that the Great Depression fell especially severely on them. Ottawa's view was that, since the Inuit obviously were not culturally Indians, they were not embraced by section 91(24) of the BNA Act and the federal government was not responsible for them. Conversely, Quebec City held that Inuit were in a manner of speaking "Indians," and they were therefore a federal responsibility under the Confederation statute, a rare instance of Quebec proposing the enhancement of federal jurisdiction. The

litigation over this case, known as *Re Eskimos*, involved learned
testimony from anthropologists, who explained that Inuit were
culturally different from the First Nations found in more southerly
climes. Social scientific testimony proved unavailing, however, and
in 1939 the Supreme Court of Canada ruled that Inuit were, in
fact, Indians, if only in the constitution of Canada. On the whole
the federal government persisted with its policy of malign neglect
so far as the Inuit were concerned, but increasing economic penetration of the North by the South during and after the Second
World War, not to mention the publicity given the Inuit and their
plight as American and Canadian forces moved into the Arctic
during the war, forced the government to turn its attention to
them in the 1940s and 1950s.

One of the bizarre results of this new governmental interest in
the Inuit was the disk identification system that was used in the
Arctic between 1941 and the early 1970s. It would be hard to find
a more egregious example of government "labelling" of Native
people than this identification system. The disk, which bore the
coat of arms of Canada, was a system of identification whose
principal purpose was the simplification of government record-
keeping for Inuit.[25] The Inuit way of identifying themselves
resembled nothing that non–Native administrators understood,
and an identification disk was deemed to be an effective alternative to a system of surnames and given names. Although identification and record-keeping were the government's purpose, the
disks evolved into a proof of Inuit status, distinguishing those
who wore them from "Nomads," by which term government officials usually meant northerners of mixed Inuit or Indian blood.
Since the Inuit, who were considered "Indians" under the 1939
Supreme Court ruling, were eligible for programs offered by
Indian Affairs, while "Nomads," like Metis, were not, the distinction was important. However, the social reality in the North defied
bureaucratic simplicity: some possessors of disks were demonstrably the offspring of at least one non–Aboriginal parent, and
some of these people resisted bureaucrats' efforts to stop treating

them as Inuit once their parentage became known. One Indian Affairs director claimed that by the mid-1960s "Ownership of a disc number defines a person of Eskimo Status," a statement that demonstrated bureaucratic stubbornness rather than social reality.[26] Departmental dissatisfaction with the complex and often indefensible disk system, combined with growing attacks on it and other manifestations of Ottawa's treatment of Inuit as an administered people, brought about its replacement by a system that bestowed surnames on all Inuit. Thus, the temporary disk system had served both to create a type of Inuit status in government eyes and to provoke indigenous political opposition.

In many ways it was fitting that increasing political organization by the Inuit helped to bring on the demise of the disk system, because from the 1960s onward political organization by Aboriginal communities increasingly brought them into the consciousness of non-Native society in Canada. In 1971 the Inuit formed a pan-Arctic political body to represent them in the form of the Inuit Tapirisat of Canada. While pan-Inuit organization was important, and while it would take on international dimensions with the creation of the Inuit Circumpolar Conference, which joined indigenous peoples from Greenland to Siberia in 1977, political activities by specific groups of Inuit also helped to raise their profile in southern Canada. The activities of the Eastern Arctic Inuit, for example, helped them to achieve their objective of a land claim and plan for self-government when the Tungavik Federation of Nunavut signed an agreement in principle with Canada to recognize their land claim and to create a new northern territory, Nunavut, by 1999. Nunavut, which means "Our Land" in Inuktitut, was carved out of the former Northwest Territories after the division was approved in a territorial plebiscite in 1992. Since the Inuit dominate the new territory numerically, the creation of Nunavut effectively provided for Aboriginal self-government over a wide territory for the first time in recent

Canadian history. Naturally, the process of pursuing and then implementing this new northern territory helped to entrench the image of Inuit as a distinctive people in the minds of the southern Canadian majority.

Similarly, the process of political organization and participation in key public issues has helped since the 1960s to establish Indians and Metis as distinct social entities. Status Indians had tried on and off since Frederick Loft's initiative in the 1920s to forge a pan-Canadian political organization for themselves, but had been defeated by Indian Affairs opposition and their own straitened financial circumstances. Finally, in 1961 status Indians, together with some non-status groups and Metis, formed the National Indian Council (NIC). However, differences of interest among these groups made the NIC unstable, and by the late 1960s the Council had subdivided amicably into the National Indian Brotherhood (NIB), a status Indian organization, and the Canadian Metis Society. In the 1980s a further evolution occurred, thanks in part to constitutional developments in Canada. The NIB renamed itself the Assembly of First Nations, a title that jettisoned the "Indian" in their name and simultaneously distinguished them from Metis as peoples who were in Canada "first." For their part, the Metis and non-status Indians received encouragement of a sort from the 1982 constitutional renewal that both recognized the rights of Aboriginal people as protected by the Constitution and said explicitly that the Aboriginal peoples included "Indians," Inuit, and Metis. Since the new constitution's language did not distinguish between status Indians and non-status Indians, the implication seemed clear that both communities, hitherto treated very differently by Indian Affairs, enjoyed the same constitutional protections. In the 1980s and 1990s further organizational evolution produced the Metis Nation of Canada to represent the Metis and the Congress of Aboriginal Peoples to speak on behalf of non-status Indians.

As the foregoing summary of Aboriginal political evolution reveals, status and recognition in law continued to be important issues for Aboriginal peoples in the last quarter of the twentieth century. No issue enjoyed a higher profile than gender discrimination against Indian women who "married out." This discriminatory policy had been introduced in the Gradual Enfranchisement Act of 1869, was embodied in the Indian Act of 1876, and maintained in every revision of the latter statute down to and including the major overhaul of 1951. However, by the 1960s the combination of accelerating Native political organization and growing support for women's liberation in Canada meant that the policy, which stripped an Indian woman of her status for marrying a non-Indian while allowing an Indian man who married a non-Indian woman to retain his status, was doomed. Yet domestic developments seemed to suggest that there was no solution within Canada. Jeannette Lavell, an Anicinabe woman from Manitoulin Island, Ontario, discovered after her marriage to a non-Native student in Toronto that she had been stripped of her Indian status by Indian Affairs. She fought the decision in court, arguing that the gender discrimination in the Indian Act on which it was based was a violation of the Bill of Rights, a statute that the Diefenbaker government had enacted in 1960. After split decisions in lower courts, the Supreme Court of Canada ruled 5–4 in 1973 that the Bill of Rights did not nullify the Indian Act. Lavell, like thousands of other status Indian women, found herself without Indian status thanks to the discrimination in the Indian Act. Developments on both the international and Canadian scenes would in time prevent Canada from simply resting on this Supreme Court ruling.

The gender discrimination of the Indian Act was exposed to international scrutiny and disapproval in the Lovelace case. Sandra Lovelace, a Maliseet woman from the Tobique reserve in New Brunswick who had married an American air serviceman, took her case against loss of status to the Canadian public and to the Human Rights Committee of the United Nations. In July 1979 a group of women from Tobique undertook a highly publicized march from Oka to Ottawa, a distance of more than 160 kilometres (100 miles) to draw attention to the Indian Act's discriminatory policy. Lovelace and her supporters then took their protest to the UN Committee, which decided in 1981 that the discrimination was a denial of Sandra Lovelace's rights under the UN's International Covenant on Civil and Political Rights. By itself, this international condemnation probably would not have forced Canadian governmental action, in part because of bureaucratic inertia and in part because of opposition in status Indian political organizations, which were dominated by men, to tackling the issue without safeguards for their communities. However, the renewal of the Canadian constitution in 1982 included a Charter of Rights and Freedoms that explicitly outlawed discrimination on several grounds, gender among them. In contrast to the Lavell case, in which the Supreme Court upheld the Indian Act in spite of its gender discrimination, now any court would have to strike down that portion of the Indian Act because of the gender equality guarantee of the Charter. The constitutional deal that brought about the Charter in 1982 included a provision, known as delayed justiciability, that provided for a three-year period during which these equality rights could not be litigated. The thinking behind this was that three years would give both federal and provincial governments time to examine their legislation for now-prohibited grounds of discrimination and to deal with it.

The federal government's "solution" to gender discrimination in the Indian Act, Bill C-31 in 1985 conferred a minimum of relief and a maximum of difficulty. While the amendment to the Indian Act did cut out the language that discriminated against Indian women who married out, it introduced many other problems. First, to appease Indian leadership that worried about being inundated by vast numbers of returnees who, having reacquired status, would want to go back to their reserve communities and claim their rights, Ottawa created new rules. In part, the problem with restoring status was the sheer number of women who could potentially return and put greater stress on programs and facilities that were already inadequate. In part, leaders feared the return of people who had been separated from reserve communities so long that they had lost all connection with or sense of identity as an

Indian. In the case of a few oil-rich bands in Alberta there was even the danger that returnees would overwhelm the reserve community and use their political power to strip the reserve of its resources by voting for distribution of band resources to individual members. The government's response to the leadership's concerns was to distinguish between Indian status, which under Bill C-31 could be granted by Ottawa, and band membership, which was the conduit through which individual Indians gained access to services such as housing, educational assistance, and welfare. Bands were given a limited period in which to develop their own membership codes, after which status would be determined according to Indian Affairs criteria. The consequence of this cynical ploy of separating status and band membership has been the creation of large numbers of "C-31s" who exist in limbo, their Indian status restored by the federal government but their band membership denied by on-reserve leaders enforcing narrow criteria for band membership.

Although the precise number of those Indian women and their offspring who found themselves in legal limbo between restored Indian status and full band membership is not known, it is clear that there have been many such cases. The Royal Commission on Aboriginal Peoples (1996) reported at some length on this problem. It quoted one woman, Florence Boucher of Lac La Biche, Alberta, whose experience was poignant:

> I thought by applying and receiving my [Indian Act status under Bill C-31] I would have the same benefits as other status Indians. [But] I don't have equal rights and, in fact, I have less identity than before . . . I can't have a home on the reserve. . . . The reserves at present could possibly house us, the Bill C-31 minority Aboriginal people, but refuse to . . . I will probably have a resting place when the time comes, but why should I accept to be buried on reserve land after I die, when I could also enjoy sharing all the services that are being kept away from me today . . .

> [The problem is] coming from . . . Chief and Council.
> I know they are really against Bill C-31s. They have, I
> guess, no use for [us].[27]

For people such as Florence Boucher, Bill C-31 was a hollow victory over gender discrimination.

The other major complication that C-31 introduced was a mechanism that seemed designed to continue Indian Affairs' campaign to limit the numbers of status Indians in Canada. Now federal legislation focused not on inducing or forcing individuals with status to surrender it, but on preventing those who had lost it from regaining it. Whether the focus was on preventing individuals from acquiring status or on taking it away, the central purpose of Indian Affairs policy seemed consistent. It aimed to shrink the number of "Indians" in Canadian society in order to reduce the government's obligations and liabilities to the status community. Indians were divided into those who had possessed status prior to 1985 and those who acquired it afterwards by Bill C-31. The latter group was subjected to invidious treatment by a series of complex requirements that amounted to a system in which the offspring of post-1985 status Indian families who have "married out" for two consecutive generations will not have status. This provision is often referred to as the "double grandmother rule." (For more detail, see the account in Royal Commission on Aboriginal Peoples, *Final Report. Volume 4*, 33–53.) This mechanism led the former president of the Congress of Aboriginal Peoples, Harry W. Daniels, to dub C-31 "the Abocide Bill."[28] By about 2025 – two generations after passage of Bill C-31 – the full impact of this provision will begin to hit home, as the offspring of marriages outside the magic circle of full status will lose their Indian status. Needless to say, Bill C-31's Machiavellian "solution" to the gender discrimination problem in the Indian Act has caused turmoil and hardship, and will inflict more before too long.

The sorry history of Bill C-31 demonstrates two points: issues of Native identity continue to be major public disputes; and these issues help to maintain the identity of Native peoples as both a matter of public policy importance and a cause of confusion for the non-Native public. So far as issues of identity and status are concerned, the various problems with C-31 – the distinction between Indian status and band membership, or the "double grandmother rule" – are only part of the agenda. Non-status Indians, Metis, and urban Natives all continue to face discrimination at the hands of the government of Canada.

Both non-status Indians and Metis have not as yet been able to match their constitutional gains of 1982 with legislative benefits. Although the Constitution now includes them as one of the Aboriginal peoples whose Aboriginal and/or treaty rights are "hereby recognized and affirmed," Ottawa continues to deny responsibility for delivering programs or program funding to them as it does to on-reserve status Indians. The federal government's desire has always been to force provincial governments to make provision for these groups by denying the special federal services that Indian Affairs and other branches of the federal government provide to status Indians on reserve. Canadians can expect more negotiation and litigation on these matters, as groups such as the Metis Nation of Canada and Congress of Aboriginal Peoples continue to press for treatment similar to that enjoyed by status Indians. To take only one example, in both Manitoba and Saskatchewan, Metis have resorted to the courts in an effort to enforce land claims based on their Aboriginal status. Canada faces the prospect of more such initiatives, with consequent recriminations and expense, in the coming decades.

Another disadvantaged Native group, band members who live in cities, has already used the courts to force governments to accord them political rights. The problem with urban status Indians has been that in many cases their bands deny them the right to vote for a chief and councillors because they live away from their home reserve. Since decisions on the distribution of meagre band resources are made by chief, council, and their employees, this political exclusion has induced bands to deny services to their members who live in town. However, in 1999, the Supreme Court of Canada in the Corbiere decision required that off-reserve Indians belonging to bands that elected their officers under the Indian Act be allowed to vote for chief and council. Hitherto the language of the Indian Act had been understood to bar off-reserve members from voting, but the Court now ruled that the provision was void because it violated the equality rights of the Charter of Rights and Freedoms and was unconstitutional. If urban Indians avail themselves of the restored franchise, the consequences for band politics are likely to be dramatic.

The advance made by urban status Indians in the Corbiere decision stands in stark contrast to other aspects of the lives of urban Natives. As the Royal Commission on Aboriginal Peoples pointed out in 1996, the proportion of Aboriginal peoples, including status Indians, who live off-reserve or away from the Native settlement is high, about half, and rising. The growth in the urban Native population is fuelled by a high birth rate and inadequate economic opportunities on reserves and in Metis communities. Here, too, the federal government has attempted to minimize financial liability by denying responsibility for urban dwellers of Native ancestry, attempting to force provinces and cities to absorb the costs of providing public housing, social assistance, employment help, and child welfare to groups that are disproportionately undereducated and economically disadvantaged. As the socio-economic problems of these groups, particularly in western Canadian cities, explode, the issues associated with a burgeoning urban Native population will also loom large both as matters of public policy and in the consciousness of non-Native Canadians. Again, issues of economic responsibility that are rooted in Native identity and federal government evasion of its role seem likely to keep Native matters front and centre in Canadian public life.

Who are the Aboriginal peoples? Historically, they are a variety of distinctive groups who share Aboriginal origins. In other words, whether Inuit, Indian, or Metis, they all trace their ancestry back to peoples who were present in Canada when European new-comers began to arrive and establish permanent settlements in the seventeenth century. In the face of this newcomer intrusion they have shown an amazing adaptability and resilience in the face of adversity. Whether the problems the strangers brought were undermining traditional economies, introducing epidemic dis-eases to which the indigenous peoples had little or no resistance, or subjecting them to a barrage of cultural denigration and assim-ilation at the hands of Christian missionaries and bureaucrats, the Native groups have prevailed. Part of the secret of their persist-ence has been their flexibility and adaptability. They adjusted to the presence of European fishers, fur traders, and merchants; they often intermarried with the strangers, especially in the fur trade; and they usually demonstrated a generous inclusiveness in accept-ing outsiders into their communities.

It was not Native groups but governments that defined "Indian" and sought by a variety of means to limit the numbers of Native people for whom government could be held responsible. For example, "Indian" was never a racial category so long as First Nations were defining themselves. The acceptance by Kahnawake Mohawk of Caucasian captives and, in some cases, their elevation to positions of leadership is one proof of this. The Blood nation's acceptance of the descendants of Henry Mills, the "Black White man" from the United States, as members of their community is another. First Nations' requests to Canadian treaty commissioners that the Queen's representatives look after their Metis kin in treaty talks made the same point. In contrast to the inclusive and non-racial approach to identity that Native peoples, most noticeably First Nations, took, Canadian governments have treated these terms as racial categories. For a long time, the Indian Act contained a blood quantum as part of its definition of "Indian." Government also imposed an artificial distinction between status Indians, for whom they would accept responsibility, and non-status Indians, for whom they did nothing. The Department of Indian Affairs sought by ways from gender discrimination in the Indian Act to enfranchisement, both voluntary and involuntary, to limit and reduce the number of status Indians. The federal government saw the scrip system as a means of dealing with the Aboriginal title rights of Metis without incurring ongoing obligations. And the Inuit disk system, a failed attempt to impose the bureaucrat's order on social reality, was a means to determine who qualified, and who did not, as an Inuit in the middle of the twentieth century. Through devices of these kinds and various sorts of designer labels the government of Canada effectively racialized Native categories, principally to limit and reduce state financial responsibility.

Through all of this, Native communities have persisted and prevailed, and in the twenty-first century once more occupy a prominent place in Canadian public life. As recent censuses have shown, their numbers have grown dramatically since the 1940s, and the Indian and Metis groups in particular continue to have birth rates well above those of non-Native Canadians. All Aboriginal groups in Canada now have well-organized and effective political leadership, leadership that over the past thirty years especially has reversed many of the setbacks they suffered at the hands of a parsimonious government and unsympathetic public. They are now numerous, confident, effectively led, and ready to confront the rest of Canadian society. The remaining chapters in this volume will explain the background of some of these issues in an effort to reveal why they have become as complex and troubled as they are now.

Notes

1 Jean Teillet, "Metis Harvesting Rights in Canada: *R v Powley*," *Indigenous Law Bulletin*, 5, no. 12 (Oct. 2001), 16, 19 n 5

2 Interview with Brian Johnston, June 27, 2002, Saskatoon. Mr. Johnston did receive documentation of "Metis Citizenship" (The Metis Nation of Saskatchewan "To Whom It May Concern," April 12, 1996) that enabled him to play in a local Aboriginal hockey tournament, but quit the reserve team to pursue another hockey opportunity before team officials procured

for him documentation of Indian status that would have permitted him to play in a larger, regional Aboriginal hockey tournament.

3 Jose Brandão, *"Your fyre shall burn no more": Iroquois Policy Towards New France and Its Native Allies to 1701* (Lincoln and London: University of Nebraska Press 1997)

4 Joseph-François Lafitau, *Customs of the American Indians compared with the customs of primitive times* 2 vols., translated and annotated by W.N. Fenton and E.L. Moore (Toronto: Champlain Society 1974-7; first French edition Paris 1724), vol. 2, 171

5 James Axtell, *Natives and Newcomers: The Cultural Origins of North America* (New York and Oxford: Oxford University Press 2001), 201. This paragraph on the treatment of captives relies heavily on Axtell's chapter, "The White Indians," 189-213.

6 *Ibid.*, 207

7 See John Demos, *The Unredeemed Captive: A Family Story From Early America*, (New York: Vintage Books 1995; 1st ed. 1994), *passim.*

8 Report of the Department of Indian Affairs for 1883, Canada, *Sessional Papers* (No. 4) 1884, 72

9 Arthur J. Ray, Jim Miller, and Frank Tough, *Bounty and Benevolence: A History of Saskatchewan Treaties* (Montreal and Kingston: McGill-Queen's University Press 2000), 196

10 Hugh A. Dempsey, *The Amazing Death of Calf Shirt and Other Blackfoot Stories* (Calgary: Fifth House 1994), "Black White Man," 103

11 Quoted in J.R. Miller, *Skyscrapers Hide the Heavens: A History of Indian-White Relations in Canada* 3rd ed. (Toronto: University of Toronto Press 2000; 1989), 124

12 John Leslie and Ron Maguire, eds., *The Historical Development of the Indian Act*, 2nd ed. (1975: Ottawa: Indian Affairs and Northern Development 1983), 23-4

13 For information on this important point I am greatly indebted to Professor Theodore Binnema of the University of Northern British Columbia, "Women and the Canadian Government's Definition of *Indian*," (unpublished paper presented at a joint session of the Canadian Historical Association and the Canadian Women's Studies Association, University of Toronto, May 29, 2002).

14 John L. Tobias, "Protection, Civilization, Assimilation: An Outline History of Canada's Indian Policy," J.R. Miller, ed., *Sweet Promises: a Reader on Indian-White Relations in Canada*, (Toronto: University of Toronto Press 1991), 130

15 *Ibid.*, 141

16 D.B. Sealey and A.S. Lussier, *The Métis: Canada's Forgotten People* (Winnipeg: Pemmican Publications 1975), 1

17 Alexander Morris, *The Treaties of Canada with the Indians* (1880; Saskatoon: Fifth House 1991), 123

18 Trudy Nicks and Kenneth Morgan, "Grande Cache: The historic development of an indigenous Alberta métis population," Jacqueline Peterson and Jennifer S.H. Brown, eds., *The New Peoples: Being and Becoming Métis in North America* (Winnipeg: University of Manitoba Press 1985), 163-81. See especially 168, 176, and 177 (quotation).

19 Evelyn Plaice, *The Native Game: Settler Perceptions of Indian/Settler Relations in Central Labrador* (St. John's: ISER Books 1990). The quotation is from 123.

20 Leslie and Maguire, *The Historical Development of the Indian Act*, 53. This account of the evolution of enfranchisement is based on Leslie and Maguire, and on J.R. Miller, *Canada and the Aboriginal Peoples, 1867-1927* (Ottawa: Canadian Historical Association 1997).

21 Report of the Deputy Superintendent-General of Indian Affairs, Annual Report for 1870 of the Indian Branch, Department of the Secretary of State for the Provinces, *Canada Sessional Papers (No. 23) 1871*, 4

22 Leslie and Maguire, *The Historical Development of the Indian Act*, 113

23 D.C. Scott, quoted in Leslie and Maguire, *The Historical Development of the Indian Act*, 114

24 W.J. Calihoo, Michel band, quoted in Leslie and Maguire, *The Historical Development of the Indian Act*, 116

25 This account is based on Derek G. Smith, "The Emergence of 'Eskimo Status': An Examination of the Eskimo Disk List System and Its Social Consequences, 1925-1970," Noel Dyck and James B. Waldram, eds., *Anthropology, Public Policy and Native Peoples in Canada*, (Montreal and Kingston: McGill-Queen's University Press 1993), 41-74.

26 Quoted *ibid.*, 61

27 Royal Commission on Aboriginal Peoples, *Report. Volume 4: Perspectives and Realities* (Ottawa: RCAP 1996), 43

28 See his "Bill C-31: The Abocide Bill" on the web at http://wwwabo-peoples.org/programs/dnlsc-31html.

CHAPTER 2

"According to Our Ancient Customs":

Self-Government

Kahkewaquonaby was an Anicinabe man with heavy responsibilities. Son of an Aboriginal woman and a Welsh-Canadian father, he had always moved easily between their two worlds. Educated in part in a boarding school, he converted to Christianity at a Methodist camp meeting, and by 1830 was an ordained Methodist minister and chief of the Credit River band. He identified with both the Aboriginal and Euro-Canadian societies, and he often sought to combine the best features of the two cultures when he operated as leader of his people. For example, the "Bylaws and Regulations" for the Indian Village at the Credit that he drafted in 1830 expressed a desire to organize their local government "According to our ancient customs," but included a number of innovations – such as elected chiefs – that accorded more with the ways the newcomers did things than with the Anicinabe system of choosing leaders from certain clan lines. Yet Kahkewaquonaby, or Peter Jones, as he was known to non-Natives, felt no discomfort about combining the two ways of life in laying out rules of government for his people, any more than he felt any antagonism between his own profound

Christian faith and his affinity for his Aboriginal roots. In the code
of government that he laid out in 1830 he was adjusting Aboriginal
ways to the changed circumstances that non-Native newcomers
had surrounded his people with in an era of rapid immigration.
Kahkewaquonaby saw his version of self-government as a modification of Aboriginal tradition, not the abandonment of it.[1]

In the closing decades of the twentieth century Canadian
political leaders wrestled with many of the same problems of constitutional continuity and change through which Peter Jones
attempted to lead the Credit River band early in the nineteenth
century. Modern leaders found their efforts enveloped in recur-
ring debates involving both Aboriginal and non-Aboriginal
society. The most immediate cause of these discussions was constitutional change, which, having preoccupied Canada on and off
since the 1960s, culminated in the entrenchment of a Charter of
Rights and Freedoms and a number of clauses that bore on
Aboriginal rights in 1982. In particular, section 35 of the 1982
Constitution asserted that "the existing Aboriginal and treaty
rights of the Aboriginal peoples of Canada are hereby recognized
and affirmed." The constitutional framers adopted this statement
of principle knowing full well that it left open the question,
"What *are* these existing Aboriginal rights that are recognized and
affirmed?" It was this uncertainty that drew Aboriginal groups
and first ministers from the federal and provincial levels into
repeated talks that attempted to define those "existing Aboriginal"
rights, first in a series of First Ministers Conferences (FMC), and
then in broader talks that fashioned the agreement, aborted by
voters in a 1992 referendum, known as the Charlottetown Accord.
In the negotiations at both the First Ministers Conferences of the
1980s and at the Charlottetown talks, leaders from First Nations,
Metis organizations, and Inuit bodies attempted to secure constitutional recognition of a right of Aboriginal self-government that
they contended had always existed and was unextinguished. The
protracted and difficult nature of these talks revealed that non-
Native political leaders had great difficulty accepting Aboriginal

self-government as an "existing" entity in the late years of the twentieth century.

Canadians at large frequently found themselves baffled by the debates over defining and entrenching Aboriginal self-government in the country's constitution. In part, their bewilderment stemmed from a simple lack of knowledge of Aboriginal peoples and their social and political institutions. In part, an obstacle to understanding was that many Canadians could not fathom how there could be governmental entities within a political system that was divided sharply into federal and provincial levels. Many feared that recognizing Aboriginal self-government would be tantamount to enshrining a notion of racially based politics, something for which Canada and other nations of the Commonwealth had condemned South Africa during apartheid. As it was, a national newspaper referred editorially to reserves as "small, geographically isolated Bantustans."[2] Finally, other observers of the on-again, off-again talks dealing with constitutional recognition of Aboriginal self-government in the 1980s and 1990s wondered about the practicality of the proposal. If there were over six hundred reserves, to say nothing of Metis settlements, and Inuit towns and hamlets in the Arctic, did Aboriginal self-government mean a bewildering, and probably expensive, multiplicity of tiny Native governments with expanding socio-economic needs and woefully limited resources?

Examining how Aboriginal peoples have governed themselves in the past can cast light on the history of the issue of Aboriginal self-government and suggest ways in which the concept might be both politically palatable and practicable in twenty-first-century Canada. Such a review illustrates that Aboriginal people were organized in self-governing communities long before Europeans turned up, and that they continued to exercise effective control of their own affairs for some time after contact. Although non-Natives made strenuous efforts to limit indigenous self-government, Aboriginal groups often continued, as Peter Jones and the Credit River band showed, to exercise these powers as much as their circumstances allowed. In other words, the demands for recognition of the right of self-government that became audible in the latter decades of the twentieth century were not novel, not recent inventions. Rather, the drive for recognition of Aboriginal self-government, which has been a feature of public policy discussions in the last two decades, is well rooted in Aboriginal societies themselves.

European newcomers did not recognize the indigenous societies they met from the sixteenth century onward as coherent, self-governing communities. The French, for example, were wont to refer to the First Nations they encountered as peoples *ni foi, ni roi, ni loi.* The phrase literally meant that the French viewed Algonkians and Iroquoians as lacking religion, government, or a legal system. Other European sojourners, such as the English in the Thirteen Colonies to the south or, later, in the western interior and on the Pacific coast, similarly tended to take a dim view of Aboriginal peoples' political and religious sophistication. Over time, however, particularly in the realm of theology, newcomers usually came to appreciate that First Nations did have a system of religious belief, even though the strangers tended to think it was misguided at best, and inspired by the devil at worst. Newcomers were slower to appreciate that Indian societies were organized to regulate their own affairs, although as a result of increasing involvement with Native societies in diplomacy in the eighteenth century Europeans began to recognize that First Nations certainly did have governance. A major reason for the Europeans' initial ignorance of the state of Aboriginal political organization was that both the mechanics and the spirit of indigenous government were dramatically different from their counterparts in European societies.

European incomprehension aside, however, there was no doubt that Aboriginal self-government existed at contact. The case of the Mi'kmaq of Maritime Canada, for example, illustrates that a First Nation occupying an extensive territory had a system of government that looked strikingly like federalism. The Mi'kmaq, an Algonkian people who relied on fishing, hunting, gathering, and trade to support themselves, were distributed over much of the

Maritimes, with groups located on Prince Edward Island and Cape Breton, as well as in peninsular Nova Scotia and the northern portions of New Brunswick. The Mi'kmaq lived in communities that could range in size from fifty people up to several hundred, and the communities were organized into seven districts, each with its own name and governing council. Cape Breton, for example, was known as *Unama'kik* and had a district council in addition to the local community chief and council. Each Mi'kmaq district had a council composed of a district chief, Elders, village chiefs, and some wise, elderly people. In addition to the community leadership and district chiefs and councils, the Mi'kmaq could also claim a grand council composed of the seven district chiefs, a body that dealt with major issues assigned to it by the districts. The grand council frequently played a mediating role with districts whose interests clashed, and also handled issues of general import for the Mi'kmaq across the region. Finally, the extended and complex Mi'kmaq government was also part of a regional grouping known as the Wabanaki Confederacy, whose principal purpose was organization for self-defence against attacks from other groups, particularly Iroquoian peoples from the St. Lawrence region or further inland in the interior. Clearly, the Mi'kmaq example shows that Aboriginal self-government was far from unknown when the Europeans began to reach the shores of North America in the sixteenth and seventeenth centuries.

Another impressive example of Aboriginal governance was found in a people who often were in rivalry or conflict with the Mi'kmaq, the Iroquois. When Europeans began to establish themselves in the eastern parts of Canada in the early 1600s, the Iroquois were known to newcomers as the Iroquois Confederacy or the Five Nations. The Iroquois referred to themselves, as noted in the previous chapter, as "the people of the longhouse" in recognition of the distinctive residences in which they lived. Geographically, the Five Nations were located south of Lake Ontario in what is now the Finger Lakes district of New York state, but they ranged widely to hunt, gather, trade, and make war. Their title, the Five Nations, referred to the fact that they were a grouping of five peoples, known from east to west as the Mohawk (Keepers of the Eastern Door), Oneida, Onondaga (Keepers of the Council Fire), Cayuga, and Seneca (Keepers of the Western Door). Because they were sedentary horticulturalists they resided in one location for many years and congregated in relatively large population clusters. These social characteristics distinguished them from hunter-gatherers, among whom the necessity to follow a seasonal pattern of migration to harvest the game, fish, and other resources available at separate locations at different times of the year necessarily limited the size of their communities. In contrast, Iroquoian populations were concentrated. They lived in semi-permanent villages, and those features of their life had important governance implications.

Simply put, the Iroquois developed complex and sophisticated institutions of government because their social circumstances required that they have mechanisms for regulating relations among large numbers of people normally resident in one location. Like the Mi'kmaq they had local systems of government in the villages, but, more so than was common among Algonkian peoples, the women of their communities had prominent political roles. For example, clan mothers were responsible for selecting a new chief, and deciding to make war or peace also fell within their jurisdiction. Iroquoians were matrilineal and matrilocal peoples, meaning that they traced kinship through the mother's family, and when a man married he relocated to the longhouse of his bride's family. Much of the prominence of Iroquois women's public role seems to have stemmed from their contribution in agriculture. In short, farming was women's work, with the result that women controlled the food supply and thereby gained great influence.

The uniqueness of Iroquois governance also manifested itself in the role and procedures of the grand council. This body, which met at Onondaga, in the land of the Keepers of the Council Fire, consisted of fifty chiefs or sachems, distributed roughly according to the size of the five nations, and selected by clan mothers in the various nations. When a sachem died and was succeeded by a new appointee, an elaborate ceremony was held by another nation, at which the nation that had lost a leader would be condoled with speeches and belts of wampum, and where a new chief would be raised to office – or requickened – to replace the departed, again with songs, speeches, and wampum belts. In these ways the Iroquois recognized the permanent quality of their leadership – the occupant of an office died and was replaced, but the office itself endured – and bound nations together through rituals of commiseration and celebration. Although the Iroquois League or Confederacy was a relatively new alliance when Europeans arrived in eastern North America (anthropologists estimate that it emerged sometime between 1450 and 1650), it had developed elaborate and sophisticated institutions and practices that bound its disparate elements together and provided for stability of leadership.

Vitally important to the Iroquois, as it was to most First Nations in eastern North America, wampum was a crucial economic and political tool. Wampum at its simplest level was merely a string of white or purple shell beads that represented a store of value, but in the public life of the Iroquois wampum's role extended well beyond this economic feature. (For a time in seventeenth-century New England, when circulating currency was scarce, wampum was legal tender among the colonists.) Politically and diplomatically, wampum served as a mnemonic device, as evidence that a speaker was telling the truth, and as an invocation of the sacred. No major public ceremony – from receiving wartime captives into the community to condoling the loss of a chief to undertaking negotiations towards an alliance or conclusion of a peace – was held by the Iroquois without the use of wampum. The belts were used to "wipe away the tears," or to "wipe the rust from the chain" of alliance, or to record through the symbols worked into its beadwork agreements that had been concluded. A body of wampum deposited at Onondaga represented "the national archives of the Confederacy," and specially chosen men were charged with the duty of remembering the event or agreement associated with a particular belt, or retelling that belt's meaning when necessary, and of passing the communal historic information down to later generations by instructing a successor in the role of keeper of a belt's meaning. By the eighteenth century European military leaders who entered into negotiations with eastern First Nations found that they had to follow the protocol of presenting wampum, offering gifts, and making speeches that were part of First Nations political and diplomatic practice.[3]

A widespread First Nations custom of governance that European newcomers did not understand and certainly did not practise was the use of consensus in decision-making. A striking example of the desire for consultation and compromise was found in the informal rules of the Iroquois Confederacy: decisions had to be unanimous. Lengthy periods of speech-making and consultation were required to reach a decision with which all the nations of the League felt they could live. In reality, an issue that particularly touched one nation, the Mohawk say, more than the others would likely lead to a conclusion that the Mohawk favoured, but issues on which the several nations' interests diverged could prove problematic, even destructive, to the League. At the outset of the American Revolutionary War in the mid-1770s, for example, the League found itself divided over what role it should play in the family quarrel between Britain and its American colonies. The Mohawk, who were close geographically, economically, and socially to the British in New York, favoured supporting the mother country, but others who had been influenced by Protestant missionaries from the Thirteen Colonies were inclined to side with the Continental Congress, and still others preferred a position of neutrality. The result of this disagreement on an issue of fundamental importance to the future of the member nations of the League was that no consensus could be reached. The League's council fire at Onondaga was extinguished, signifying that the League was ended – temporarily as it later proved.

The search for political consensus was a product of some of the deepest values of indigenous society. Unlike the Europeans, who came from societies in which political and even individual power was exercised coercively, Aboriginal peoples placed great value on non-interference in the affairs of others. Whether the Europeans were governed by an absolute monarch, a parliament, or a republican assembly, their deliberative bodies reached decisions that favoured the most powerful element in their system. On a more personal level, at the family hearth, Euro-Americans similarly had authoritarian male leaders and submissive spouses and children. The ethos of Aboriginal society differed from the European or Euro-American from top to bottom. Newcomers were aghast at the freedom that Indian children enjoyed in their own societies, and the men among them were appalled by the autonomy, influence, and status that Native women enjoyed.

As far as First Nations' leadership was concerned, Europeans tended to dismiss it as not amounting to leadership at all. An early French missionary noted disapprovingly, "All the authority of their chief is in his tongue's end; for he is powerful in so far as he is eloquent and, even if he kills himself talking and haranguing, he will not be believed unless he pleases" them.[4] The priest meant to disparage the fact that an Aboriginal leader could lead only if he could persuade his supposed followers of the wisdom of his proposed course of action. To the European this was not leadership, but in Native society leadership was a form of service, if not servitude. A chief was expected to offer wise counsel, provide prudent direction, and be generous to his followers. It was his responsibility to ensure that the distribution of the fruits of the hunt would include the elderly and ill, so that no member of the community would be in want. Very often the chief provided for dependent members of the group from his own resources. A chief had more obligations than rights, provided more service than received benefits, and constantly had to ensure that the course of action he desired to follow was explained to the community so that they would support it. Although Europeans did not understand this style of direction, Aboriginal leadership that emphasized giving and consensus-building perfectly reflected the value system of

Aboriginal societies, which placed a premium on mutual support, generosity, and non-interference in the affairs of others.

Although First Nations communities in other parts of Canada did not share the use of wampum found in the northeast, they usually did subscribe to a role for their chief that emphasized service rather than enjoyment, as well as consensus in making decisions for the group. Among Plains societies, for example, peoples with whom fur traders came into contact frequently in the eighteenth century, there were elaborate political and military mechanisms, but underlying them was the same emphasis on individual autonomy and communal support. A chief among the Plains Cree or Blackfoot bore the same onerous burden of providing for his followers and building consensus found in the political system of the Iroquois to the east. A Plains chief was not chosen by clan mothers, but community opinion determined whether the son of a departed chief had the requisite qualities or if someone else should take up the mantle of leadership. A chief of a prairie band was aided by a council, in which older men had more influence than younger, but in which the search for consensus was extremely important. Plains leadership was also divided into civil chiefs, who led in normal times, and war chiefs and warrior societies that made the decisions in times of crisis, such as attack by an enemy. The specific military and economic needs of the Blackfoot of southern Alberta encouraged the development of an even more extensive governance structure than was typical of western First Nations.

In southern Alberta the dominant group was the Blackfoot Confederacy, which was composed both of ethnic Blackfoot and other nations. It consisted of three Algonkian Blackfoot nations: the Siksika or Blackfoot, the Kainai or Blood, the Piikuni or Piegan – an Athapaskan people; the Tsuu T'ina or Sarcee; and a Siouan group, the Stoney of the foothills of the Rockies. These diverse groups often co-operated militarily in spite of their ethnic distinctions, a pattern that was exceptional more in degree than in quality from other associations on the prairies. The Cree and Assiniboine, for example, had often co-operated in trade and in warfare, although they did not develop as great a degree of co-operation as the Blackfoot Confederacy. Nonetheless, these groupings were indications of how powerful forces, such as trade and warfare, could foster greater integration among otherwise proudly independent nations.

Among Plains peoples the greatest promoter of co-operation was the buffalo, which was also the foundation of the Plains economy and culture. Plains societies either hunted the buffalo on foot, luring or driving the animals into an enclosure (pound) or over a cliff; or, after acquiring horses early in the eighteenth century through trade with Indian nations in the south, they ran the animals down on horseback and shot them with bow or musket. Either way, the hunt promoted a high degree of co-operation among the Plains peoples to locate, pursue, and harvest the shaggy animals. While on the hunt, they were under the direction of the Warrior Society, both for vigilance against enemies and to enforce the discipline that buffalo hunting required. Similarly, war, whether trade-related or arising from quarrels over the diminution of the buffalo resource in the nineteenth century, handed group leadership to the war chief and the Warrior Society. Such economic and military considerations among the Plains peoples worked to promote the development of relatively sophisticated institutions of governance. It was a system in which the arrangements for times of war or emergency were largely in the hands of relatively young males, while the civil leadership that dominated in peacetime was made up of older band members.

The same dependence on the buffalo was found among the western Metis, who were, of course, closely related biologically and culturally to the Plains peoples. Metis reliance on the buffalo hunt, particularly in the first half of the nineteenth century, encouraged the development of the governance system known as captains of the hunt. An especially gifted leader and hunter, such as Gabriel Dumont, for example, would be in charge of a Metis buffalo-hunting expedition as it headed out from Red River, and he would be assisted by captains who enforced a rigid code of behaviour designed to avoid alerting either enemies or animal prey. The easy translation of the quasi-military structure of the Metis buffalo hunt into governance was demonstrated both in the Metis conduct of the Red River Resistance of 1869–70 and in an experiment in local self-government in Saskatchewan in the early 1870s. At Red River in 1869 Riel's followers naturally turned to the organizational structure of their buffalo hunt to provide the military decision-making and muscle that backed up their challenge to Canada's presumptuous behaviour. Similarly, among Red River Métis who relocated to the St. Laurent district of Saskatchewan after 1870, it was natural to form a local government to regulate the buffalo hunt in an effort to conserve the animal resource on which they were so dependent. In the case of "the little republic of St. Laurent" the experiment led to a clash with non-Native sports hunters, and subsequently to an interview between Métis leaders and a Mounted Police officer that resulted in an agreement by Dumont and other leaders to dissolve their local institution. However, Metis political and military behaviour during the Red River Resistance and the creation of the St. Laurent government demonstrate that the western Metis, like Plains First Nations, developed effective institutions of governance in the post-contact period.

On the Northwest Coast the most dramatic example of Aboriginal self-government that existed before the newcomers arrived was an institution that in some ways did not look like governance at all. The Potlatch is best known for the manner in which it regulated status relationships between families or villages. It was a celebration in which vast quantities of goods, especially blankets, were given away to those in attendance. The status-related function of Potlatching could be found in the institution's use to rise above another individual, family, or village – a practice that is sometimes described as "warring with property." The Potlatch was also an effective means of redistributing wealth within communities, and for the very poorest members could be an essential material support. However, the Potlatch had other social purposes as well, functions that are sometimes summarized under the heading "to make my name good." What this phrase signified was that the ceremony served to validate rites of passage and movements in the social hierarchy, such as a member of a noble family reaching adulthood and taking a new name, or someone achieving a new title within the social grouping. Recognition of proper names, titles, and ranks in Northwest Coast societies was of extreme importance as is demonstrated by the fact that participants in a Potlatch studied long and hard to learn all the names, in their proper ranked sequence, of principal participants. To get one of the names or titles wrong, a Kwagiulth man recalled, would attract ridicule from the community.[5] In this respect, the Potlatch regulated relations within the group, ensuring recognition and peaceful acceptance of adjustments in relations internal to the group. In effect, then, Potlatching provided social regulation and the maintenance of peace. In that sense, the Potlatch was a system of governance among Northwest Coast peoples that existed prior to the coming of Europeans in the 1770s.

As these several examples show, the French notion that First Nations at contact were *ni foi, ni roi, ni loi* was well off the mark. They all had mechanisms for regulating their internal affairs to avoid conflict and bloodshed. These things might range from chiefs and councils whose leadership roles boiled down to taking opinions and seeking to establish consensus within the group to formal decision-making institutions. In some cases, such as the Mi'kmaq and the Five Nations, there were more elaborate governance arrangements that covered larger populations and more extensive territories. In both these instances, the structures of the broader governmental regime was what Europeans later would recognize as a federal one, with local governments for local affairs, and another level of decision-making for issues that affected the population as a whole. Usually, these more generalized issues were matters of external affairs, external, that is, to the Mi'kmaq or Iroquois. In the case of the western Metis, the emergence of governance arrangements, like the emergence of the Metis themselves, was something that developed after the arrival of the Europeans. Among the Metis the development of such institutions as the leader and captains of the hunt was a spontaneous response to the needs of the buffalo hunt, and one that obviously was influenced by the practices of the Plains First Nations of the region. In short, then, Aboriginal groups developed the institutions and practices of governance that were appropriate to their circumstances and sufficient to their needs, whatever Europeans raised with different practices and institutions might think of them.

In the early phases of contact between Natives and newcomers in Canada, the strangers had little desire to interfere with indigenous self-government. The reason for this forbearance was found in the Europeans' small numbers and their motives for entering Indian country. Until late in the eighteenth century in Maritime Canada, and later in other regions, Europeans were outnumbered by the Native population. Any inclination towards interference or coercion would have been resisted, at considerable cost to the newcomers. In any event, there really was no reason for Europeans to want to change the governance practices of First Nations in the early periods of contact and interaction. Europeans came to the northern half of North America for fish, whales, or furs, and none of these objectives required any great change, certainly no political change, in Aboriginal societies. Europeans relied upon First Nations' expert knowledge of fishing and hunting and were content to stay out of their affairs. The one possible exception to this generalization were the Christian missionaries, and they were so few in number relative to the people they were attempting to proselytize that they had to accommodate their Native hosts to get permission to work among them. Neither Europeans' numbers or motives, in other words, led them to try to interfere with the ways in which indigenous populations regulated their own affairs in the early decades after contact.

Even when European motivation for interacting with First Nations underwent modification in the eighteenth century, the restraints on political interference persisted. From about 1700 to 1817 in eastern Canada, French and British were increasingly concerned about securing the friendship and alliance of First Nations because of the intensifying rivalry between the two European states for dominance in North America. Since conflict was viewed as inevitable in this confrontation, Europeans sought the diplomatic and military support of First Nations, often relying on the fur-trade relationships they had developed with them to form the basis of an alliance. After France lost to Britain by 1760, the same dynamic continued to work, as Britain now found itself increasingly at odds with its Thirteen Colonies, and later with the United States of America. In other words, the same territorial rivalries, now played out within the Anglo-American family alone, ensured that reliance on First Nations' friendship and support remained a high priority for the Europeans and Euro-Americans who were active in the eastern half of the continent.

As in the earlier commercial period when the fishery and the fur trade dominated, so too, in the period of alliance and diplomacy from 1700 to the end of the War of 1812 the newcomer societies found that they had little incentive to interfere with First Nations' arrangements for conducting their own affairs. Whether the European diplomats were French, British, or American, they all sought active alliance or at least the friendly neutrality of First Nations in the newcomers' military rivalries. They were concerned less with how the Iroquois or Algonkin regulated their own affairs than they were with the kind of decisions on external relations the governments of those societies made. In other words, European and Euro-American dependence on the diplomatic and military support of First Nations continued to ensure that the newcomers would not try to interfere with the Native societies whose help the strangers wanted.

European attitudes towards First Nations began to shift once a settler society emerged in eastern North America. The end of the War of 1812 and the signing of the Rush–Bagot Agreement demilitarizing the Great Lakes in 1817 ushered in a long peace between

British North America (BNA) and the United States that led to the British Indian Department's no longer worrying much about maintaining diplomatic and military relations with the Indians. Simultaneously, the 1821 union of the Hudson's Bay Company and the North West Company, and the resulting termination of the Montreal-based fur trade symbolized the collapse of the commercial motive for Native-newcomer interactions in eastern BNA. In the eyes of Indian Department planners, First Nations were losing both their political and their commercial importance. The indigenous populations were no longer essential for the successful pursuit of newcomers' goals.

The emergence of an agricultural society, especially in the central colonies of BNA, in the first half of the nineteenth century also had the effect of altering how First Nations were viewed by the newcomers. Rather than being seen as people whose co-operation was essential, now they increasingly were perceived as people who could be an obstacle to the newcomers. The immigration and settlement of large numbers of agriculturalists placed a premium on acquiring access to First Nations lands to establish farms and towns. First Nations did not resist this process, but after access to lands was acquired by treaty in central BNA, the Indians' presence began to be a problem. To the extent that they were hunter-gatherers who used territory in an extensive fashion, following a seasonal migratory pattern to harvest resources, they came into conflict with the now numerically dominant Euro-Canadian population. In this novel relationship, the old incentive to maintain good relations by following a policy of non-interference disappeared. The result, as already noted in the case of 1850s legislation that dealt with Indian status and enfranchisement, was a growing willingness to interfere with the way that First Nations conducted their own affairs. One very obvious area where this was true from the 1820s onwards, particularly in the future Ontario, was Christian evangelization. Missionary activity now became more intense and more focused on altering Native societies than had ever been the case before.

The same phenomenon – a growing tendency to reject Indian ways and attempts to suppress them – developed in governance from the 1860s onward. Now, of course, Canada was a newly fashioned federal state in which responsibility for "Indians and lands reserved for the Indians" was assigned to the federal, or central, level of government. It was not long after Confederation that Parliament began to implement the system of political tutelage for which Canadian Indian law would become notorious. The Gradual Enfranchisement Act of 1869 took the first steps down the road of interfering with First Nations governance. In addition to introducing gender discrimination in status legislation, the 1869 statute also purported to confer on First Nation communities the blessings of British Canadian municipal government arrangements. Besides empowering the cabinet to require that chiefs be elected by adult male band members for three-year terms, the 1869 Act authorized the federal cabinet to remove Indian leaders for "dishonesty, intemperance or immorality," a broad category of deficiencies that required interpretation and application – by the minister responsible for Indian Affairs, of course. Ordering the use of elections was a discretionary matter, not a mandatory requirement, and the statute also said that "all life Chiefs now living shall continue as such until death or resignation, or until their removal by the Governor for dishonesty, intemperance, or immorality." It was not a coincidence that the Gradual Enfranchisement Act, in addition to injecting gender discrimination and providing a mechanism for altering First Nations governance, also created "location tickets," by which individuals on reserves could establish their claim to a specific share of community land. What these measures on status, governance, and land-holding had in common was that they reflected the new willingness of a numerically dominant Euro-Canadian populace to meddle with First Nations' internal affairs by means of legislation that emanated from a parliament in which First Nations had no representation.

Over succeeding decades, federal legislation increasingly interfered in First Nations governance, as it did in other areas of Indian communal life. The 1876 Indian Act, which consolidated previous legislation that dealt with First Nations, broadened the grounds on which a chief might be removed by Ottawa to embrace "dishonesty, intemperance, immorality, *or incompetency*," the nature of the last deficiency remaining undefined and subject to interpretation by federal officials. The 1876 statute spelled out the jurisdiction of band governments in terms that were essentially municipal: "The chief or chiefs of any band in council may frame, subject to confirmation by the Governor in Council, rules and regulations for the following subjects: . . . care of public health, the observance of order and decorum at assemblies of the Indians . . ., the repression of intemperance and profligacy, the prevention of trespass by cattle, the maintenance of roads, bridges, ditches, and fences, . . . etc." While the Indian Act purported to grant reserve communities local self-government, it was limited government and "subject to confirmation" by the federal cabinet. Another amendment to the Indian Act in 1880 – the statute was amended frequently in the late decades of the nineteenth century – renewed the government's announced desire to interfere in band governance, providing the newly created Department of Indian Affairs (DIA) with the mandate to impose an elected band council on a First Nation whether a band wanted the change or not. "Life chiefs" were to retain their offices, subject, of course, to the now extended power of the Superintendent General of Indian Affairs to remove them for "dishonesty, intemperance, immorality, or incompetency." If the Indian Affairs minister ordered the use of elections for band government, the Act now said explicitly that life chiefs lost their authority after the commencement of elections.

The process of interfering with First Nations governance continued in the 1880s. The Indian Advancement Act of 1884 provided for annual elections of councillors and expanded the areas in which they might legislate, but it retained the provisions for imposition of elective institutions at the discretion of the Indian Affairs minister and the powers to depose chiefs whose behaviour or performance Ottawa deemed offensive or incompetent. Indian agents, the DIA officers supervising a particular band, had a stranglehold on First Nations' decision-making under the 1884 statute, with the agent responsible for calling a council meeting, presiding, keeping a record of discussion and decisions, and forwarding the deliberations of the band council to Ottawa for its inspection and approval. Band council decisions that were disapproved by the DIA were a nullity. The other significant, though short-lived, governance measure that parliament introduced in this era was a clause in the 1885 Franchise Act that gave the vote in federal elections to adult Indian males residing east of Manitoba. The rationale for this, Prime Minister Macdonald explained, was that eastern Indians were acculturated and worthy of the franchise. "Indians living in the older Provinces who have gone to school – and they all go to school – who are educated, who associate with white men, who are acquainted with all the principles of civilization, who carry out all the practices of civilization, who have accumulated round themselves property, who have good houses, and well furnished houses, who educate their children, who contribute to the public treasury in the same way as the whites do, should possess the franchise," the Prime Minister argued.[6] The measure was harshly criticized by the Liberal opposition, and within two years of their obtaining power in 1896 this provision of the Franchise Act was repealed.

By the end of the nineteenth century Canada had fashioned an extended system of regulations to interfere with First Nations' management of their own political affairs. Ottawa signalled clearly that it preferred elective leadership to chiefs chosen by clan mothers or according to the hereditary principle, and Indian Affairs, while tolerating "life chiefs" for the time being, reserved the power to remove them and elective chiefs of whom the department disapproved. Indian agents had extraordinary powers to shape local deliberations and decisions, and the wishes of an Indian council were not effective unless and until approved by the Superintendent General of Indian Affairs in Ottawa. There were only two factors that mitigated the severity of this new coercive governance system. The Indian Act and the Indian Advancement Act (the latter's provisions were folded into the larger Act in 1906) still kept the implementation of the elective system as a discretionary power of the Indian Affairs minister. By the latter part of the 1890s it was obvious that the DIA was becoming impatient because few bands had requested elections. In 1895 an Order in Council applied the three-year elective system to forty-two bands in Ontario, six in Quebec, and seven in New Brunswick, none of whom, apparently, had asked for the change. In 1899 another Order applied three-year elective institutions to all bands in Ontario east of Treaty 3 (northwestern Ontario), Quebec, and the three Maritime provinces.[7] The other factor that lessened the severity of Ottawa's interfering ways was resistance from First Nations communities. Many groups who had developed their own governance systems, including the Credit River group led by Kahkewaquonaby, saw no reason to abandon them. The successive legislative measures that tried to foist elective institutions on band councils evoked protests from various Indian groups, although as time passed Ottawa showed itself less and less receptive to Indian opinion. Other instances of resistance to interference on governance would be more dramatic than protests or petitions, although not always any more effective.

First Nations responded to Ottawa's interference with defiance, resistance, and evasion. Defiance is hardly surprising, bearing in mind that many of the bands that Canada sought to control from the 1880s on, especially in the West, were self-regulating groups who had no experience dealing directly with European or Euro-Canadian governments. Accordingly, it was a senior chief from the first generation of those who signed western treaties in the 1870s who provides one of the sharpest examples of First Nation defiance of the federal government's interfering ways.

Wahpeemakwa, whom Europeans knew as White Bear, was chief of a band in the Moose Mountain area of southeastern

Saskatchewan. On behalf of his followers he adhered to Treaty 4
in 1875 and chose a reserve with lightly wooded areas that contained a large lake well stocked with fish. The fact that this land
was not well suited to agriculture did not worry Wahpeemakwa
and his people, because they pursued an economic strategy that did
not rely on the growing of crops. In the difficult period after the
collapse of the buffalo economy in 1879 they did well economically with hunting, gathering, and fishing, with some gardening
and the sale to local homesteaders and villagers of fish, seneca
root and other medicinal plants, firewood, and hand-produced
goods such as tanned hides. This harvesting strategy, in concert
with casual employment by nearby farmers, served them well. In
fact, in the eyes of the Department of Indian Affairs, it served
Wahpeemakwa's community too well. As Indian agent J.J. Campbell
complained to Ottawa in 1887, "White Bear's Band . . . have
steadily resisted every effort to make them work properly; a large
lake on their reserve providing them with sufficient fish in addition to the game and fur which they obtain, to render them more
independent of the Department's wishes, than are the [neigh-
bouring] Assiniboine bands."[8] Compounding the offence was the
fact that Wahpeemakwa and his followers rejected the overtures
of Christian missionaries and withheld their children from the
missionary-run residential schools that Ottawa was establishing
in the west from 1883 onward. Obviously, such a recalcitrant leader
had to be removed, even if his leadership was making his band
the economically self-sufficient community that the DIA said was
its objective.

A struggle between Wahpeemakwa and the Department of
Indian Affairs ensued that lasted from 1887 until 1900. Agent
Campbell asked his superiors in 1888 to depose the chief, offering
by way of justification: "White Bear is law abiding in his inter-
course with the settlers, and is an industrious fisherman, but he is
very obstinate and prejudiced, and resents anyone but himself controlling his band."[9] The government quickly acceded to the agent's
request, but then found that it had created a problem bigger than

the one they had been attempting to remove. Through the 1890s Wahpeemakwa, his sons, and their supporters effectively fought back, opposing farming and raising crops, and continuing their refusal to allow their children to be taken away to distant residential schools that had already acquired a reputation as places that often mistreated children and jeopardized their health. By late 1897 the DIA official nominally in charge of the reserve capitulated to the band, who, he reported, "want the old Chief reinstated. They also want a day school placed on the Reserve." The official explained, "Old White Bear cannot live, in my opinion, more than two or three years and should the request of himself and his sons and others be granted I am of opinion it would be a good thing for the reserve. I mean I should have a hold upon them in the way of getting work done on the reserve."[10] The victory of the traditionalists proved short-lived. They got their chief and a day school, but Wahpeemakwa died before long, and the Department of Indian Affairs engineered the closure of two neighbouring Assiniboine reserves and dumped the population from those reserves onto Wahpeemakwa's reserve. The result was economic hardship and social turmoil that set the band back until late in the twentieth century.

Resistance to the Indian Act's interference with Aboriginal self-government also developed in central Canada, where two of the most noteworthy examples were the Mohawk reserve of Akwesasne, near Cornwall, Ontario, and the Six Nations community near Brantford. These peoples were descendants of the League of the Iroquois who had always insisted that they were self-governing nations, not communities dependent on the Crown or Euro-Canadians. For example, when Britain betrayed the interests of the Mohawk at the end of the American Revolutionary War by surrendering Six Nations lands south of Lake Ontario to the United States, a Mohawk protested, saying "They were allies of the King, not subjects."[11] And throughout the nineteenth century, as settlement swept over their new homes in southern Ontario, they had persisted in retaining control of their own affairs.

One instance of the Mohawk drive for autonomy took the form of resisting DIA imposition of elective government. Akwesasne had an elaborate governance system whose complexity was made more tangled by the fact that the reserve straddled the border between New York, Ontario, and Quebec. In the New York portion of the reserve the prominent men of the community elected five trustees. In the part located in Ontario and Quebec the traditional governance of a chief selected for life by clan mothers prevailed until 1888 when the federal government imposed elective institutions on the "Canadian" portion of the reserve by Order in Council. The community lived with the imposition for about ten years. However, in 1898 those who favoured the appointive system succeeded in getting support for a movement to resist elective leadership. The clan mothers politely informed the Governor General that they had selected their life chiefs and consequently would have no need for the elections that the DIA had planned. When Indian Affairs ignored the expression of local opinion, those who opposed elections seized the polling place in an effort to prevent the vote from taking place. The following year, in 1899, there was another disturbance at voting time, and this time Jake Ice, brother of a traditional chief, was shot dead by the Dominion Police. Contention continued, and, when they were consulted in 1904, the community informed Ottawa that it favoured the traditional system by a margin of two to one. Nonetheless, by 1908 the elective system was back in operation. Akwesasne, like most Mohawk reserves in Quebec and Ontario today, suffers from political factionalism that makes community action difficult.[12]

The resistance on the Six Nations reserve in central Ontario was more extensive and longer lasting than that at Akwesasne. The grand council at Six Nations effectively maintained its own governance system in the face of increasing pressure from both the Province of Ontario and the Dominion of Canada. It functioned as both a legislative body and a judicial institution, and it had its own "forest bailiffs" to enforce its decisions, especially those involving territory and resources such as wood. On one occasion the grand council ruled against Jonas Baptiste, who then threatened to bring suit in a provincial court against the person he claimed had wronged him. When, despite the council's ruling, Baptiste went to the civil court and lost, he returned to the grand council with a request for help paying his court-ordered costs. The council refused, allowing Baptiste to go to jail for failing to pay the court what he owed.[13] The episode demonstrated the persistence of traditional self-governing institutions in an era when the Euro-Canadian state was attempting to impose its ways on First Nations.

At Six Nations after the First World War, the community's desire to maintain political autonomy brought it into sharp conflict with the federal government. In part the quarrel arose from resentment at the DIA's imposition of elections, because, apparently, a majority at Six Nations favoured traditional appointment. A second element was added to what was becoming a confrontation when the Indian Act was amended in 1920 to provide for involuntary, or forced, enfranchisement at the discretion of the Indian Affairs minister. Six Nations leaders saw coerced enfranchisement as one part of a larger policy that aimed to control and assimilate them. Finally, by the 1920s a movement had arisen under the leadership of Deskaheh, or Levi General, in pursuit of recognition of the traditional Six Nations claim that they were a sovereign people, "allies, not subjects of the King." The sovereigntists tried to achieve their aims by negotiation with Ottawa, and, when those talks were unsuccessful, employed a lawyer, petitioned, and generated supportive newspaper comment in opposition to compulsory enfranchisement. When all these actions made no impression on the DIA, Deskaheh and his followers moved their lobbying efforts to London, Canada still being technically a colony and the First Nations insisting on their direct relationship with the Crown. When the London effort proved unavailing, Deskaheh shifted to the new League of Nations at Geneva. At the League Deskaheh succeeded in garnering enough support from countries such as

Holland, a sixteenth-century ally, and a clutch of states recently emerged from European tutelage – Persia, Estonia, Ireland, and Panama – to get the Six Nations' request on the agenda of the Assembly of the League. Only when Great Britain weighed in, diplomatically twisting the arms of the "minor powers," who were presuming to meddle in the internal affairs of a British dominion, did these former subjects of imperial states back down.[14]

The setback did not deter the Six Nations in the long term. The deputy minister of Indian Affairs, infuriated by their campaign against involuntary enfranchisement in the press, cracked down on the reserve by stationing a permanent mounted police detachment at Ohsweken, the town on the Six Nations reserve. Ottawa continued to combat the Six Nations, although, as noted, a change in government in 1921 led to rescinding the compulsory provision in enfranchisement; the federal government also persisted in thwarting their assertions of a right to be recognized as a sovereign people. However, like the Mohawk at Akwesasne who continued to protest against interference symbolically by their annual celebration of Jake Ice Day, the Six Nations in the latter decades of the twentieth century continued to act like an autonomous people. The Six Nations, like the Haida on the Queen Charlotte Islands of British Columbia and the Nishnawbe-Aski nation of northwestern Ontario, frequently travel internationally with passports issued by their own governing bodies, and find that this documentation is usually accepted by the immigration authorities of other countries.

Finally, some First Nations responded to the imposition of elective political institutions with evasive tactics. Perhaps it was easier and just as effective to appear to comply with the desires of the Department of Indian Affairs without in reality giving ground. So, some communities simply elected the people who would have held office on the appointive principle anyway when pressed to elect their leaders by the agent or chose men who lacked prestige and who they knew would not interfere with the desires and activities of band members.[15] It was fear that the Blood would "probably elect an agitator" opposed to DIA policy if the department imposed elective institutions on them that led the Indian agent to recommend against imposition.[16] A Cree community on the prairies simply continued their tradition of having policy issues talked over by the adult males until agreement was reached, the "chief" then announcing the decision.[17] In an exceptional case in central Saskatchewan in 1907 a Dakota band that was reportedly divided between two candidates, turned to their Indian agent to make the choice. What makes the episode look more like a community conciliating officialdom by appearing to defer to the agent is the fact that, according to the resident Presbyterian minister, the "selection . . . met with the approval of all the Indians," and the unsuccessful candidate made a gracious speech expressing satisfaction with the agent's choice of his rival.[18]

In the face of First Nations' reluctance, and in spite of DIA impatience, the spread of the elective system was slow. By 1951 only 185 bands operated under the three-year elective system, and nine conducted their affairs under the one-year provisions that had originally appeared in the Indian Advancement Act. Four hundred bands still adhered to tribal custom. Following the amendment of the Act in 1951 there was an upsurge in interest in elections, with sixty-nine bands adopting the elective system, for a Canada-wide total of 263. By 1971 384 bands, 71 per cent of all bands in the country, followed elective practices.[19]

Through the twentieth century First Nations had slowly gathered the strength to promote their case for self-government on their own terms. In most instances they had not lost their desire for the political autonomy they had enjoyed before the coming of the Europeans, but a combination of factors deterred them from asserting themselves. For one thing, the oppressive tactics of the Department of Indian Affairs was a deterrent to political organization and assertion of rights, including an Aboriginal right of self-government. The same spirit that had animated the Department's crackdown on the Six Nations sovereignty movement and its institution of involuntary enfranchisement in 1920 continued to characterize its approach to Aboriginal political movements. Meetings of the fledgling League of Indians of Western Canada were subjected to RCMP surveillance in the 1920s. And, according to some western First Nations political leaders, the continuing use on the Prairies of the pass system, a policy that the DIA had implemented in 1885 that required Indians who wished to leave their reserve to obtain prior approval from the agent, also was inhibiting.

Sheer poverty also limited First Nations leaders' ability to carry out political organization in the first half of the twentieth century. Dynamic spirits such as Andy Paull of British Columbia, James Gladstone in Alberta, or John Tootoosis in Saskatchewan had to depend on their own meagre resources or whatever supportive relatives and friends could spare to cover their transportation costs as they travelled from reserve to reserve trying to raise political consciousness and forge organizations that could promote First Nations' issues with the Department of Indian Affairs. That leaders such as these managed to develop organizations by the 1950s is testimony both to their perseverance and their communities' support, but their exploits also help to explain why it took so long for coherent campaigns for Aboriginal self-government to emerge. Finally, the problems of widespread disease and death that resulted in a declining Aboriginal population throughout Canada until approximately 1930 also go far to explain why there was relatively little assertiveness from First Nations and so little interest or sympathy from the non-Native population. For the latter, for example, it did not seem worth worrying about future relations with First Nations if, as the experts predicted, Indians were "a vanishing race" that was doomed to disappear.

The same problems of DIA opposition, poverty, and lack of a national organization also explain why, even after political organizations began to emerge, it took some time for these bodies to begin arguing for government recognition of a right of self-government. The repeal in 1951 of a number of repressive features of the Indian Act, such as the 1927 ban on fundraising for claims, certainly facilitated the formation of First Nations organizations. However, the emergence of a national body took longer than provincial organizations largely because of the scope of the challenge. Although Andy Paull fashioned a North American Indian Brotherhood (NAIB) in the 1940s, in reality the body was primarily a British Columbian organization animated principally by Paull's drive for Aboriginal justice. The inclination of groups such as the provincial organizations and Paull's NAIB, on the infrequent occasions when an opportunity arose to present their program publicly, was to press for practical, concrete solutions to immediate problems. So, for example, when the Liberal government of Louis St. Laurent set up a joint parliamentary committee to investigate and recommend changes to the Indian Act, the First Nations groups who appeared or submitted briefs in 1946–48 were far less likely to discuss issues of political autonomy than they were to talk about land, housing, and educational matters. There were, however, many complaints at the post-war hearings about the interfering behaviour of Indian agents, as there were about Canada's failure to honour the treaties it had made with First Nations. The same emphasis on the concrete and practical largely held true of the hearings of another joint parliamentary committee that sat from 1959–61. Given the dire conditions in most First Nations communities, this emphasis on the practical was to be expected.

However, a remarkably short time after the emergence in the 1960s of a durable national political First Nations organization, talk began to turn to considerations of governance. One example was the Dene Declaration of 1975, which asserted, "We the Dene of the N.W.T. insist on the right to be regarded by ourselves and the world as a nation. . . . What we seek then is independence and self-determination within the country of Canada. This is what we mean when we call for a just land settlement for the Dene Nation."[20] First Nations groups that were in treaty tended in the early years of governance discussion to emphasize their treaties. The leader of the Federation of Saskatchewan Indians in 1980 opened the volume *The First Nations: Indian Government and the*

Canadian Confederation by saying, "Indian Nations are sovereign by virtue of their aboriginal rights to the land," and ended his introduction with "But we will not be limited by the treaties. Our sovereign aboriginal rights give us greater scope than the treaties."[21] Such general statements were typical of Aboriginal organizations newly emerged. Those that had treaties tended to be fixated on their treaty rights and treaty problems. Those, like the Dene of the North, who were not in treaty tended to express their aspirations in fairly broad terms. Soon external events would help the political organizations focus on articulating their vision of self-government.

A series of actions by non-Native governments in the 1970s and 1980s drew Aboriginal political organizations into a debate on constitutional change that embraced the idea of entrenching Aboriginal self-government in a reformed constitution. The stimulus to pursue constitutional renewal came from the election of a separatist Parti Québécois (PQ) government under René Lévesque in November 1976. The desire to thwart the sovereignty-association agenda of the PQ spurred Liberal prime minister Pierre Elliott Trudeau to initiate talks with the premiers of the provinces. Trudeau had his own agenda, which included patriation of the amending power and inclusion of a bill of rights that protected language rights and fundamental civil and political rights in any new constitution. Given Trudeau's individualist political philosophy and his public utterances on Aboriginal issues after his ascent to power in 1968, it is certain that that agenda did not include constitutional recognition of group rights such as Aboriginal self-government. When talks among first ministers ensued on and off between 1977 and 1981, Aboriginal political organizations sought unsuccessfully to be included in the deliberations. Worse still, what emerged as a constitutional reform package in November 1981 was a set of provisions, including a Charter of Rights and Freedoms, that decidedly did not include any Aboriginal rights. During the talks the first ministers had considered inclusion of an explicit recognition and affirmation of "Aboriginal and treaty rights," but provincial opposition, particularly from western premiers, led to its being dropped late in the talks.

Along with another major excluded group – women – Aboriginal political organizations were able partially to undo the constitutional snub. Like women's groups, they lobbied ferociously for reinsertion of recognition of their rights in a last-minute amendment of the constitutional package. Both women's groups and Aboriginal organizations succeeded. In the case of the latter, the final 1982 constitutional package that was implemented contained two clauses of vital importance. One said that "The existing Aboriginal and treaty rights of the Aboriginal peoples are hereby recognized and affirmed," and the other declared that the "Aboriginal peoples" included the "Indian, Inuit, and Métis peoples of Canada." This constitutional formulation was definitely a good news/bad news development. The bad news was that the adjective "existing" had been inserted before "Aboriginal and treaty rights" to restrict the constitutional recognition to those rights that existed – and could be demonstrated in a court of law to exist – in April 1982. Rights developed in future would not enjoy constitutional protection by this wording. On the other hand, the generality of the formulation – "Aboriginal and treaty rights" – clearly necessitated further discussions to answer questions such as "What Aboriginal rights?" and "What treaty rights?" are protected by the Constitution? Indeed, the 1982 constitutional package stipulated that a first ministers conference had to be held. In fact at that gathering in 1983, first ministers, recognizing the scope of the task of defining these rights, agreed to hold three more conferences with Aboriginal leaders by 1987 to hammer out the details. What this meant was that Aboriginal political organizations would have three meetings over four years to push for constitutional entrenchment of Aboriginal self-government.

The apparently encouraging nature of these constitutional developments in 1982–83 was enhanced by another breakthrough in Ottawa in the same period. The Penner Committee, a Commons committee charged with investigating and recommending on Aboriginal self-government, in 1983 brought down a report that essentially endorsed First Nations' understanding of self-government. In contrast to previous parliamentary bodies, the Special Committee of the House of Commons on Indian Self-Government both included representatives from Native political bodies as non-voting members and carried out extensive hearings to collect Native testimony. The result was that the *Report* of the Penner Committee spoke of the government's *recognizing* the Aboriginal right of self-government, a dramatically different approach than the traditional attitude, which had usually involved talk of *conferring* self-government on First Nations groups, for example by the Indian Act. The implication of the Penner Committee's choice of words was that the Aboriginal right of self-government was *inherent*, rather than *delegated* by non-Native governments. Second, the *Report* advocated that this recognition of the inherent right of Aboriginal self-government should be entrenched in the Canadian constitution, shielding the right from future legislative assaults. Finally, the Penner Committee made it clear that it was recommending a form of Aboriginal government that went beyond the limited, municipal-style arrangements that hitherto had been made available by the Indian Act. "Indian First Nations," the Committee's *Report* urged, should "form a distinct order of government in Canada."[22] This formulation left much to be negotiated – how "distinct" an "order of government in Canada," for example? – but the Penner Committee had given official endorsement to a view of self-government that was close to the version that the national status Indian body, the Assembly of First Nations, was proposing.

Another influence on the constitutional talks on Aboriginal self-government in the 1980s and early 1990s was an emerging consensus among English-Canadian academic lawyers about the inherent rights of First Nations to governance and other Aboriginal rights. The case for this academic position was largely historical, relying on a new reading of the history of Native-newcomer relations that tended to emphasize those pre-contact powers that had not been expunged or extinguished through contact, rather than an older view that had tended to argue, or at least to assume, that pre-contact powers such as self-government were diminished by interaction with Euro-Canadians and the state. The new argument had two parts, depending upon whether the Aboriginal group in question was in treaty or not. For those who had not taken treaty, such as most First Nations in British Columbia, parts of the Far North, and large segments of Quebec and Atlantic Canada, the contention was simply that rights such as self-government were unextinguished and intact because the Native groups had never been conquered in war or persuaded to give up their rights in a treaty.

For those who were in treaty, largely in the region from Ontario to the Rocky Mountains, the lawyers' argument was significantly different. In these instances, the case for self-government stressed that the version of treaty making on which the state relied to argue that Aboriginal rights such as self-government had been extinguished was the government's written text. The oral history of treaties that First Nations held contained none of the references to giving up powers to manage their own affairs found in the government's text. Sometimes even the government's own version of events lent support to the First Nations' view. For example, during the negotiations for Treaty 10 in 1907, Treaty Commissioner Thomas Borthwick told a group of Dene "that the Chief and his Headmen would be expected to look after the interest of their Band, and therefore it would be well for them to select for office the best self-governing men among them."[23] In northern Saskatchewan, the oral tradition of the Peter Ballantyne Cree Nation concerning their adherence in 1889 to Treaty 6 held that taking treaty meant that Canadian law and police would henceforth protect the Cree, not diminish their right to govern themselves. That was why the Peter Ballantyne people were happy when each year at treaty celebrations an RCMP officer explained Canadian law to young people, but on another occasion, in 1924, when Mounties arrested some Cree trappers for taking beaver, Chief Cornelius Bear stripped the policeman of his coat because, according to the community tradition, the RCMP didn't have the chief's permission.[24] The coat was a symbol of office and authority. After this altercation the police detachment was moved off the reserve.

From the 1980s onward the academic community was familiarizing itself with Aboriginal history, largely oral, and incorporating its insights into their scholarly writings. As noted political scientist Alan Cairns has pointed out, academic lawyers in particular used these new insights from history, anthropology, and their own discipline to fashion arguments in support of Aboriginal assertions, including the assertion of a continuing right of Aboriginal self-government, in the process becoming something of "an intellectual vanguard in the service of a social movement."[25] Such intellectual underpinnings, along with the buttressing support of the Penner Committee *Report* and their own growing strength, placed the Aboriginal political organizations in a promising position when the Canadian political leadership turned in 1983 to the task of defining in constitutional language the "existing Aboriginal rights" that the 1982 constitutional settlement had "recognized and affirmed."

In spite of the auspicious conditions in which the series of constitutional talks began, they ended in failure and frustration. At the conferences in 1984, 1985, and 1987 leaders of First Nations, Metis, and Inuit organizations argued for redress of their land claims, respect for their treaties, and constitutional entrenchment of their continuing right of self-government. Support from the first ministers of non-Native governments was minimal. During the 1984 gathering, Pierre Trudeau, in what was his swan song as prime minister, urged the premiers to accept Aboriginal self-government in principle, leaving the working out of the details of the concept until later. However, the provincial leaders were having no part of that approach, and they continued to stonewall Aboriginal arguments in 1985 and 1987 as well. A major part of the reason for provincial opposition was found in the western

Canadian provinces, where large numbers of Indians and Metis lived. Western premiers feared the impact of constitutional recognition of broad rights of self-government on politics in their home communities. The fear probably was sharpest in British Columbia, most of which was not covered by treaties. The final conference in the series, the 1987 gathering, was noteworthy for televised clashes between Native leaders and western premiers. It ended in well-publicized acrimony.

The understandable disappointment of Native leaders was aggravated and turned into bitterness not long after the failure of the 1987 conference. They had entered talks in 1983 buoyed up by the 1982 assurance that their "aboriginal and treaty rights" were "recognized and affirmed," got a boost from the Penner Committee and increasing support from elements of the academic community, only to fail in the face of provincial premiers who pleaded that they could not agree to a concept like Aboriginal self-government because it was too vague. They needed specifics of what recognizing Aboriginal self-government would mean in practice before they could agree, some of the premiers said.

However, less than two months after the collapse of the 1987 conference on entrenching Aboriginal rights, the same prime minister and provincial premiers – minus the Indian, Metis, and Inuit representatives, of course – got together at the federal government's conference centre at Meech Lake in the Gatineau Hills of western Quebec and quickly hammered together the Meech Lake Accord. From the viewpoint of Native political leaders there were a number of things wrong with the Meech Lake deal. For one, it proposed a new constitutional requirement that any territory would have to secure the agreement of all provincial governments before it could become a province. This had never been the case in the past, when no fewer than six new provinces were created between 1870 and 1949. However, from now on territories such as Yukon and the Northwest Territories, which just happened to have large Aboriginal populations, would have to run the gauntlet of provincial leaders who had shown little sympathy or interest in Native people and issues in recent years. More offensive still for Native leaders, the Meech Lake Accord, whose purpose was to overcome Quebec's alienation from the 1982 constitutional settlement that had been fashioned at the last minute without its approval, did for *la belle province* what Canada's politicians said they could not do for Aboriginal people. The Accord recognized Quebec as "a distinct society" and affirmed that it was the role of "Quebec to preserve and promote the distinct identity of Quebec."[26] What did that mean? No one could say with certainty, and that lack of certainty underscored the humiliating treatment to which Natives had been subjected in recent constitutional talks. While Native leaders could do little about the insult in 1987, they got a chance for revenge in 1990, when an Oji-Cree member of the Manitoba legislative assembly, Elijah Harper, was able to hold up that province's ratification of the Accord and thereby kill the Meech deal. The anger in Quebec at rejection of the Accord was profound; it dangerously fanned the fires of political separatism.

The failure of the Meech Lake Accord and the ensuing crisis in relations with Quebec ensured that the country would soon embark on another round of constitutional talks, negotiations that this time would apparently achieve endorsement of the Aboriginal right of self-government. The Charlottetown round of talks, named for the location of the critical negotiations, was, in Prime Minister Mulroney's words, "a Canada round." What this meant was that the constitutional interests of other segments of the country as well as Quebec would have to be taken into account. With the death of Meech at the hands of Elijah Harper, not to mention the Oka crisis in which Mohawk Warriors and Canadian forces faced each other in a tense seventy-seven day standoff during the summer of 1990 that attracted worldwide attention and galvanized First Nations' anger across the country, it was obvious that the "Canada round" would have to be an Aboriginal round, too.

Although the Charlottetown Accord of 1992 advanced the cause of Aboriginal self-government substantially, the progress was short-lived. One important improvement occurred in the process: leaders of Canada's Aboriginal political organizations joined the first ministers of the country's twelve senior governments in Charlottetown to hammer out the agreement. Moreover, this Accord included a Canada Clause, a definition of the country's constitutional nature, which stated that "the Aboriginal peoples of Canada, being the first peoples to govern this land, have the right to promote their languages, cultures and traditions and to ensure the integrity of their societies, and their governments constitute one of the three orders of government in Canada." In addition, the Charlottetown agreement said that "the Constitution should be amended to recognize that the Aboriginal peoples of Canada have the inherent right of self-government within Canada," and that "the recognition of the inherent right of self-government should be interpreted in light of the recognition of Aboriginal governments as one of the three orders of government in Canada."[27] At the same time, the Accord placed definite limits on the Aboriginal right of self-government. The Accord's reference to Aboriginal peoples having an inherent right of self-government "within Canada" precluded an independent international status for Aboriginal governments, and a separate clause in the draft agreement required that any legislation that future Aboriginal governments might pass "may not be inconsistent with those laws which are essential to the preservation of peace, order and good government in Canada." The last phrase referred to Parliament's fundamental jurisdictional right, implicitly constraining Aboriginal legislatures within whatever legislative regime Ottawa prescribed.

As it turned out, a limit on jurisdiction was the least of the problems that Aboriginal self-government faced in 1992. In a national plebiscite on the Charlottetown Accord held in October, the deal was rejected by Canadian voters. What perhaps was more surprising was that of those Aboriginal people who voted in the plebiscite – and some First Nations abstained – more spurned the Accord than supported it. Some Native groups distrusted the generality of the pact's language on self-government, or distrusted their leaders who had negotiated it or the Native leaders who would govern them in future. Certainly one major source of Native opposition came from some First Nations women. Many women leaders had been alienated by the behaviour of male First Nations leaders on Bill C-31, viewing the chiefs' stance as hostile to Native women. More particularly, the Native Women's Association of Canada (NWAC) opposed the Accord because they had been frozen out of the discussions leading up to it, when male politicians, both Native and non-Native, rejected their demand for a place in the Charlottetown talks. NWAC's unhappiness resulted in a failed court challenge to the process of constitutional renewal.

The other major support for a broad national endorsement of Aboriginal self-government was the Royal Commission on Aboriginal Peoples (RCAP), which was appointed by the Mulroney government in 1991 to investigate and recommend ways of improving the lot of Aboriginal groups in Canada. RCAP's view of the Crown-First Nations relationship historically was what is sometimes referred to as the "two-row wampum" interpretation. The term derives from a seventeenth-century wampum belt commemorating an agreement between the Dutch and First Nations in New Amsterdam (later New York), in which two parallel lines symbolized the parties' intent to sail on together in friendship and co-operation, but without interfering with one another. The two-row wampum view of Crown-First Nations relations was a metaphor for continuing First Nations political sovereignty in the Canadian state.

Essentially, RCAP argued that Aboriginal peoples, having had the right to govern themselves at contact, maintained that right through at least the end of the eighteenth century. Accordingly, it claimed, the practice had hardened into a common law right and "formed a tacit promise of many treaties." Moreover, RCAP contended that there were "persuasive grounds for concluding that the right of self-government continues to exist today as a matter of constitutional common law and qualifies as an existing Aboriginal or treaty-protected right under section 35(1) of the

Constitution Act, 1982."[28] Although the RCAP statement had a fair amount of history in its favour, not everyone agreed with the Commission's interpretation of early Canadian history. Other skeptics who were not moved by the historical argument tended to wonder why it was only after the failure of the political process to enshrine Aboriginal self-government in the Constitution by the Charlottetown Accord that RCAP discovered that Aboriginal self-government was a constitutional common law right that was already protected in the Constitution. In any event, by 1992–93 Canadians were so exhausted and disillusioned by the constitutional scraps that had gone on from the late 1970s until the 1992 plebiscite that voters wanted to hear nothing more on the subject. When the Royal Commission on Aboriginal Peoples recommended sweeping proposals to advance Aboriginal peoples' political rights, including by means of a constitutionally entrenched agreement, the country ignored the recommendations. The federal government's January 1998 response to RCAP, *Gathering Strength*, had nothing concrete to say on the governance recommendations of the RCAP report.

Although two decades of attempts to define and implement Aboriginal self-government by constitutional change at the national level thus ended in failure and frustration, there were a few small-scale advances by individual First Nations or regional groupings of Native people towards the goal of self-government. To date, groups in northern Quebec and coastal British Columbia have fashioned agreements on governance that provide them with a measure of political autonomy and control, and individual bands in Yukon are entitled to negotiate self-government arrangements under the Umbrella Final Agreement signed in 1993. A 1975 treaty between First Nations and Inuit in the James Bay watershed of Quebec provided a measure of self-government to the Native signatories. This agreement was repeated in 1978 in a pact that covered another area of northeastern Quebec. Although both these deals provided for a measure of local autonomy and control of programs, it was not until 1984 that the Cree-Naskapi Act finally laid down a legislative regime to implement the commitment. This federal legislation provided for limited First Nations self-government in areas such as education, local taxation, public works, and land use over a limited portion of the territory covered by the two 1970s land agreements. In the sense that the Cree-Naskapi Act removed the First Nations involved from the coverage of the stultifying Indian Act, it represented progress, but the distance advanced in the direction of self-government by the statute was quite limited.

Getting out of the restrictions of the Indian Act was the primary goal of British Columbia's Sechelt First Nation, which negotiated a self-government pact in 1986. The year before the Conservative government of Brian Mulroney had announced that it was prepared to enter into agreements with specific bands or regional organizations that would, like the Cree-Naskapi Act, take the First Nations out from under the Indian Act and provide a measure of self-administration, if not self-government. The Conservative initiative was obviously a major step back from the Penner Committee's recommendations of only two years earlier, which had called for the recognition of Aboriginal governments as a distinct order of government in Canada. However, for the Sechelt the opportunity had much to commend it.

Stan Dixon, the feisty leader of the Sechelt in the mid-1980s, by his own account came to the struggle for self-government by a roundabout route. He was "more aggressive" than most band leaders, having "been out in the white world since 1961, drove a dump truck, a contractor, I sold jewelry, I was a logger, I was a shop steward, I was a IWA [International Woodworkers Association] member." After his brother died, he returned to Sechelt and ran successfully for chief in 1983. Since the band had been exploring ways to free itself from the restrictions of the Indian Act for over a decade, he leapt at the chance apparently offered by the Mulroney government's policy change in 1985. He used his good personal relations with David Crombie, minister of Indian Affairs, to secure a statute in 1986 that set the Sechelt band up as a legal corporation with the usual powers to own and sell property, borrow and invest, and pursue economic development without the restrictions of the Indian Act. According to Dixon, the Minister of Indian Affairs who soon followed Crombie had second thoughts and wanted to undo the agreement, but the Sechelt insisted that the legislation stand.[29] The Sechelt elected council possesses a somewhat broader jurisdiction than would be the case under the Act, but, again, similarly to the Cree-Naskapi Act's provisions, the powers conferred on the First Nation are modest, essentially a range of municipal-style functions.[30] The limited nature of this self-government regime has led to criticisms from the national First Nation political organization, the Assembly of First Nations. However, the Sechelt community has expressed itself as pleased with the change in legislative powers, and some other bands have contemplated following this example.

Somewhat more latitude than the Sechelt enjoy is provided in the self-government provisions of the Yukon comprehensive claims agreement of 1993. This pact, which covers fourteen individual Yukon First Nations, permits individual bands to negotiate their own self-government packages with the federal government. The legislative scope of these potential governments is relatively large, including province-like powers such as education and training, health services, the administration of justice, and the maintenance of law and order, although the framework agreement specified that any negotiated agreements "shall include provisions respecting the status of a Yukon First Nation as a municipality or public body performing the functions of government or a municipal corporation under the *Income Tax Act*."[31]

Eight Yukon First Nations negotiated self-government agreements between 1993 and 2003. To judge by the example of the Tr'ondëk Hwëch'in Self-Government Agreement of 1998, the jurisdiction of self-governing Yukon First Nations embraces such matters as spiritual and cultural beliefs and practices, the Han language, health care, welfare services, training programs, citizenship, education, solemnization of marriage of their own "Citizens," and "resolution of disputes outside the courts," among others. These powers clearly exceed those of Canadian municipalities, in some cases approximating those of provinces. On the other hand, where legislation passed under this self-government agreement is inconsistent with federal or territorial legislation, the legislation of Yukon Territory or Canada prevails. These self-government arrangements, while surpassing those of Sechelt, are a long way from constituting the type of Aboriginal sovereignty that the Royal Commission on Aboriginal Peoples favoured.[32]

Another First Nation has attempted to pursue its own self-government arrangement with Indian Affairs through legislation. The Sawridge Cree of northern Alberta, however, have found themselves frustrated by the experience. In 1988 Sawridge entered into discussions with Indian Affairs with the objective of securing federal legislation recognizing what they considered their inherent right of self-government. Sawridge had both advantages and disadvantages entering these talks. It was an unusually wealthy band holding great oil riches, and its chief, Walter Twinn, enjoyed a high profile in Ottawa thanks to his status as a member of the Senate of Canada. On the other hand, Sawridge was in disfavour with powerful interests in Ottawa, having launched a challenge to Bill C-31, the measure that provided for restoration of status to some women and their descendants, on the grounds that the legislation infringed Sawridge's long-standing right as an autonomous community to determine its own membership. Although talks appeared to proceed well at first (the Sawridge negotiators believing that by 1989 they had agreement in principle to pass a comprehensive statute and that federal cabinet approval was secured in 1991), the discussions then bogged down and progress ceased. Through the 1990s the band faced one obstacle after another, and finally, in December 1998 launched a lawsuit in the Federal Court of Canada charging that Canada had displayed bad faith and was in breach of its fiduciary duty to Sawridge to carry out the agreement to pass legislation recognizing Sawridge's right of self-government. To date neither the action concerning the self-government issue nor the litigation in which Sawridge is engaged with two other First Nations against Bill C-31 has reached a decisive stage in the court.[33]

The experience of the James Bay Cree, Sechelt, Yukon First Nations, and Sawridge raises the question of what the Government of Canada's policy is on Aboriginal self-government and how it differs from the position that Aboriginal organizations take. The pattern, even over recent decades, is by no means consistent. The federal government under Pierre Trudeau did not show much sympathy for recognizing Aboriginal self-government, although in his final year in office Trudeau did support constitutional recognition of the right in principle at the 1984 meeting of first ministers and Aboriginal leaders. Initially, Conservative prime minister Brian Mulroney showed no more interest in dealing with Aboriginal organizations than his Liberal predecessor had, but the twin shocks of Meech Lake in June 1990 and the Oka standoff from July to September of 1990 led to a change in the federal government position. One difference relevant to the governance issue was the creation of the Royal Commission on Aboriginal Peoples, which, as noted, offered substantial support for a broad constitutional recognition of Aboriginal self-government. Another shift in policy was the Mulroney government's willingness to include Aboriginal leaders in the constitutional talks that led to the failed Charlottetown Accord. Mulroney's government lost power within a year of the Charlottetown failure.

The government headed by Jean Chrétien that took power in 1993 has cautiously begun to depart from the policy of implementing local-government arrangements as in Sechelt. In its 1993 election manifesto known as the Red Book, the federal Liberal Party committed itself to the recognition of an Aboriginal right of self-government under section 35 of the Constitution, and following its sweeping victory proceeded to declare that to be federal government policy. The policy insists that "Aboriginal government and institutions exercising the inherent right of self-government will operate within the framework of the Canadian Constitution," and "is committed to the principle that the *Canadian Charter of Rights and Freedoms* should bind all governments in Canada," including future Aboriginal governments.[34] Following a series of consultations, Canada initiated new approaches to the implementation of self-government in Manitoba and Saskatchewan. In Manitoba the government entered into a general discussion with Manitoba First Nations, which was supposed to implement self-government generally in that province. However, the Manitoba initiative stalled in the face of the chiefs' distrust and suspicion.

From 1996 on, a different process was attempted in neighbouring Saskatchewan. There Canada and the Federation of Saskatchewan Indian Nations (FSIN) agreed upon the creation of a federally appointed treaty commissioner to facilitate talks between Canada and FSIN. The talks, in which the province had observer status, aimed to modernize and implement treaty commitments made with Saskatchewan First Nations between 1874 and 1906.[35] The focus in the Saskatchewan process is on negotiating agreements on seven mutually agreed upon treaty issues, the idea being that Saskatchewan First Nations will acquire a larger role in these areas of responsibility. If the process works out as its promoters, both governments and First Nations, hope, it will result in yet another approach to Aboriginal self-government.

Although Chrétien implied after the Royal Commission on Aboriginal Peoples that he was open to turning control back to First Nations — "We've made enough mistakes for them. It's time for them to make their own mistakes," he told a reporter[36] — his actions belied his words. In 1999 the Chrétien government embarked on a third approach to the governance issue with First Nations that in some ways looked like an effort to turn back the clock. While continuing its support of the treaty-based approach in Saskatchewan, and ostensibly remaining willing to negotiate individual self-government arrangements under its 1995 policy, the federal government began to offer bands the opportunity to remove themselves from the limitations of the Indian Act in some areas, while attacking the statute itself in others. In 1999 Bill C-49 permitted individual bands greater control over property on their reserves, an opening that several bands took. In 2001 Indian Affairs minister Robert Nault promised to introduce a First Nations Land Management Act to confer the land-management powers enjoyed by fourteen bands in the western provinces and New Brunswick on eighty more bands that had filed letters of interest with the government. The future of the legislation is somewhat unclear. While bands that are under the 1999 statute are pleased with the greater autonomy they enjoy, the statute is being opposed in court by the Native Women's Association of Canada. NWAC charges that the legislation violates the Charter of Rights and Freedoms because it does not ensure Indian women will enjoy equal treatment with regard to property when a marriage ends.[37]

The First Nations Land Management Act, viewed together with other federal government initiatives, has provoked disquiet among some First Nations leaders, who suspect that the government is intent on eliminating the Indian Act by stealth. While Indian leaders have their own quarrels with the confining Indian Act, they fear that sweeping it away will destroy their special relationship with the federal Crown. This has been a lively fear ever since 1969, when the Liberal government of Pierre Elliott Trudeau, with its Indian Affairs minister Jean Chrétien, proposed a White Paper that would have eliminated the Indian Act, the Department of Indian Affairs, treaties, and would have turned provision of services for First Nations communities over to the provinces. Intense anger and lobbying by First Nations political organizations in 1969–70 persuaded the Trudeau government to promise not to proceed with the White Paper. However, ever since that episode many Indian political leaders have suspected that the White Paper approach remains the secret operator's manual for federal Indian Affairs policy. The First Nations Land Management Act of 1999, the government's role in litigation leading to the Corbiere decision of 1999 that allowed off-reserve Indians to vote in band elections, and measures undertaken in 2002–03 lend support to the suspicion. In the legal action that produced the Supreme Court decision that upheld the political rights of off-reserve band members, the government of Canada supported financially those who were pushing the action, while refusing to provide any financial support to the Batchewana band in Ontario, which was effectively the defendant in the litigation. This stance is taken by some as proof that Ottawa supported the weakening of reserve-based political leadership.

The Liberal legislative agenda announced in 2001 and introduced in 2002 strengthened the suspicion that the federal government was attacking the Indian Act. Indian Affairs minister Robert Nault refused to deal exclusively with reserve-based chiefs in their national organization, the Assembly of First Nations, in carrying out consultations with First Nations individuals and groups prior to launching sweeping new legislation. The AFN leadership wanted the process of legislative revision to tackle a wider range of issues, but the government refused to modify its agenda. While the process for developing the legislation left much to be desired, the contents of the measures introduced in Parliament in June 2002 (the legislation was reintroduced later in 2002 after a new session of Parliament began), the screams of protest from Aboriginal political leaders notwithstanding, were not as alarming as feared. A bill for a First Nations Governance Act required First Nations to develop their own codes on how to select leaders, operate their band governments, and spend their money, subject to minimum standards established by the federal government. (At the same time Nault also introduced a bill to improve the procedures for resolving specific claims.) A provision reminiscent of part of Bill C-31 in 1985 warned that if First Nations did not develop such codes within two years, Ottawa's own set of "default rules" would automatically be in place. The proposed Act also would also make the Indian Act subject to the Canadian Human Rights Act, and give off-reserve members the right to vote in elections as the Corbiere decision required.[38]

Despite the vociferous lobbying against the legislation that the AFN organized in early 2003, the legislation per se was not all that ominous. First Nations would develop their own codes of practice, although the practicality of 633 individual bands doing so within two years seemed doubtful. The experience with developing band membership codes under Bill C-31 after 1985 did not augur well for these proposed band governance codes. The provisions requiring stricter codes of financial management were viewed positively by many non-Natives who had been conditioned by several years of media criticism of selected reserves' financial woes to perceive First Nations as deficient in financial accountability. Although a variety of First Nations leaders attacked Nault's legislative program and promised organized resistance, none of them addressed what the Canadian public considered an important issue: the necessity that on-reserve governments account for the expenditure of between four and five billion dollars of federal taxpayers' money annually.

The future of Nault's legislative package seemed uncertain in the late spring of 2003. Introduced late in the session in 2002, it fell off the legislative table when Parliament recessed. Its reception in the new parliamentary session in 2002–03 has been stormy, although the government promises to persist with it. In addition to attacking the legislation during hearings of the Aboriginal Affairs Committee in Ottawa, some First Nations have launched legal challenges to it. The AFN in particular refuses to engage the legislation on its merits, preferring resistance through political action, the courts, and international censure. What has largely been overlooked in the fireworks generated by the AFN and the government is the quiet support for the legislation among significant numbers of urban Indians and First Nations women. Neither group has had any great reason to view on-reserve leaders with much confidence, and they have largely declined to follow band chiefs and the AFN in strident opposition to the Nault legislation. In any event, the measure again was postponed in the autumn of

2003, a victim of AFN opposition and the transition to a new government led by Paul Martin.

The stance of the Indian Affairs department over Minister Nault's legislation raises obvious questions about the future of First Nations self-government. In some ways Minister Nault's failure to modify his approach in light of the views of First Nations leaders and his determination to legislate in governance areas now covered by the Indian Act is merely a continuation of the high-handed behaviour in political matters that characterized the Department of Indian Affairs from its inception in 1880 until the controversy over the White Paper in 1969–70. Early in the twenty-first century, an Indian Affairs minister was still trying to criticize and undermine First Nations leadership and political organizations, as deputy minister Duncan Campbell Scott did, particularly in the 1920s and 1930s.[39] And the government of Canada, albeit with input from First Nations individuals collected by the government itself, attempted to dictate what legislation was appropriate for their communities. This is how the federal government behaved in all policy areas affecting First Nations, including governance, down until recent decades. In the past the government's aggressive behaviour has usually resulted either in the government's backing down in face of Aboriginal protest or in legislation that does not work because it lacks legitimacy in the eyes of First Nations leaders.

However, it is not clear at the time of writing if the federal government's current agenda of legislative change will repeat the historic pattern. For one thing, a very large proportion – about 50 per cent – of First Nations people nationwide live off-reserve. The full impact of the Corbiere decision has not yet been felt, and these off-reserve band members still often feel little empathy with chiefs and councils that fail to pay much attention to their needs. Moreover, in a number of western Canadian First Nations communities a movement of disgruntled band members calling itself the First Nations Accountability Coalition has been criticizing what it sees as waste and corruption by reserve-based political leaders and demanding action both to end financial misdeeds and provide greater accountability of chiefs and councils. This group, a minority though a loud one that has attracted considerable media attention, is a constituency ready-made for the federal government's initiatives. It has potential allies in urban Indians and some Indian women's organizations. These First Nations critics are joined by a large number of non-Native Canadians who, as a result of a succession of media blitzes about particular reserves over the past few years, are also concerned with what they see as grave fiscal shortcomings in reserve administrations. While some of these critics might be motivated by hostility to Native people, many more appear to be moved by the serious economic plight of many on-reserve residents and by frustration that annual infusions of large amounts of federal funds are not alleviating the problem.

The commitment of non-Native Canadians to grappling with Native poverty should not be underestimated. An end-of-year poll in December 2001 revealed that "86% of Canadians believe that the need to respond to terrorism after the September 11 attacks should not interrupt the federal government's agenda of improving the environment and the living conditions of aboriginal people."[40] Such a high degree of support for maintaining the federal government's financial commitment to Native peoples is striking, in light of recent events, the destruction of the World Trade Center and the military campaign in Afghanistan, which caused the federal government to reorder its spending priorities. It is proof of the Canadian electorate's continuing concern with Aboriginal problems. If the federal government can convincingly portray its 2002–03 legislative initiatives as a likely answer to some of the problems on First Nations reserves, there is a good chance that the Indian Affairs minister will enjoy widespread support for his campaign for some new version of the First Nations Governance Act.

However, even if the recent federal government campaign to dismantle the Indian Act in stages is successful, it will not constitute effective implementation of First Nations self-government, let alone the broader requirement for Aboriginal self-government that includes the Metis and Inuit. A widespread demand in First Nations and other Native communities for greater control over their own affairs, as well as the knowledge that they were offered some sort of Aboriginal self-government in the Charlottetown Accord, will remain. Providing self-government to the Metis will be the biggest challenge, because they are scattered, highly diverse, and lack the political infrastructure enjoyed by First Nations that will be needed as a foundation for any system of self-government. The Metis are probably furthest away from achieving self-government, in part because they have other more pressing practical needs. Providing meaningful self-government for the Inuit will be simultaneously easy and extremely difficult. It will be easy in the Eastern Arctic, because a form of it exists in the recently created territory of Nunavut. Although Nunavut has a "public government," that is a territorial government open to all long-term residents of the territory, the heavy numerical domination of Inuit effectively makes it an Inuit state. In the Western Arctic, where relatively significant numbers of Dene and Metis exist alongside the Inuit, the challenge is obviously greater, if only because a "public government" there will not secure self-government for any single Aboriginal group. The same is true of northern Quebec and northern Labrador. It might well be the case that Inuit in these communities might not want extensive self-governing powers, or at least not want them for a long time to come.

Because First Nations are so diverse, it seems obvious that the nature and extent of self-government for First Nations will vary across the country. It might be possible in relatively remote areas, where compact groups of Indians live in a region little populated by non-Natives, that self-government on an extensive land base might be feasible. A version of this solution to the need for First Nations self-government is provided by the Nisga'a Treaty that deals with the Nass River valley of northern British Columbia. Perhaps similar solutions might be fashioned in northern British Columbia, the Far North, northern Quebec, and Labrador. However, in more southerly, more densely settled parts of the country such as the heavily populated and agriculturally well-developed Lower Fraser valley in B.C., a separate First Nations territory with self-governing institutions is impossible to achieve. However, there are other ways of maximizing the ability of First Nations to exercise control over those areas that most matter to them without disrupting existing political boundaries. In many parts of the country individual First Nations bands have joined in urban or district tribal councils to pursue common objectives. There is no reason why similar bodies crafted for a specific purpose should not administer services such as education, social assistance, and child welfare for First Nations in an extended area. These suggestions contemplate a highly diversified approach to First Nations self-government, but variety is at the heart of Canadian political arrangements. Diversity, after all, is one of the primary reasons Canada is a federal state. Just as the architects of Confederation in the 1860s adopted and modified the American model of federalism to accommodate strong local feeling in the Maritime colonies and concern for protecting cultural institutions such as religion and education in French Canada, Canadians in the twenty-first century are capable of reorganizing their governance structures to deal with the diversity that is needed to provide effective self-government for those First Nations that desire it.

As this brief rehearsal of the issues associated with Metis, Inuit, and First Nations self-government illustrates, the challenges Canada faces in implementing Aboriginal self-government are many and varied. However, since the Charlottetown Accord and the federal government's decision in 1993 to proceed with the implementation of First Nations' inherent right of self-government as a section 35 constitutional right, the question is *when* and *how*, not *if*, Aboriginal self-government will be created. The earlier, unhappy period in which Aboriginal people were either ignored, like the Metis and

Inuit, or legally infantilized and politically patronized, like the Indians, was one in which the results were not good, either for Aboriginal or non-Aboriginal Canadians. Whatever system – or, more likely, systems – of Aboriginal self-government Canada develops, it is essential that it or they be fashioned co-operatively and consensually. Any other approach, history would suggest, is unlikely to work or to last.

Notes

1 Mark Walters, "According to the Old Customs of Our Nation": Aboriginal Self-Government on the Credit River Mississauga Reserve, 1826–1847," *Ottawa Law Review* 30, 1998–99, 1-45. I am also indebted to Professor Walters's "How to Read Aboriginal Legal Texts from Upper Canada" (unpublished paper, Canadian Historical Association Annual Meeting, 2003).

2 *National Post*, December 17, 2001, "Debunking native myths." The phrase occurred in the sentence deriding what the editorial writer considered intellectual and political orthodoxy on dealing with First Nations' poverty. "For more than two decades, the orthodox view in this country has been that pumping billions into small, geographically isolated Bantustans will, through the magic of 'self-actualization,' spawn economic growth."

3 On the Iroquois League and wampum see the brief account in Barbara Graymont, *The Iroquois in the American Revolution* (Syracuse: Syracuse University Press 1972), 14-17

4 R.G. Thwaites, ed., *The Jesuit Relations and Allied Documents* 72 vols. (Cleveland: Burrows Brothers 1897), vol. 6, 243

5 Clelland S. Ford, *Smoke from Their Fires: The Life of a Kwakiutl Chief* (New Haven, Conn.: Yale University Press 1941), 56

6 Canada, House of Commons, *Debates*, May 4, 1885, 1575

7 Wayne Daugherty and Dennis Madill, *Indian Government Under Indian Act Legislation, 1868-1951* (Ottawa: Indian and Northern Affairs Canada 1980), part one, 6. These extensions did not apply to the Six Nations and Oneidas of the Thames in Ontario that kept their hereditary system, but it did cover the Mississaugas of the Credit and the Iroquois of Kahnawake who had been under the Indian Advancement Act.

8 Report of the Department of Indian Affairs for 1887, Canada, *Sessional Papers* (No. 15) 1888, 82

9 National Archives of Canada, Records of the Department of Indian Affairs [RG 10], vol. 3940, file 121,698-13, J.J. Campbell to Indian Commissioner, December 10, 1888

10 RG 10, vol. 3940, file 121,698-13, H.R. Halpin to DIA, November 16, 1897

11 Quoted in D.C. Scott, "Indian Affairs, 1763–1841," in A. Shortt and A.G. Doughty, eds., *Canada and Its Provinces* (Toronto: Glasgow, Brook and Co. 1914), vol. 4, 708

12 Thomas Stone, "Legal Mobilization and Legal Penetration: The Department of Indian Affairs and the Canadian Party at St. Regis, 1876–1918," *Ethnohistory* 22, no. 4 (fall 1975), 380

13 Sidney L. Harring, *White Man's Law: Native People in Nineteenth-Century Canadian Jurisprudence*, (Toronto: University of Toronto Press 1998), 149

14 E. Brian Titley, *A Narrow Vision: Duncan Campbell Scott and the Administration of Indian Affairs in Canada* (Vancouver: University of British Columbia Press 1985), chapter 7

15 R.W. Dunning, *Social and Economic Change among Northern Ojibwa* (Toronto: University of Toronto Press 1959), 184-5

16 RG 10, vol. 3939, file 121,698-3, R.N.Wilson to J.D. McLean, DIA, June 4, 1909

17 Niels Braroe, *Indian and White: Self-Image and Interaction in a Canadian Plains Community* (Stanford, CA: Stanford University Press 1975), 60-1

18 United Church of Canada Archives, Toronto, Records of the Presbyterian Church, Foreign Mission Committee, Western Section, Indian Work in Manitoba and the Northwest, box 5, file 99, Jonathan Beverly to W.E. Armstrong, July 1, 1907

19 Daugherty and Madill, *Indian Government*, part one, 74, 81

20 Reprinted in J.R. Ponting and R. Gibbins, *Out of Irrelevance: A Social-political Introduction to Indian Affairs in Canada* (Toronto: Butterworths 1980), 351-2

21 *The First Nations: Indian Government and the Canadian Confederation* Delia Opekokew, ed. (Saskatoon: Federation of Saskatchewan Indians 1980), v, vii. The FSI later renamed itself the Federation of Saskatchewan Indian Nations.

22 House of Commons, Special Committee on Indian Self-Government, *Second Report* (Ottawa: Queen's Printer 1983), 44

23 RG 10, vol. 4009, file 241,209-1, "Memorandum, Re: Indians of Treaty No. 10," (Dec. 1907)

24 Interview of Elder Ely Custer, December 28, 1998, by Tracy Strom; quoted in Tracy Strom, "When the Mounties Came: Mounted Police and Cree

Relations on Two Saskatchewan Reserves," (unpublished M.A. thesis, University of Saskatchewan, 1999), 160.

25 Alan C. Cairns, *Citizens Plus: Aboriginal Peoples and the Canadian State* (Vancouver: University of British Columbia Press 2000), 187. Cairns's section on "Academic Activism and Legal Scholarship" is 175–88.

26 Dave De Brou and Bill Waiser, eds. *Documenting Canada: A History of Modern Canada in Documents* (Saskatoon: Fifth House 1992), 635

27 Clause 2(1)b of "People and Communities" section of the Charlottetown Accord

28 RCAP, *Partners in Confederation: Aboriginal Peoples, Self-Government, and the Constitution* (Ottawa: RCAP 1993). This paper was one of several interim statements that RCAP issued along the way to its *Final Report.*

29 Interview with Stan Dixon, Sechelt, BC, September 11, 2002

30 Details on the Sechelt self-government provisions are taken from the Web site of Indian and Northern Affairs Canada: www.ainc-inac.gc.ca/pr/info/info20_e.html

31 Chapter 24 of the Yukon Umbrella Final Agreement, "Yukon Indian Self-Government"

32 *The Tr'ondëk Hwëch'in Self-Government Agreement* (Ottawa: Public Works and Government Services 1998), espec. 3, 7, and 15–18. See also "The Champagne and Aishihik First Nations Self-Government Agreement," 1993 on the Indian Affairs Web site: www.inac.gc.ca. The Tr'ondëk Hwëch'in First Nation was formerly known as the Dawson First Nation.

33 This account is based on information and documents provided by the Sawridge band. Readers should be aware that the author is acting as a consultant for the Sawridge band.

34 Canada, Indian Affairs and Northern Development, *Aboriginal Self-Government: The Government of Canada's Approach to Implementation of the Inherent Right and the Negotiation of Aboriginal Self-Government* (Ottawa: Public Works and Government Services 1995), espec. 1, 3–4

35 Hon. David M. Arnot, *Statement of Treaty Issues: Treaties As A Bridge To the Future* (Saskatoon: Office of the Treaty Commissioner 1998). Readers should be aware that the author has served as a researcher and consultant with the Office of the Treaty Commissioner in 1997–98 and 2001.

36 *Globe and Mail*, November 22, 1996

37 *National Post*, January 3, 2002

38 Canadian Press, "Indian Act changes," June 14, 2002; Linda Ward, "The First Nations Governance Act," CBC News Online, June 14, 2002

39 *National Post*, December 18, 2001, "Ottawa loses faith in Coon Come: Federal officials allege native leader is 'unable to deliver'"; *ibid.,* January 5,

2002, "National Groups too political, Nault says: Minister of Indian Affairs re-examines $350-million in annual federal funding: 'chasing the same dime'"; *Globe and Mail*, May 8, 2003, "Chiefs intimidating natives, minister says"

40   *Globe and Mail*, December 29, 2001

CHAPTER 3

"A Strong Promise":

Treaties

In January 1887 a group of Nisga'a and Tsimshian chiefs from northern British Columbia paddled all the way to the provincial capital in Victoria to meet with government representatives. Conscious that the meeting they sought was historic, they asked in advance that transcripts be made of their discussions with Premier William Smithe and other officials. For his part, Smithe was uneasy about the encounter, worried enough to arrange to meet the chiefs in the parlour of his own residence, rather than in the legislative building. Such a venue, he apparently reckoned, would preclude the attendance of the Christian missionaries who accompanied the Nisga'a, religious figures the premier suspected of concocting the journey and its anticipated complications. Robert Wilson, Tsimshian chief, told Smithe and his colleagues, "What we want . . . is, to be free as well as the whites." John Wesley, one of the Nisga'a leaders, was more explicit: "We want you to cut out a bigger reserve for us, and what we want after that is a treaty." When the premier asked what he meant by "a treaty," Wesley responded, "I have mentioned after a certain amount of land is cut out for the Indians, outside of that we want such a law as the law of England and the Dominion Government which made a treaty with the Indians." The premier denied that there were treaties. With the discussion degenerating into misrepresentation and misunderstanding, Smithe bluntly told the Indian delegates, "When the whites first came among you, you were little better than the wild beasts of the fields," and, obviously, they had no land rights. A Nisga'a chief shot back: "I understand. As I said before, we have come for nothing but to see about the land which we know is ours."[1]

A few months later it was the Nisga'a's turn to play host to visiting government officials, but the results were no more positive than those of the Victoria meeting. Nisga'a leaders were first amused and then dumbfounded when royal commissioners sent to look into Native lands told them that they had no rights to the territory they were standing on in Nass Harbour. Nisga'a Charles Russ responded that "We took the Queen's flag and laws to honour them. We never thought when we did that she was taking the land away from us." He and his colleagues emphasized that they were not opposed to sharing their territory with non-Natives, but first they wanted a treaty that would protect their rights. "We want," Russ explained, "the words and hands of the chiefs on both sides, Indian and Government, to make a promise on paper – a strong promise – that will be not only for us, but our children and forever." If the government would do that, "it will be finished," he said.[2]

It would be a long, long time before the Nisga'a quest for "a strong promise," a treaty, was successful. They formed a Nisga'a Land Committee in 1907 and petitioned London for recognition of their ownership in 1913. They were active in a movement called the Allied Tribes of British Columbia that worked for recognition of Aboriginal title. They were part of a First Nations delegation that appeared before a joint parliamentary committee in 1926 to argue unsuccessfully for recognition of their title, an episode that led the following year to amendment of the Indian Act to outlaw raising or giving money for pursuit of an Indian claim. Once that

extraordinary provision was repealed in 1951, the Nisga'a returned
to the struggle, and in 1973 it was a case on behalf of one of their
number, Frank Calder, on which the Supreme Court of Canada
handed down a ruling that held that Aboriginal title existed in
Canadian law as some form of property right. After that mixed
judicial result, Canada and the Nisga'a in 1976 began lengthy negotiations that culminated in agreement on a treaty early in 1996.
Little wonder that Joseph Gosnell, one of the Nisga'a principal
negotiators, a man who frequently pointed out that he had grown
grey sitting at the negotiating table, exulted to reporters when bargaining concluded, "At 8:27 a.m., our canoe arrived. The journey
our ancestors began more than a century ago ended."[3] It had,
indeed, been a long journey – lengthy in both distance and time –
from the meeting in Premier Smithe's parlour in January 1887 to
the final negotiations in Terrace, B.C., in February 1996.

Canadians' confused reactions to the draft Nisga'a Treaty that
Gosnell celebrated revealed wildly divergent understandings of
treaty making. Critics of the agreement charged that the government of Canada went too far in *granting* extensive powers of
self-government to the First Nation, bestowing on the Nisga'a
what the critics condemned as a "race-based fishery," and *giving*
the Nisga'a control of too vast a territory. Representatives of the
Nisga'a, for the most part, left the task of responding to specific
complaints about governance or land use to members of the
provincial or federal government. When they spoke in defence of
the treaty, it was generally to emphasize how long they had waited
for its conclusion, to point out that it allowed them to maintain
their hold on a comparatively small portion of what had once
been their vast patrimony, and to stress that the recently concluded
treaty was best understood as a simple matter of justice. The
difference in tone and content of the arguments between the
Nisga'a and their opponents was all too typical of discussions of
Aboriginal issues, including treaties. Canadians do not understand
the history of treaties between the Crown and First Nations, nor
the implications of these agreements for contemporary society.

The Nisga'a struggle for recognition of their land rights embodied many of the misunderstandings and clashes of value that are associated with the history of treaty making. Critics who saw in the treaty such governance issues as local jurisdiction and access to a share of the fishery as Canada's *giving* advantages to the First Nation were reacting from historically conditioned positions. Their opposition reflected beliefs about who owned the land and its resources. It assumed that the liberal democratic form of government with which non-Natives were familiar was the only valid system of governance. And it espoused liberal democratic values that implicitly held individualism, individual property rights, and representative legislative institutions up as the ideal. Their First Nations opponents, perhaps appreciating that what divided their adversaries and themselves were the conditioning forces of history and ideology, declined to engage in a debate on the critics' terms. Instead, they emphasized the moral rightness of their case, as well as the patience and forbearance they had shown until their "canoe arrived." They also implied that their generosity, patience, and tolerance were not being reciprocated by their adversaries. The dissonance in the comments of champions and foes of the Nisga'a draft treaty, like many contemporary disputes, had its basis in a lengthy history during which differing interests, values, and aspirations had hardened into contrasting and antagonistic positions.

How have these differing interpretations and attitudes about treaties been shaped by historical forces? What are treaties? Or, more usefully, what are the various understandings of treaty that are found among Native and non-Native groups? Why are treaties perceived so differently in the twenty-first century? And what, if any, are the common elements in this clash of perception and outlook on which a consensus might be fashioned?

Treaties and treaty making are probably as old as interactions between indigenous and immigrant peoples in the northern half of North America. Naturally, the character of the agreements that early European adventurers and Mi'kmaq or Algonkin made was determined by the reason that they had for interacting. Form followed function, as it were. Generally, the accommodations in the early interactions between European and North American revolved around the commercial association that they had in the fur trade, although other pacts were possible, too. The Mi'kmaq of Cape Breton, for example, contend that the 1610 baptism of their venerable and influential chief, Membertou, was in fact the creation of a *concordat*, or church-state agreement, between themselves and the Roman Catholic church.[4] Although that interpretation of Membertou's conversion was not shared by the Vatican, the Mi'kmaq believe it nonetheless. More likely than *concordats*, if only because there were material reasons for pursuing them, were commercial pacts governing the trade relations between newcomers and Native fur suppliers. It would have been sensible for traders from both sides to parley and agree upon the terms and manner in which commercial exchange was to take place. There do not appear to be extant examples of these early pacts, particularly from the French activities in New France, where the French state's use of a monopolist private company to carry on the trade lessened the chances of formal accounts surviving. However, from the Hudson's Bay Company in the late seventeenth century there is evidence that European traders considered commercial agreements – trade treaties, in other words – important preludes to bartering with North American Indians effectively and profitably.

Although the English Crown presumed to confer on the Hudson's Bay Company (HBC) a monopoly of trade in the region drained by rivers flowing into Hudson Bay and James Bay, the Governor and Committee of the HBC instructed their principal agent in James Bay to make prudent arrangements with the local inhabitants:

> There is another thing, if it may be done, that wee judge
> would be much for the interest & safety of the Company.
> That is, in the severall places where you are or shall settle,

you contrive to make compact wth. the Captns. or chiefs
of the respective Rivers & places, whereby it might be
understood by them that you had purchased both the lands
and rivers of them and that they had transferred the
absolute propriety to you, or at least the only freedome of
trade, And that you should cause them to do some act
wch. by the Religion or Custome of their Country should
be thought most sacred and obliging to them for the
confirmation of such Agreements.[5]

Two years after this instruction was issued, in 1682, the Company
repeated it to their agent at York Factory, at the time known to the
English as Port Nelson: "Endeavor to make such Contracts with
the Natives for the River in & above Port Nelson as may in future
times ascertain to us a right & property therein and the Sole
Liberty of trade & Commerce there, and to make Leagues of
friendship & peaceable Cohabitation with such Ceremonies as you
shall finde to bee most Sacred and Obligatory amongst them."[6] As
these and other Hudson's Bay Company records indicate, the giant
English trading company favoured routinely making compacts
with the First Nations in the northern regions to which they sent
traders from the late seventeenth century onward. Apparently a
version of these agreements that recognized First Nations' territorial rights lasted into the nineteenth century. When the Bay
wished to open a year-round post on the North Saskatchewan
River at Fort Carlton, they "gave the Indians one boatload of goods
for the use of the Saskatchewan River."[7]

Although such commercial agreements were important early
forms of treaty, they were by no means the only ones used in the
colonial period during which France and Britain contended for
secure footing in North America. In both the seventeenth and
eighteenth centuries treaties of alliance, peace, and friendship were
commonly employed to regulate relations between Europeans and
First Nations, and also between and among the Indian nations
themselves. Probably the most famous example of the early treaty

system in extensive and elaborate form was the "Covenant Chain" that the Iroquois League (or Iroquois Confederacy) fashioned with the Dutch and British. Using the metaphorical language typical of Native diplomacy, the Iroquois described their ties to Europeans and to fellow North American nations as a chain. When the Iroquois thought their allies were neglecting their obligations, for example, Iroquois negotiators would speak at conferences of how the chain was rusting, and they would call for greater effort to make it, once more, shine brightly. At its height, their alliance system embraced most of the eastern half of the North American continent, with the Iroquois influencing dozens of other nations and sometimes shaping their diplomatic behaviour.[8] The enormous amount of skill, material resources, and military muscle that the Iroquois had to mobilize to keep the system effective was truly mind-boggling.

More directly relevant to the history of treaty making in Canada was a peace agreement that the Iroquois concluded with the French in 1700–01. This pact was unusual, for the French normally did not make formal treaties with First Nations, relying instead upon their extensive fur-trading network and regular giving of presents to maintain harmonious relations. However, this case was special because it regulated relations with the Iroquois League. The Treaty of Montreal came at the end of six decades of on and off warfare between the Iroquois Confederacy and New France. The Iroquois were simply exhausted by the struggle, particularly as a consequence of the last phase of conflict from the 1680s onward. Moreover, they were concerned about the expansionist tendencies of the French, who had built Fort Frontenac near Kingston in 1673 in what was Iroquois hunting hinterland, and also by the unreliability of their English allies, on whom they had found by bitter experience they could not rely. From the French and Canadian standpoint, the 1701 Treaty of Montreal promised in future to spare them the punishing Iroquois raids on their settlements and to separate the Five Nations from the Covenant Chain alliance. The latter consideration was an important one for French planners, who had begun by 1700 to prepare for a showdown with the English for control of the eastern half of North America. By the Montreal treaty the Iroquois secured a commitment to peaceful coexistence with the French and, perhaps more important, assurances of Five Nations neutrality in the event of war between the French and the English, at a cost of sharing traditional hunting territories north of the lower lakes with Indian allies of the French and tolerating the existence of the French Fort Detroit to the west.

As important to the Iroquois Confederacy as the gains realized by the Treaty of Montreal was their simultaneous conclusion of another treaty with their long-time allies, the English at Albany, in 1701. In parleys with the English the Five Nations ceded control of hunting territories north of the lower Great Lakes that they had wrested from the Huron Confederacy and other nations in the seventeenth century, and in return the English promised the Iroquois protection against the French and their Indian allies who in the past had sometimes threatened the Five Nations. These provisions, taken together with the pact with the French, provided the Iroquois with as much security as European imperial rivalries permitted in the North America of the early eighteenth century. The two sets of treaties shielded the Five Nations from attacks by the French and their Indian allies, secured trade prospects at Fort Detroit and with western nations for the Iroquois, and drew the English into playing the role of potential protectors of Iroquois hunting rights in territories between Lake Huron and Lake Erie.[9]

The two-handed treaty making in which the Iroquois Confederacy engaged with England and France in 1701 serves as an excellent example of Aboriginal diplomacy in North America. The Five Nations undertook protracted and extensive negotiations with representatives of the European powers because of pressing reasons – war exhaustion and insecurity about French expansion – and achieved complex results. They secured accommodation and neutrality with the French and their allies and promises of English protection north of the Great Lakes in future, which they considered vital to their survival and economic prospects. The 1701 treaties reveal not only the skill of Native diplomats, but also the determined way in which they adhered to bargaining strategies that defended the people they represented and advanced their interests. Like the best of European diplomats, the most skilful Aboriginal emissaries were expert at analyzing their situation to define the principal threats they faced and the optimum means to counteract the menaces, and then adroitly pursuing their goals.

While the two 1701 treaties were in some ways the most spectacular instance of Native diplomacy during the period of imperial warfare in North America, they were by no means the only ones. Indeed, some of the treaties concluded in Atlantic Canada in the first half of the eighteenth century, as Britain and France jostled for advantage in and, ultimately, control of North America, would have longer-lasting influence than the 1701 pacts. In contrast to the French, who concluded only one treaty with the Mi'kmaq in 150 years of close relations with them, the British entered into no fewer than thirty-two between 1720 and 1786.[10] An example was the 1725 Treaty of Boston, one of two agreements that year that ended – or, more accurately, interrupted – hostilities between the Mi'kmaq and the English. By this agreement a variety of nations in New England and the vast Maritime region that the British called Nova Scotia were guaranteed for all time "their lands, Liberties and properties not by them convey'd or sold to or possessed by any of the English Subjects as aforesaid. As also the privilege of fishing, hunting, and fowling as formerly."[11] The long-term implications of undertakings such as those in the Treaty of Boston were made manifest in 1997, when a New Brunswick Court of Queen's Bench judge upheld a lower court acquittal of a Mi'kmaq man who had been charged with cutting valuable bird's-eye maple on Crown land in violation of provincial statute. The Queen's Bench justice declared flatly: "I am of the opinion that the Indians of New Brunswick do have land rights and that such are treaty rights. . . . It does not matter what such rights are called. It is not a right restricted to personal use, but a full-blown right of beneficial ownership and possession in keeping with the concept of 'This is our land — that is your land.'"[12]

Also important to the legacy of the eighteenth-century Maritime treaties was the 1752 Treaty of Halifax between Britain and the Shubenacadie Mi'kmaq, which by renewing the 1725 provisions of the Boston treaty not only repeated the acknowledgements of "free liberty of Hunting and Fishing as usual," but also explicitly guaranteed to the Mi'kmaq "free liberty to bring to Sale to Halifax or any other Settlement within this Province, Skins, feathers, fowl, fish or any other thing they shall have to sell" and introduced the concept of annuities, or annual payments to the Indians, as part of treaty. In order "to Cherish a good harmony" between Indians and Crown, said the treaty, as "long as they shall Continue in Friendship," the Mi'kmaq would receive "gifts of Blankets, Tobacco, some Powder & Shott."[13] Although the Treaty of Halifax was repudiated by the British in 1756 because of ongoing hostilities with some Mi'kmaq groups in Nova Scotia, it was succeeded in 1760–61 by several treaties that the British made with Mi'kmaq following the conclusion of the Seven Years' War (1756–63).[14]

The 1760–61 Mi'kmaq treaties are now indelibly associated with Donald Marshall in the minds of most Canadians. Donald Marshall, Jr., as he was known in his home community on Cape Breton, was the son of a prominent Mi'kmaq leader. He first came to notice in 1971 when he was wrongly accused of murdering another young man and served eleven years in penitentiary before his case was re-examined and he was released. In spite of chronic lung problems Donald Marshall associated himself with a test case designed to establish the 1760–61 agreements as treaties that overrode federal fishing regulations. Convicted of several fisheries offences, Marshall appealed the rulings until in the autumn of 1999 the Supreme Court of Canada *R. Vs. Marshall* upheld the 1760–61 treaties as treaties protected by section 35 of the 1982

constitution, treaties that defend Mi'kmaq fishers from most regulation by the federal Department of Fisheries and Oceans. (The
constitution overrides federal and provincial statutes.) Although
the decision touched off violence between Mi'kmaq and non-
Native fishers, most people in the Maritime region learned to live
with the result over the next few years. There was even a happy
personal ending for Donald Marshall, Jr. In May 2003 he underwent a successful double-lung transplant operation in Toronto, and
seemed to be on his feet once again.

In most of the eighteenth-century treaties, including the
Mi'kmaq pact of 1752, the Crown promised to provide gifts
regularly to the First Nation with which it concluded the treaty.
Gifts were an important element in the emerging tradition of
treaty making; moreover, they were a harbinger of annuities, the
annual payments that would become part of treaty-making practice in the future. As was noted earlier in relation to the Iroquois
Covenant Chain system, First Nations welcomed the receipt of
presents, which might burnish a chain of friendship and alliance
that had been allowed to grow dull and rusty from lack of attention. The French in particular used the giving of presents, usually
annually, to their Indian allies very effectively, particularly in the
Maritime theatre during the long confrontation with the British
after 1713 that culminated in British victory. From the Indians'
perspective, presents were welcome both as material gifts and as
tokens of an enduring association with the European donors. The
annual giving of presents was a symbolic renewal of the alliance, a
renewed pledge of friendship and support. So important was this
symbolic role of presents in Indian diplomacy that a decision by
the British commandant to cease giving presents to interior
Indians who had been allies of the French after Britain's conquest
of New France in 1760 was interpreted as proof of the redcoats'
hostility. After all, the Indians reasoned, if Britain chose not to
renew friendly association annually by giving presents, the decision proved Britain harboured hostile intentions towards the
First Nations. The cessation of gift-giving in the interior was an

important factor in a rising of Indians under Pontiac that shook British control between 1763 and 1765.

Treaty making in the northeastern part of North America in the eighteenth century took a change of direction and gathered impetus as a result of the Royal Proclamation of 1763, the single most important document in the long history of Canadian treaty making. The Proclamation's significance was that it set the stage for agreements concerning territory, which non-Natives viewed as land surrenders. In fact, the Royal Proclamation was only incidentally about the territorial rights of First Nations. More pressing from the point of view of the British Crown that issued it in the autumn of 1763 was creating institutions of government in Britain's newly acquired North American territory and making arrangements to discourage Aboriginal armed resistance to British settlers in the region west of the Thirteen Colonies. Having defeated France in the Seven Years' War and obtained rights to almost all of the North American territories the French king claimed, Britain had to create boundaries and establish institutions of government and law in regions such as the St. Lawrence colony that Versailles had called Canada, and the British now styled Quebec. In addition, however, British government planners had to be concerned about the restiveness of First Nations in the interior who either had been allies of the defeated French or feared the expansionist tendencies of American agricultural settlers who coveted their lands. Making these strategic concerns all the more pressing was the bloody reality of Pontiac's rising, or the Beaver War as many of the First Nations involved called it, that had led to the deaths of over two thousand Anglo-American settlers and the loss of most of the British forts south of the lower Great Lakes after the conclusion of the Seven Years' War.

The Royal Proclamation tried to ensure peace with the Indian nations of the interior by discouraging incursions on their lands by agricultural settlers. For a long time in the Thirteen Colonies a major irritant in Native-colonial relations had been the land hunger of the settlers, who now expected that they would be able to flood westward into prime agricultural lands since the French, who along with their Indian allies had kept them out of the interior, had been defeated militarily. However, the Royal Proclamation thwarted those settler ambitions in the interests of restoring and maintaining peace with First Nations in the interior. The Proclamation drew the western boundary of Quebec well north of the coveted lands below the Lakes, forbade entry on and settlement in the regions beyond the western boundary, and even sought to regulate traders' penetration of western lands by requiring a license from the colonial administration to legalize commercial activity there. More significant still, the Proclamation referred to these western regions as Aboriginal lands, "reserved to them . . . as their Hunting Grounds."[15]

The most significant of the Proclamation's measures that aimed at heading off conflict with First Nations, however, were the provisions limiting the ways in which Aboriginal lands could be obtained by non-Natives. Here the objective was to put an end to what is sometimes called "the deed game," a device for fraudulently dispossessing Native people by obtaining a deed of sale from an individual or group of unrepresentative people, probably by the use of bribes or liquor. Too often Thirteen Colonies purchasers could brandish their "deed" and insist that the state help to enforce their spurious title against indigenous resistance. The Royal Proclamation aimed to prevent such outrages by decreeing that private citizens could not obtain Native land.

> And Whereas Great Frauds and Abuses have been committed in purchasing Land of the Indians, to the Great Prejudice of our Interests, and to the great Dissatisfaction of the said Indians; In order, therefore, to prevent such Irregularities for the future, and to the End that the Indians may be convinced of our Justice and determined Resolution to remove all reasonable Cause of Discontent, We do, with the Advice of our Privy Council strictly enjoin

and require, that no private Person do presume to make
any Purchase from the said Indians of any Lands reserved
to the said Indians . . .

Only the Crown could legally get land from Aboriginal people.
And, even then, the Crown's representative had to do so in a
public way. Said the Proclamation, if "any of the said Indians
should be inclined to dispose of the said Lands, the same shall be
Purchased only for Us in our Name, at some public Meeting or
Assembly of the said Indians, to be held for the Purpose by the
Governor or Commander in Chief of our Colony."

The Royal Proclamation sought to regulate Euro-American
access to Aboriginal lands to head off conflict between Natives
and newcomers. The boundary definition and restrictions on trade
closed the hinterland to agricultural expansion and regulated
access for commerce. More important, the provisions spelling out
the only way lands could legally be obtained from First Nations –
by the Crown at a public meeting called specifically to acquire
land – were aimed at putting an end to "the deed game," which
threatened peace by increasing Natives' insecurity about their land
tenure. In the opinion of at least one legal scholar, the British
Indian Department went even further in an effort to ensure that
the Proclamation maintained peaceful relations. According to this
view, the head of the northern section of the Indian Department,
Sir William Johnson, acquainted over two thousand Native leaders
with the Proclamation's provisions, assured the leaders that Britain
would not interfere in their affairs, and secured their agreement to
the arrangements.[16]

Whatever awareness First Nations leadership had of the Royal
Proclamation's protections in the short term, over time these guarantees would have profound implications for Aboriginal control
of their territories. Episodically, during an interval that stretched
over two centuries, the courts would erect a structure of legal
recognition of Aboriginal title that by the end of the twentieth
century represented a defensive bulwark against future depredations

on Native lands. And, not incidentally, the procedures that the Royal Proclamation prescribed for legal acquisition of First Nations lands would prove to be precisely the methods that the state in colonial and post-Confederation Canada would use to make land-related treaties.

Between the 1770s, when the British Crown began making territorial treaties pursuant to the Royal Proclamation, and the 1870s, when the Dominion of Canada put into operation a fully developed system for making treaties, the implications of the Royal Proclamation for non-Native access to Aboriginal lands were refined. The immigration of Loyalists, both First Nations and Euro-American, into Upper Canada following their defeat in the American Revolutionary War forced Britain in the 1780s to negotiate with the Ojibwa for access to their lands north of the upper St. Lawrence River and the lower Great Lakes to accommodate the newcomers. The process of Crown-initiated negotiations to gain access to Aboriginal lands continued into the 1790s and early years of the nineteenth century in Upper Canada (the future Ontario) to provide homesteads for land-hungry immigrants from the republic to the south. By means of treaties, then, Britain and its colonists obtained access to large tracts of what is now southern Ontario without bloodshed and at relatively low cost. One important development in this period was Britain's deviation from the earlier practice, first noted in the 1752 Halifax treaty, of compensating the Aboriginal vendors with annuities. During the period of treaty making from the Royal Proclamation to the War of 1812, the Crown provided compensation in the form of one-time payments only.

Following the War of 1812 the Upper Canadian pattern of treaty making again underwent modification. While some lands were secured for Indian refugees, as had been the case following the American Revolution, now most of the land covered by treaties was to be settled by British immigrants. Indeed, from the 1820s to the 1860s, a vast immigration of Britons transformed the face of the Great Lakes basin, pushing First Nations communities in the region to the margins of society and the economy. The change was captured eloquently in a letter that Shingwaukonse, chief of the Garden River Ojibwa near Sault Ste. Marie, wrote to the Governor. He reminded the queen's representative that when British immigrants first came to his region, the Native people were strong and the newcomers weak, "But did we oppress them or wrong them? No."

> Father, time wore on and you have become a great people, whilst we have melted away like snow beneath an April sun; our strength is wasted, our countless warriors dead, our forests laid low, you hunted us from every place as with a wand, you have swept away all our pleasant land, and like some giant foe you tell us 'willing or unwilling, you must now go from amid these rocks and wastes, I want them now! I want them to make rich my white children, whilst you may shrink away to holes and caves like starving dogs to die.'[17]

The other big difference between treaty making before and after the War of 1812 was that the Crown again changed its preferred method of compensating First Nations for lands negotiated. Principally in the interests of economy, British officials reverted to the annuities system of paying First Nations with whom they negotiated for land after 1818. The theory now was that the Crown would obtain revenue from the lands by selling them to non-Native settlers, and the settlers' annual payments for the land would fund the payment of annuities to the First Nations from whom the land had been obtained. By this means, government secured most of the land in what is now southern Ontario at minimal cost and established a population of over a million in the region before Confederation.

One feature of modern treaty making that was not systematically developed in the pre-Confederation period in Ontario was reserves. Today most people think of treaties and reserves as two sides of the same coin: reserves are created for the Aboriginal signatories after a treaty is made with them. However, down to 1850 there was no necessary connection between reserves and treaties, and many treaties were negotiated that made no mention of reserves at all. Historically, the first reserves had been created in New France as refuges for First Nation allies of the French who had been bested in warfare or for Native converts to Catholicism who now found life difficult in their home communities, dominated as they were by religious traditionalists, or "pagans" as the Europeans described them. In nineteenth-century Ontario, Quebec, and the Maritimes reserves were often created by the colonial state or Christian missionary bodies, or by the two acting in concert, to respond to problems of poverty and demoralization that beset First Nations communities as the regions they inhabited were taken over by non-Natives. Consequently, while treaties and reserves had become much more common in the colonies of British North America by 1850, there was no necessary connection between treaty making and reserve creation. Nova Scotia, New Brunswick, and Lower Canada had reserves, although no land treaties had been made in these colonies. Upper Canada had treaties and reserves, but the latter, such as the Credit Mission reserve established by the Methodists in the 1820s, where Peter Jones experimented with self-government, or the Coldwater-Narrows reserves set up by the Indian Department and Christian missions co-operatively in the 1830s, were not dependent on the former.

As the absence of a link between treaties and reserves in British North America suggested, nothing resembling a coherent treaty system developed in the first eighty years following the Royal Proclamation. Britain might have decreed that Aboriginal lands were to be obtained only in a certain way, but there was no guarantee that the prescribed procedure was followed consistently or universally. The background to two important nineteenth-century treaties, the Selkirk Treaty (1817) in present-day Manitoba, and the Robinson treaties (1850) in Ontario, illustrates clearly the disorganized and inconsistent character of treaty making in the British colonial period.

The Selkirk Treaty was negotiated in the region around what is now Winnipeg for reasons that had nothing to do with the Royal Proclamation. This was hardly surprising, because the region in which the Selkirk Treaty fell had been part of Rupert's Land, the empire given to the Hudson's Bay Company by the English Crown in 1670, and Rupert's Land was explicitly exempted from the limitations and obligations that the Crown laid out in the Royal Proclamation of 1763. Lord Selkirk, a Scottish peer with a strong interest in promoting immigration and settlement in British North America, had obtained land from the Hudson's Bay Company on which to settle Scottish emigrants. Only when the Selkirk Settlement ran afoul of the interests of a fur-trading rival of the Hudson's Bay Company, the North West Company, and of some Metis hunters and traders whose livelihood relied on trade with the Nor'Westers, were the conditions created for treaty making. In 1817, significantly following the bloody clash in 1816 at Seven Oaks between Metis and a party of Selkirk settlers, Selkirk's representative negotiated with local Saulteaux (western Ojibwa) and Cree leaders for access to lands along the Red and Assiniboine rivers. In return for an annual "present or quit rent consisting of one hundred pounds weight of good and merchantable tobacco" to each of the Indian nations, Selkirk obtained land extending "two English statute miles back from the banks of the said rivers."[18] According to a later Canadian treaty negotiator, the extent of the land covered by the Selkirk Treaty was explained as "the greatest distance, at which a horse on the level prairie could be seen, or daylight seen under his belly between his legs." The Selkirk Treaty had been inspired not by Royal Proclamation requirements but by indigenous, specifically Metis, resistance to settlement. And not surprisingly, given the fact that traditional Aboriginal lifeways and economic pursuits were still viable in a vast region with little European agricultural settlement, no provision was made for reserves.

While the Robinson treaties, the other major agreements from the pre-Confederation era, were also grounded in Native resistance rather than royal decree, these 1850 pacts in what would soon be Ontario did contribute substantially to the treaty-making system in a number of ways, including the development of an explicit provision for creating reserves.[19] The background to the Robinson treaties lay in Native resistance to mining on their lands in the latter part of the 1840s. Alarmed that the colonial government had authorized exploration and mining on a large number of tracts near the upper Great Lakes, Chief Shingwaukonse of the Garden River Ojibwa, and local Metis first petitioned and later threatened to eject the entrepreneurs when their objections were not heeded. Eventually the Governor dispatched William B. Robinson northward to make agreements. In due course, the treaty commissioner concluded pacts known as the Robinson-Huron and Robinson-Superior treaties for large areas in Northern Ontario adjacent to Lake Huron and Lake Superior respectively.

The Robinson treaties set the pattern for post-Confederation agreements in western Canada. In the 1850 pacts, for the first time coverage of large areas, provision of reserve lands, annuities, and promises of continued rights of hunting and fishing were all combined in a single treaty. Particularly important was the Crown's agreement that Natives would enjoy "the full and free privilege to hunt over the territory now ceded by them, and to fish in the waters thereof as they have heretofore been in the habit of doing, saving and excepting only such portions of the said territory as may from time to time be sold or leased to individuals, or companies of individuals, and occupied by them with the consent of the Provincial Government."[20] All these elements – extensive territory, annuities, reserves, and continuing hunting and fishing rights – would figure prominently in later treaty negotiations, not to mention a large body of litigation and volumes of public controversy that flowed from the Natives' exercise of continuing Aboriginal rights.

By Confederation a treaty-making system was well developed. Although the Royal Proclamation had not always and everywhere been followed to the letter, in general it provided a template for Euro-Canadian treaty negotiators. Prior to incursions on Aboriginal lands, the Crown's representative would bargain publicly with Native leaders for access to extensive tracts. While Aboriginal people would continue to enjoy hunting-gathering rights on the lands covered by treaty until they were occupied by non-Native settlers or entrepreneurs, they would have the option of taking up reserves under treaty. In any event, the Crown would provide annuities as part of the compensation for the lands whose exclusive control First Nations agreed to give up.

The Canadian predilection to negotiate for access to Native lands was transformed into an imperative in the early post-Confederation years by the demands of a project that lay at the heart of national unification: the acquisition of the Hudson's Bay Company lands in the West. Acquisition and integration of Rupert's Land were critical to Confederation in at least two ways. First, the dominant political party of Ontario, George Brown's Liberal forces, made obtaining the western lands a precondition of their support for Confederation, a political venture in which they felt Ontario was sacrificing a great deal. Brown insisted that a clause providing for the addition of the western territories to Canada be included in the resolutions approved by the Fathers of Confederation. Second, Ontarians thought that the new Dominion could not succeed unless it rapidly became a transcontinental state in imitation of its American neighbour. These expansionist sentiments became part of a nationalist ideology centred in populous Ontario.

If Ontario's expansionism made acquisition of western lands an imperative, the bungling manner in which the Canadian government annexed Rupert's Land simply underlined the necessity to negotiate with the indigenous populations in advance of moving into their territories. In 1869 Canada obtained the Hudson's Bay Company (HBC) lands for £300,000 ($1,500,000), the trading company retaining one-twentieth of the lands around their posts, thanks in no small part to the pressure that the British government exerted on the Company. Unfortunately, in its rush to clear HBC interest in Rupert's Land, Canada ignored the rights and sensitivities of the local population. In the region in which Lord Selkirk had established his settlers earlier in the century, a mixed population had developed in a series of parishes along the Assiniboine and Red rivers. The greatest part of the population of Red River – probably half the total of about twelve thousand – were Métis, the descendants of Francophone fur traders and their Native wives. The second largest group were the mixed-blood communities descended from Native and Anglophone ancestors, a population of perhaps five thousand known as country born. The remainder were Ontario immigrants and other non-Native people. The mixed-blood community, and the Métis in particular, took exception to Canada's insensitive manner of dealing with the Bay, and under the astute leadership of Louis Riel they resisted Canada's assertion of control following transfer of the region from the Hudson's Bay Company. The Red River Resistance during the winter of 1869–70 forced Canada to negotiate belatedly with representatives of the local community and to concede their inclusion in the Dominion of Canada on terms more congenial to the westerners than Canada had originally intended.

Riel's Resistance was a sobering reminder of the importance of negotiating in advance with indigenous populations in the West. Canada's failure to consider Metis concerns had delayed the Dominion's expansion and sent an unfortunate signal to American expansionists that Canada's reach might exceed its grasp in Rupert's Land. For Prime Minister John A. Macdonald, who disliked and feared Americans for what he considered their insatiable imperialism, this was a salutary warning. However, the lessons of Red River did not end there. Macdonald also knew that Canada

was not prepared to fight its way into control of the West. For one
thing, there were no transportation links through Canadian territory suitable for moving troops. For another, Canada did not have
the military forces to impose the nation's will on western peoples,
even if troops could have been transported in large numbers to
the plains. Finally, Canada could not afford to fight, rather than
negotiate, its way into the West. In the early 1870s the total annual
expenditure of the government of Canada was about $19 million.
In this same era, the United States was spending $20 million a year
on its Indian wars alone.[21] All these difficulties had the effect of
underscoring the legal fact that the Deed of Surrender by which
the Hudson's Bay Company had transferred its rights in Rupert's
Land contained a clause that made it Canada's responsibility to
satisfy any Indian claims on the land. "Any claims of Indians to
compensation for lands required for settlement shall be disposed
of by the Canadian Government . . . [T]he Company shall be
relieved of all responsibility in respect of them." That there would
be "claims of Indians to compensation for lands" was guaranteed
by Aboriginal assertion of their ownership of the land and by government recognition of the validity of their claim.

The confrontation at Red River had produced evidence of First
Nations, as well as Metis, insistence on respect for their rights.
The Ojibwa occupying the territory between Rainy River and
Lake of the Woods had made clear their opposition to Canadian
intrusions, such as a proposal to build a road over the Dawson
Route from the lakehead to what became Manitoba. They had
proclaimed both their resentment of Canadian intruders and their
willingness to negotiate in 1869:

> We are not afraid of the white man; the people whom you
> go to see at Red River [i.e. the Metis] are our Cousins as
> well as yours, so that friendship between us is proper and
> natural. We have seen evidence of the power of your
> Country in the numerous warriors which she has sent

forth. The soldiers have been most orderly and quick and they have held out the hand of friendship to the Indians. We believe what you tell us when you say that in your land the Indians have always been treated with clemency and justice and we are not apprehensive for the future, but do not bring Settlers and Surveyors amongst us to measure and occupy our lands until a clear understanding has been arrived at as to what our relations are to be in the time to come.[22]

The reality of Ojibwa control of this strategically important section of northwest Ontario was underlined by the fact that Colonel Garnet Wolseley, the British officer in command of the expeditionary force that Canada sent to Red River after the Resistance, encountered First Nations disgruntled at his passage through their territory. Wolseley was compelled to distribute presents to the local Indians to secure peaceful transit of the region.[23]

The same reality was acknowledged and accepted, implicitly at least, by the government of Canada in the immediate aftermath of the Red River Resistance. The negotiated conclusion of the confrontation took the form of the Manitoba Act (1870), a Canadian statute that spelled out the terms on which a small portion of Rupert's Land entered the Dominion as the Province of Manitoba. One clause noted, "And whereas, it is expedient, towards the extinguishment of the Indian Title to the lands in the Province, to appropriate a portion of such ungranted lands, to the extent of one million four hundred thousand acres thereof, for the benefit of the families of the half-breed residents . . ." the Act provided a land base for the Manitoba Metis in the future. In explaining this controversial measure to the House of Commons, Prime Minister Macdonald made it clear that the underlying reason was found in Aboriginal, or, as he styled it, Indian title. Referring to the lands set aside "for the benefit of the families of the half-breed residents" as "a reservation," Macdonald explained, "This reservation, as I have said, is for the purpose of extinguishing the Indian title and all claims upon the lands within the limits of the Province. . . . It is, perhaps, not known to a majority of this House that the old Indian titles are not extinguished over any portion of this country, except for two miles on each side of the Red River and the Assiniboine."[24] However belatedly, Canada did recognize the existence of "Indian title," in this case as it was shared in by the mixed-blood population of Manitoba.

While Canada did not acknowledge the territorial rights of the First Nations of Rupert's Land in the Manitoba Act, the Indians quickly made it known that they could no more be taken for granted than the Metis could. Besides the Ojibwa on the Dawson Route, other First Nations made it clear during the early 1870s that they were aware of and insistent upon their territorial rights. Saulteaux on the west side of the new Province of Manitoba warned settlers who had located around Portage la Prairie not to cut wood or take possession of further lands until the rights of the Saulteaux had been dealt with by negotiation. A notice posted by Chief Yellow Quill and others on a church door told the settler community that "we have not yet received anything for our lands, therefore they still belong to us." In 1875, in what is now central Saskatchewan, Cree along the South Saskatchewan River stopped the work of a party of the Geological Survey of Canada, as well as the activities of a construction crew that was erecting a tele-graph line across their territory. And the powerful Blackfoot Confederacy of southern Alberta in the mid-1870s sent a message to the government of Canada objecting to the fact that traders and settlers were using their land, firewood, and the diminishing buffalo resource without paying compensation to the Blackfoot.[25]

On the other hand, in 1871 a group of Cree chiefs representing the region along the North Saskatchewan River between Fort Edmonton and Fort Carlton and led, significantly, by the venera-ble and powerful Chief Sweet Grass, sent a message to Canada through the HBC Chief Factor at Edmonton:

Great Father, – I shake hands with you and bid you welcome. We heard our lands were sold and we did not like it; we don't want to sell our lands; it is our property, and no one has a right to sell them.

Our country is getting ruined of fur-bearing animals, hitherto our sole support, and now we are poor and want help – we want you to pity us. We want cattle, tools, agricultural implements, and assistance in everything when we come to settle – our country is no longer able to support us.

Make provision for us against years of starvation. We have had great starvation the past winter, and the small-pox took away many of our people, the old, young, and children . . .

We invite you to come and see us and to speak with us. If you can't come yourself, send some one in your place . . .[26]

The message from Sweet Grass and the other Cree was a reminder both that First Nations believed the lands that Canada thought it had acquired from the Hudson's Bay Company were Aboriginal lands – "no one has a right to sell them" – and that the First Nations of the region were willing to negotiate – "come and see us and to speak with us" – just like those in Blackfoot country, in central Saskatchewan, around Portage la Prairie, and in north-western Ontario.

These messages from First Nations leadership in the 1870s raise the important question of Aboriginal motivation. Unlike the earlier treaties, in the case of the numbered treaties that Canada negotiated in the former Hudson's Bay Company lands in the 1870s it is possible, thanks to both documentary and oral evidence, to piece together the assumptions, anxieties, and aspirations of the First Nations negotiators. The indigenous populations of the West were motivated principally by unease, both about their present situation and their future. And they were also apprehensive about the recent and future behaviour of the non-Native population that was obviously taking a great interest in their territories.

The economic underpinnings of the woodlands peoples of northwestern Ontario and the Plains nations further west were in great jeopardy by 1870. In the case of Ojibwa and Woods Cree who had relied on trade and seasonal employment providing transportation for the Hudson's Bay Company, their anxiety was rooted in dramatic changes in the HBC transportation system that made their labour unnecessary. The Bay was shifting from boat brigades that used immense amounts of Indian labour to get trade goods into the interior and furs out, to reliance on railway and lake steamers that would bring goods into the West from eastern centres. Even more compelling was the evidence of the dramatic decline in the number of available buffalo, on which the Plains nations relied for meat, fresh and dried (pemmican); sinews for thread; dried manure for fuel; bones for implements; and hides for lodges, clothing, and trade. Decades of over-hunting, especially commercial hunting, by First Nations, Metis, and non-Natives had made visible inroads on the bison resource. The high demand and decreasing supply was the underlying cause of much of the warfare from about 1820 to 1870 that resulted in drastic loss of life in the Plains nations. Besides warfare and hunger, by the 1860s epidemic disease once again stalked the lodges, taking a shocking number of lives. The combination of these problems led the principal warring groups, the Cree and Blackfoot, to conclude peace as the era of treaty negotiations began. However, the Plains peoples faced a future that clearly was going to include the arrival of many non-Natives in their territory, at a time when First Nations were in a weakened and apprehensive state.

What they knew of the newcomers did not make them any more sanguine about the future. From HBC traders and missionaries they had heard that large numbers of people were likely to come from the east with the intention of settling and farming. The Saulteaux and Cree in Red River knew first-hand that this agricultural invasion was already becoming a reality. All Plains people were aware, as the message from Sweet Grass and the other chiefs around Fort Edmonton revealed, that these people had already made a deal with the Hudson's Bay Company to pay a large sum of money for lands that the Cree, Saulteaux, Blackfoot, and others considered theirs. However, they also knew that the newcomers would come from the Queen's Canadian territories to the east, and in this they found some solace. To western First Nations the Queen's people had long been represented by the personnel of the Hudson's Bay Company, men with whom they had conducted business profitably for close to two centuries. Equally important, the Queen's people were not Americans. The Queen's people would not come from the south, the territory Plains First Nations called the Land of the Long Knives. The term "long knives" referred, of course, to the sabres of the American cavalry, a force that had wrought havoc among other First Nations south of the "medicine line," the international boundary. The expected newcomers, then, were people of the Queen, with whom it probably would be easier and more productive to negotiate terms to govern the entry into First Nations lands of the thousands that missionaries in particular advised First Nations would come.

The combination of insecurity about their future and uneasy belief that an association with British power held promise of a better future largely explained western First Nations' reasons for entering into treaty talks in the 1870s with the Canadian representatives of Queen Victoria. During the discussions that occurred between 1871 and 1877 in the vast portion of Rupert's Land that stretched from northwestern Ontario to the Rockies, and from the international boundary in the south to a point roughly midway up the future prairie provinces, the First Nations' motivation for dealing with the Europeans became apparent. Fortunately, in the case of one of the seven treaties that resulted from these talks, Treaty 6 in central Saskatchewan and Alberta, there is a record of private talks among Native leaders at the beginning of negotiations at Fort Carlton, the Hudson's Bay Company post on the

Though both Louis Riel (above, ca. 1875) and Peter Lougheed (1980) were of Indian ancestry, culturally, they were worlds apart. (Riel: National Archives of Canada, PA139070; Lougheed: Glenbow Archives, NA-556-72c)

David Mills, whose father was African-American, married a Blood woman and was accepted into the group as one of their own. (Glenbow Archives, NA-4035-160)

James Gladstone (centre) began life as a mixed-blood child in southern Alberta, but ended his career as the first status Indian to be appointed to the Canadian Senate. With Gladstone are B.C. Nisga'a leader Frank Calder, left, and Saskatchewan premier Tommy Douglas. (Saskatchewan Archives Board, R-PS 58-523-02)

Jeannette Lavell was one of the leaders in the fight against the gender discrimination in the Indian Act, which required an Indian woman to give up her status when she married a man without status. (*Toronto Star*)

This dance was a part of a Potlatch ceremony held by the Tlingit of northern B.C. Potlatches regulated relationships among North West Coast nations. (Archives of Yukon, Anglican Diocese of Yukon Records, box G-141, album 1, #146)

Nicholas Vincent Isawanhonhi, a Huron chief, recites the meaning of the wampum belt. (National Archives of Canada, C38948, lithograph of painting by Mr. Chatfield, London, 1825)

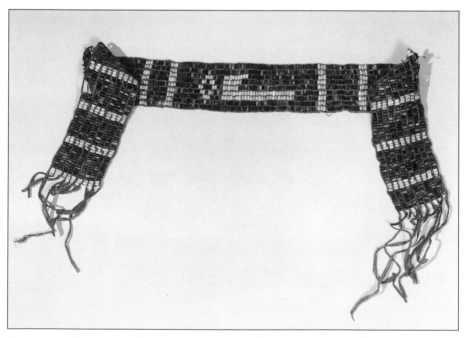

Wampum belts such as this one were a means of keeping records of important events for the Iroquois and other First Nations of the Eastern Woodlands. (McCord Museum, M20401)

Six Nations hereditary chiefs, one of the most determined of self-governing groups after Confederation, using wampum in their deliberations. (National Archives of Canada, C85137)

Prime Minister John A. Macdonald, who also served as minister of Indian Affairs from 1878 – 87, presided over many government attempts to undermine self-government in Indian communities. (National Archives of Canada, C121604)

Jean Chrétien (standing) and Pierre Elliott Trudeau (sitting, right) meet Indian Association of Alberta leaders to discuss the White Paper in 1970. (National Archives of Canada, PA170161)

Buffalo was the foundation of the Plains economy and way of life until the 1870s.
(National Archives of Canada, C403, "A Buffalo Rift," watercolour by A.J. Miller, 1867)

Parleys at the Stone Fort, which resulted in the first of the post-Confederation treaties.
(National Library of Canada, C56481. *Canadian Illustrated News*, September 9, 1871, p.172)

Many of the early Maritime treaties were concluded with the Mi'kmaq, seen here greeting European visitors. (Art Gallery of Nova Scotia, ca. 1795, slide 1994.229)

The signature panel of this 1764 Huron treaty contained both the totems of the chiefs and the signature of William Johnson of Britain's Indian Department. (National Archives of Canada, C135291)

Ahtahkakoop (left front) and Mistawasis (right front) were influential pro-treaty Cree chiefs at talks leading up to Treaty 6 at Fort Carlton in 1876. (Front centre, Chief Flying in a Circle; left rear, Chief Osoup; and right rear, Peter Hourie, interpreter.) (National Archives of Canada, C19258)

Mistahimusqua (Big Bear), in contrast to Ahtahkakoop and Mistawasis, was opposed to entering Treaty 6 because he doubted the government would honour its promises. (National Archives of Canada, C1873)

The Fort Carlton site of Treaty 6, August 1876. (National Archives of Canada, C64741)

On Treaty Day in Saskatoon (June 2003) a representative of the government pays an Indian man the five-dollar annuity promised him in Treaty 6. (*The StarPhoenix*)

An Oka chief "telling" wampum. Specially chosen members of a band were responsible for recounting the history of alliances and events recorded in the beaded belts. (McCord Museum, Notman Photographic Archives, 48,873-BI)

The construction of the Mercier Bridge, ca. 1956, from the South Shore of the
St. Lawrence to Montreal produced grievances because it cut into Kahnawake lands.
(National Archives of Canada, PA115315)

Wikwemikong, 1856, one of the first Ontario reserves. (Toronto Reference Library,
J. Ross Robertson Collection, T16028)

These photos (above and opposite) from the Department of Indian Affairs illustrate residential schooling's assimilative goal in their depiction of Thomas Moore before and after he attended Regina Industrial School. (Saskatchewan Archives Board, left: R–A8223–1, right: R–A8223–2)

Civilization and Barbarism, an 1870 drawing, embodied the entrenched Euro-Canadian attitude that Natives at best were irrelevant to newcomers' "progress." (Toronto Reference Library, *Civilization and Barbarism* by William George Richardson Hind, ca. 1870, J. Ross Robertson Collection, T-33370)

The physical sacrifice involved in the prairie Sun Dance ceremony horrified many non-Natives and led to its prohibition by the Indian Act from 1895-1951. (United Church of Canada/Victoria University Archives, Toronto, 93.049P/949, "Sun Dance: making a brave," Boorne & May, Photographers, Calgary, N.W.T., 1887)

North Saskatchewan River, in August 1876. At a caucus that First Nations leaders requested before beginning substantive talks with Canada's commissioners, the Native headmen debated their options in the presence of a Metis interpreter, Peter Erasmus, whom two senior Cree chiefs, Mistawasis and Ahtahkakoop, had hired to assist them. What Erasmus heard in the caucus and recounted later in writing provides a clear indication of the conflicting points of view within the Plains First Nations community and the reasons for the eventual triumph of those who wished to enter treaty.

At the heart of the private talks Indian leaders held at Fort Carlton lay the question of whether or not they should make treaty at all. Mistawasis and Ahtahkakoop, judging by their tactics and their words, had decided that they must overcome the objections of other, younger leaders, such as The Badger, Poundmaker, and Young Chipewyan, to taking treaty with the Crown. Both the pro-treaty speakers were experienced, respected Plains Cree leaders, and Ahtahkakoop in particular was already familiar with the agricultural and secular instruction an Anglican missionary resident in his community could provide. At their caucus, these seasoned leaders allowed the younger men to lodge their objections, and then they moved in succession to counter these arguments and promote the case for entering treaty. Mistawasis began, picking up on the widely shared concern about the dwindling buffalo:

> I have heard my brothers speak, complaining of the hardships endured by our people. Some have bewailed the poverty and suffering that has come to Indians because of the destruction of the buffalo as the chief source of our living, the loss of the ancient glory of our forefathers; and with all that I agree, in the silence of my teepee and on the broad prairies where once our fathers could not pass for the great number of those animals that blocked their way; and even in our day, we have had to choose carefully our campground for fear of being trampled in our teepees.

With all these things, I think and feel intensely the sorrow my brothers express.

I speak directly to Poundmaker and The Badger and those others who object to signing this treaty. Have you anything better to offer our people? I ask, again, can you suggest anything that will bring these things back for tomorrow and all the tomorrows that face our people?[27]

Mistawasis suggested an alternative: a relationship with the Crown secured by treaty. "I," he continued, "think that the Great White Queen Mother has offered us a way of life when the buffalo are no more. Gone they will be before many snows have come to cover our heads or graves if such should be." He explained: "I, for one, look to the Queen's law and her Red Coat servants to protect our people against the evils of white man's firewater and to stop the senseless wars among our people, against the Blackfoot, Peigans, and Bloods. We have been in darkness; the Blackfoot and the others are people as we are. They will starve as we will starve when the buffalo are gone. We will be brothers in misery when we could have been brothers in plenty in times when there was no need for any man, woman, or child to be hungry."

There was no point in dwelling on the past; they must face a worrisome future, if possible with the protection and assistance that the Crown represented.

We speak of glory and our memories are all that is left to feed the widows and orphans of those who have died in its attainment. We are few in numbers compared to former times, by wars and the terrible ravages of smallpox. Our people have vanished too. Even if it were possible to gather all the tribes together, to throw away the hand that is offered to help us, we would be too weak to make our demands heard.

Look to the great Indian nations in the Long Knives' country who have been fighting since the memory of their oldest men. They are being vanquished and swept into the most useless parts of their country. Their days are numbered like those of the buffalo. There is no law or justice for the Indians in Long Knives' country. The Police followed two murderers to Montana and caught them but when they were brought to the Montana court they were turned free because it was not murder to kill an Indian.

The prairies have not been darkened by the blood of our white brothers in our time. Let this always be so. I for one will take the hand that is offered. For my band I have spoken.

Mistawasis's message was clear: their precarious position made it prudent to look for an association with Queen Victoria and the power she commanded; the contemporary example of Indian wars in the United States demonstrated that the alternative to taking "the hand that is offered" was unthinkable.

Mistawasis's colleague, fellow Cree chief Ahtahkakoop, then took over, reiterating some of Mistawasis's key points and elaborating on the benefits that might be obtained in association with the queen's people.

Can we stop the power of the white man from spreading over the land like the grasshoppers that cloud the sky and then fall to consume every blade of grass and every leaf on the trees in their path? I think not. Before this happens let us ponder carefully our choice of roads.

There are men among you who are trying to blind our eyes, and refuse to see the things that have brought us to this pass. Let us not think of ourselves but of our children's children. We hold our place among the tribes as chiefs and councillors because our people think we have wisdom above others amongst us. Then let us show our wisdom. Let us show our wisdom by choosing the right path now while we yet have a choice.

We have always lived and received our needs in clothing, shelter, and food from the countless multitudes of buffalo that have been with us since the earliest memory of our people. No one with open eyes and open minds can doubt that the buffalo will soon be a thing of the past. Will our people live as before when this comes to pass? No! They will die and become just a memory unless we find another way.

For my part, I think that the Queen Mother has offered us a new way and I have faith in the things my brother Mista-wa-sis has told you. The mother earth has always given us plenty with the grass that fed the buffalo. Surely we Indians can learn the ways of living that made the white man strong and be able to vanquish all the great tribes of the southern nations. The white man never had the buffalo but I am told they have cattle in the thousands that are covering the prairie for miles and will replace the buffalo in the Long Knives' country and may even spread over our lands. The white men number their lodges by the thousands, not like us who can only count our teepees by tens. I will accept the Queen's hand for my people. I have spoken.

Ahtahkakoop recognized that adjusting to the twin traumas of declining buffalo resources and immigrating farmers by embracing horticulture was a potential solution. Cree were as smart as white people. If the latter could sustain themselves with crops or cattle, the Cree could learn the same. And such an adjustment in association with the government of the incoming society – "the Queen's hand" – promised more assistance and protection than the obvious alternative, a war of resistance like the one their kinfolk were suffering on the Great Plains of the United States.

The metaphor-rich language that treaty negotiators such as Mistawasis and Ahtahkakoop used was an important component of treaty making. First Nations leaders were expected to be eloquent orators who could present their case effectively, whether to other Indians or to outsiders such as a treaty commissioner. Moreover, First Nations rhetorical traditions relied heavily on metaphor, simile, and allegory, with both positive and negative results. The positive aspect of such rhetoric was the power it lent to the argument. Terms and phrases such as "long knives," "the Queen Mother has offered us a new way," and "taking the Queen's hand," were immediately understandable, at least to those listeners who came from the same culture as the speaker. And when Blackfoot chief Crowfoot in 1877 at Blackfoot Crossing praised the mounted police in rich metaphor, his words were evocative: "If the Police had not come to the country, where would we be all now? Bad men and whiskey were killing us so fast that very few, indeed, of us would have been left to-day. The Police have protected us as the feathers of the bird protect it from the frosts of winter."[28] And it is noteworthy that the treaty commissioners and Indian negotiators often adopted the same words, as when Commissioner Alexander Morris at Fort Carlton finished outlining what the Crown was offering by saying "I hold out my hand to you full of the Queen's bounty and I hope you will not put it back." And a few days after the talks at Fort Carlton Morris addressed the Willow Cree as "my brother children of the Great Queen."[29]

But the downside of oratory laced with metaphor was that it could simultaneously create and cover up misunderstanding, or different understandings, of what was being said. These pitfalls were revealed in two areas in particular: the language of childhood, and the language of an equestrian culture. Treaty talks were striking for the way that representatives on both sides referred to one another, as Morris did to the Willow Cree, in terms of kinship, usually indicating that non-Native Canadians and First Nations were all children of the Queen. However, the common use of familial language concealed the fact that the two sides often meant different things when they used the same words. As historian John Tobias has explained, childhood in Euro-Canadian society was a period of dependence, submission, and adult control; but childhood in Plains culture was a time of great autonomy for children, during which they had every right to expect and receive protection and assistance from their parents.[30] Accordingly, when a Canadian such as Alexander Morris referred to Plains people as "children" of the Queen, the implication was that they would be obedient as well as receive the Queen's "bounty," and, indeed, such language usage by treaty commissioners often occurred in a context in which there were references to obeying Canadian law. However, references by First Nations leaders to themselves and their people as "children" clearly were never meant to imply obedience to the queen's law. Inasmuch as the Parliament of Canada had passed the Indian Act, which assumed state control and First Nations submission, just a few months prior to the negotiation of Treaty 6, the difference in understanding and implication embedded in the common use of such language of childhood was pregnant with future difficulties.

The perils of these linguistic pitfalls were well illustrated by two utterances of Mistahimusqua (Big Bear), a powerful Cree leader who participated in Treaty 6 talks at Fort Pitt in September 1876. Mistahimusqua, of mixed Saulteaux and Cree descent, was a widely respected chief then at the height of his powers. He had arrived late at the talks at Fort Pitt and was chagrined to discover that the other leaders, with Sweet Grass at their head, had already agreed to treaty terms. This discomfited him, in part because he distrusted the Crown representative and in part because he did not believe he had his followers' endorsement to enter an agreement. Accordingly, he held back and refused to sign on as others had. Moreover, in the course of his brief discussions with Commissioner Alexander Morris he obliquely explained that one of his major preoccupations was to obtain from Morris a commitment "that he will save me from what I most dread, that is: the rope to be about my neck."[31] Although the interpreter translated Mistahimusqua's words as "hanging," which immediately put Morris's back up, as John Tobias has explained, the Cree leader's meaning was quite different. Coming as he did from a Plains background in which the horse was a central element, his metaphorical reference – "the rope . . . about my neck" – was to the horse's bridle, not the hangman's noose. The misunderstanding about "rope" that ensued from the speakers' different cultural backgrounds, plus the fact that Mistahimusqua declined to enter treaty in 1876, marked him as a troublemaker in the eyes of the government. Even Big Bear's assurance – "I am not an undutiful child, I do not throw back your hand" – later in the meeting did not improve Treaty Commissioner Morris's view of the holdout.

The problems that arose in treaty making from culturally based linguistic misunderstandings were not the end of the difficulties that flowed from the opposing culturally determined attitudes and expectations of the two parties. First, many problems were the result of the fact that the Crown representatives were the products of a literate society while the First Nations leaders came from an oral culture. Translation of a speaker's words, as the serious misunderstanding of Mistahimusqua's reference to a "rope" showed, could be too difficult even for an experienced translator. In addition to the language barrier First Nations as people from an oral culture considered that the treaty embraced everything *said* during the parleys, as well as what was recorded at the end of the discussions. What was *said* was what was essential.

This viewpoint was strengthened in the 1870s treaty talks by the fact that a pipe ceremony, in which a ceremonial pipe was smoked by all participants, preceded almost all the treaty talks.[32] For First Nations the significance of smoking the pipe in such a ceremony was that the action brought the Great Spirit into the proceedings and bound all those involved to speak only the truth. To put it in Judeo-Christian terms, the pipe ceremony transformed the treaty talks into the creation of a covenant, a covenant being an agreement in which two human parties and the deity are involved. This view of the pipe ceremony was widespread throughout First Nations in Canada. Mohawk elder Ernest Benedict of Akwesasne, the Mohawk reserve near Cornwall, Ontario, told the Indian Claims Commission in 1992: "I have heard the Elders say that when the terms of the treaties were deliberated the smoke from the pipe carried that agreement to the Creator binding it forever. An agreement can be written in stone, stone can be chipped away, but the smoke from the sacred pipe signified to the First Nation peoples that the treaties could not be undone."[33]

The words of Euro-Canadian negotiators in the public talks gave First Nations reason to believe the "queen's children" shared the Aboriginal view of the talks. For example, at Fort Carlton in 1876 Commissioner Alexander Morris invoked God at the end of his opening address, observing, "I will trust that we may come together hand to hand and heart to heart again. I trust that God will bless this bright day for our good, and give our Chiefs and Councillors wisdom so that you will accept the words of your Governor." The following day, a Sunday, the Anglican cleric who accompanied the treaty party held "divine service," first for the Euro-Canadians, and then, at the request of the Indians, "preaching in their own tongue to a congregation of over two hundred adult Crees."[34] However, the Canadians did not understand that the pipe ceremony and their own words and actions would be interpreted as involving God in the deliberations, as a comment by Commissioner Morris's secretary at Fort Carlton reveals. After describing the pipe ceremony that preceded talks, this man observed: "The significance of this ceremony is that the Governor and Commissioners accepted the friendship of the tribe."[35] In fact, the significance was far more profound than friendly exchanges: the pipe ceremony created a covenant.[36]

Because Plains culture was oral, and also because of the solemnity and obligation conveyed by the pipe ceremony, First Nations negotiators remembered and counted on every word the Crown representative uttered even more than the words of the written version of the treaty that resulted. From time to time the language that the Crown's commissioner used seemed to accord with the Aboriginal understanding of solemnity in treaty talks: "What we have done has been done before the Great Spirit and in the face of the people," Morris informed his audience at Fort Carlton in

August 1876.[37] Accordingly when a treaty commissioner assured his First Nations audience that the Crown had no desire to interfere with their way of life ("Understand me, I do not want to interfere with your hunting and fishing. I want you to pursue it through the country, as you have heretofore done;") his First Nations audience took it for granted that these words were every bit as binding as any provision in the government's written text. The same held for the Crown's oral assurance that it sought only to add to what the Indians enjoyed without diminishing anything they had ("What I have offered does not take away your living, you will have it then as you have now, and what I offer now is put on top of it,") or its assurance that the agreement was permanent, not transitory ("What I trust and hope we will do is not for to-day or to-morrow only; what I will promise, and what I believe and hope you will take, is to last as long as that sun shines and yonder river flows.")[38]

At the time of treaty making and since, First Nations have lamented that the government's version did not capture accurately what had been agreed in the negotiations. As early as 1727, Panaouamskeyen, a Penobscot chief, went to the trouble of having his understanding of what he had agreed to in the Treaty of Canso written out, because he had heard that British officials were claiming that he and others had agreed to submit to the authority of Britain. In particular, Panaouamskeyen denied the English claim that he accepted the authority of the officer with whom he had negotiated. Never "did I, become his subject, or give him my land, or acknowledge his King as my King. This I never did . . ."[39] Discrepancies between the First Nations' recollection of the oral treaty and the European's written version have persisted to the present.

In the 1870s First Nations negotiators quickly began to dispute what had been agreed to in Treaty 1 in 1871. Canadian officials claimed that the Crown had not agreed to provide agricultural implements and livestock to begin farming, but Native leaders clearly remembered having raised these issues and secured agreement. The problem was caused by the fact that Treaty Commissioner Wemyss Simpson, in order to achieve agreement after protracted bargaining, agreed to these items even though his mandate from the government of Canada did not stretch that far. In this case, First Nations' protest and the fact that Simpson's memorandum of the discussions contained the disputed items, led the government to concede in 1875 that what it called "outside promises" were part of Treaty 1. For the First Nations leaders there had never been anything external about the promises. Whether they were in the official text of the treaty or not, the commitments were part of the treaty, because they had been discussed and agreed upon orally. Similar difficulties have arisen in most of the prairie treaties over game, water, and subsurface rights; for example, First Nations in Treaty 4 and Treaty 6 maintain that they agreed to give up the land only to "the depth of a plough."[40]

Beyond the matter of misunderstandings about language, First Nations who entered into treaties in the 1870s or later understood the arrangements they had made in a sense that differed from the understanding that Euro-Canadian society had of the pacts. As the government's emphasis on the written version of the treaties from the immediate post-treaty days onward suggests, Ottawa regarded the ententes essentially as contracts. And, as western First Nations declined numerically and proportionally because of losses to epidemic disease and in-migration of non-Native agricultural settlers, Ottawa came increasingly to deal with treaty matters in a narrowly legalistic manner. Some examples of this attitude have become infamous. For instance, when Treaty 6 promised that the Crown would maintain a "medicine chest" in communities, the federal government refused to reinterpret that commitment as a guarantee of government-funded hospitalization and medical care. Even though Indian Affairs has paid for almost all medical costs for status Indians since the 1960s, Ottawa continues to deny that in the case of Treaty 6 Indians that coverage is a treaty right. The schooling provisions of the western treaties are an even more damning instance. The promise to create "schools on reserves" that is found in most of the western treaties was disregarded by Indian Affairs from the 1880s until the late 1960s, as Ottawa constructed off-reserve residential schools, which they often forced children from the Plains treaty areas to attend. All the same, in the latter decades of the twentieth century, as First Nations' interest and enrolment in post-secondary education began to mushroom, the government of Brian Mulroney had no compunction about capping expenditure on post-secondary education for status Indians or in shifting the administration of the limited funds to bands and tribal councils. When Indian organizations complained that such limitations violated the spirit of the treaties, maintaining that the equivalent of an elementary education in the 1870s was post-secondary instruction in the late twentieth century, the federal government denied that higher education was a treaty right. Finally, an annuity of five dollars in many of the western treaties is still paid today to every First Nations man, woman, and child covered by a treaty. Legalistically, Ottawa has made no adjustment for 130 years of inflation.

In spite of the government's penny-pinching and legalism on annuities, treaty First Nations remain devoted to the annual payment of treaty money. Treaty days are formal events in which a government official checks the name of each person attending against Indian Affairs' official register, and then gives a five-dollar bill to a red-coated Mountie to hand over to the intended recipient. Such ceremonies can last all day in some centres. While treaty days are important social occasions, a time when First Nations people can visit with friends and neighbours, some of whom they might not have seen since the last such gathering, the distribution of annuities during the events is also highly symbolic. The payment of annuities, as picayune as they are, is the twenty-first-century equivalent of the annual presents that the French and British used in colonial times to maintain their powerful alliances with Algonkian or Iroquoian groups in the northeastern woodlands. Presents were the symbolic gifts used to "wipe away the tears" of disappointed Indian allies, or to "polish the chain of friendship." Present-day payment of annuities is the symbolic acknowledgement and renewal of the covenant relationship between Crown and First Nations that is the heart of the treaty for Indian peoples. As noted earlier, when British officials ceased giving presents to the former allies of the now-defeated French, the First Nations interpreted the cessation as a sign of hostility and waged war against the newly triumphant British. Similarly, a century later, when the Indian Department stopped annual distribution of presents in Ontario, First Nations regarded the move as representing enmity towards them. First Nations reacted as they did because the gifts were symbols of a treaty relationship that extended well beyond a merely contractual tie between themselves and the Crown.

The view of treaties as the embodiments of a relationship between the Crown and the Crown's non-Native subjects is consistent with the metaphorical description of accepting "the Queen's hand" that First Nations leaders such as Ahtahkakoop used in 1876. Nowadays the same point is often contained in First Nations' references to the "spirit of the treaties" rather than the precise letter. The distinction is important to them, because they see the treaties not as contracts but covenants, the essential element of which is the relationship between the two parties in partnership.

As important to appreciating First Nations' views of the first numbered treaties is the concept of reciprocity. As historian Jean Friesen has pointed out, in the Aboriginal value system and cosmology, reciprocity was a key concept.[41] The forces of the cosmos had to be kept in balance; failure to observe the taboos or to show reverence and respect where appropriate destroyed the balance and led to illness and calamity. Mutuality or reciprocity was good, both for individuals and societies. Accordingly, because in the 1870s First Nations were surrendering the exclusive use of the territory that had given them life and a living, they expected that the Crown reciprocate by guaranteeing them protection and assistance to maintain their livelihood in a dramatically changing world. When the Indian Affairs department did little to assist them in the

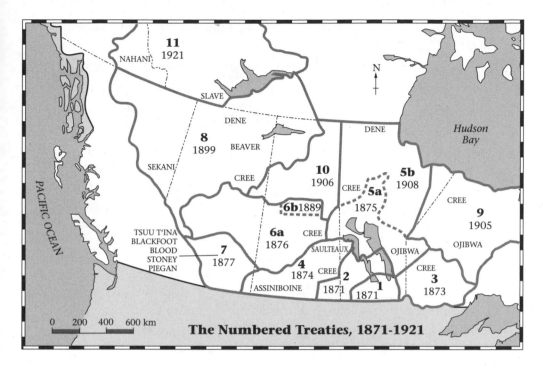

The Numbered Treaties, 1871-1921

economically and climatically harsh 1880s and 1890s, when all Plains bands suffered and many Indians died of disease and starvation, their leaders' complaints about government betrayal of the treaty relationship were sharp and loud. And when First Nations today emphasize the importance of implementing the "true spirit and intent" of the treaties, they are referring to the necessity to update the treaties in light of treaty commitments to a relationship that would ensure the maintenance of what they had, their freedom and livelihood, as well as additional benefits flowing from the "bounty and benevolence" of the Crown. Because they regard treaties not as contracts but as covenants that embody relationship and reciprocity, they want Canada to live up to what Commissioner Alexander Morris promised in the negotiations leading to Treaty 6: "What I have offered does not take away your living, you will have it then as you have now, and what I offer now is put on top of it."[42]

After Treaty 7, the last of the Plains treaties, was concluded in 1877, there was a pause in treaty making. (There were, however, many adhesions to the treaties by individual bands, and a major extension, or adhesion, to Treaty 6 in 1889.) The reason for cessation of treaty making was simple: the federal government was uninterested in First Nations' lands unless and until non-Natives showed an interest in them. When a variety of First Nations north of Treaty 6 and Treaty 5 petitioned for treaties in the 1880s because there appeared to be exploration going on for the construction of railways and agricultural settlement, and poor hunting was causing destitution, the federal cabinet declined to negotiate. These First Nations made the case that if "land within the territory inhabited by them is to be used for these purposes, it is only fair that before such appropriations of land are made treaty stipulations should be concluded with them as the owners of the soil," and because their economic hardship made them "require the annuities and other emoluments that would be secured to them under treaty to enable them to subsist." Ottawa was unmoved. "The Government," the minister of Indian Affairs reported to cabinet, "has hitherto declined to make treaties with the Indians referred to, on the ground that the lands within the regions inhabited by them were not required for settlement . . ." The cabinet saw no reason to change its policy now.[43]

When the Crown entered into four more numbered treaties between 1899 and 1921 with northern First Nations in the West, Ontario, and the territorial North, it was for motives consistent with its earlier approach to treaty making. These agreements, which covered a vast patrimony stretching from Northern Ontario to northeastern British Columbia and included a substantial part of the southern Northwest Territories, were all, as the earlier prairie treaties had also been, the product of economic interest among non-Natives in Aboriginal lands. Until southern economic interests began to covet the resources that these northern territories housed, the Department of Indian Affairs remained monumentally indifferent to appeals from northern Indians to enter into treaty with the Crown. However, when mining activities in northern British Columbia became acute in the latter half of the 1890s, and, more pointedly, when bands in northern British Columbia began to threaten retaliation against non-Native prospectors and miners invading their territory, attitudes in Ottawa changed. Hurriedly, treaty commissioners were dispatched to make a treaty with disgruntled northern bands, a pact that covered a vast territory from northeastern B.C. through Alberta to the northwestern part of Saskatchewan, in 1899 and 1900. Although the Yukon, where the Klondike gold rush had recently occurred, was not covered by Treaty 8, the important overland approaches to Yukon were.

Similar motives animated the Crown's belated interest in treaty making in other northerly regions in the early decades of the twentieth century. Treaty 9 was concluded in Northern Ontario in 1905, as southern interest in the mineral, forest, and hydroelectric potential of the territory was rising sharply. The following year, the remaining portion of northern Saskatchewan not covered by the eastern edge of Treaty 8 or the 1889 annex to Treaty 6 was embraced by Treaty 10 as economic interest in the northerly region again began to grow, and there was a desire to extend treaty coverage since a northern boundary of the province had been created at sixty degrees north in 1905. Similarly, the northerly portion of Manitoba was included in 1908 by what is known as Treaty 5b. (Treaty 5, signed in 1875, covered portions of southern and central Manitoba, as well as a small strip in east-central Saskatchewan along the Saskatchewan River.) This resource-inspired treaty movement northward culminated more than a decade later, in 1921, with the negotiation of Treaty 11, which embraced a vast portion of the southwestern N.W.T. Treaty 11, the last of the numbered treaties, demonstrated as clearly as any how the Crown's desire to make treaty was fuelled almost exclusively by southern economic interests in northern resources. Ottawa had remained indifferent to territorial First Nations' desires to enter treaty, as well as the pleas of Roman Catholic missionaries that government assist them in providing services to these groups, until oil was discovered at Norman Wells, N.W.T., in 1920. Then the federal government moved swiftly to conclude a pact.

Besides all originating in southern cupidity, the northern treaties' aftermath shared common features. Put simply, if somewhat crudely, once the treaties were made and resource-rich areas secured, Ottawa's interest in the inhabitants of the region diminished almost to zero. The examples are many and disheartening. For one thing, the federal government denied that oral promises made about tax exemption to Treaty 8 negotiators constituted part of the treaty.[44] Another instance arose in the Alberta portion of Treaty 8, where a group that would become known as the Lubicon Lake Cree were ignored by both federal and provincial governments for decades when they attempted to secure a reserve that would protect at least some of their lands from the encroachments of invading forestry and petroleum interests. In Northern Ontario an Anicinabe (Ojibwa) group who called themselves the Teme-Augama Anishnabai (Deep Water People), and whom the government referred to as the Temagami band, similarly fought long and futilely for the benefits of treaty and protection from invading forestry and commercial recreation interests. In the territorial north, missionaries, especially the Roman Catholic Oblates of Mary Immaculate, lobbied, wheedled, and complained with little effect in efforts to get Ottawa to provide services, particularly health care and education, to northern First Nations groups that were experiencing problems as the revenues of hunting and fur-trapping proved inadequate. More generally, the administration that Ottawa provided in the Treaty 11 area was so minimal that much later it would be quietly conceded that Treaty 11 was a nullity because of government inaction and would have to be redone. The treaties negotiated between 1899 and 1921 shared origins in southern economic ambition and results in southern indifference and neglect.

The same lack of interest in the well-being of northern Native peoples was also a major reason why no more treaties were negotiated for half a century after 1921. The sole exception was the Williams Treaty of 1923 signed with the Anicinabe of Christian Island, Georgina Island, and Rama; and Mississauga of Mud Lake,

Rice Lake, Alnwick, and Scugog in southern Ontario. This 1923 agreement settled a dispute over Aboriginal title, the First Nations maintaining that one parcel of land had never been covered by earlier treaties, and that some of their traditional hunting lands had been embraced by the Robinson treaties, to which they were not parties. The final settlement that Canada and Ontario drew up and then presented to the First Nations, contained one-time only cash payments. The Williams settlement has only slight claim to be considered a treaty in the full sense of the term.

Aside from the Williams Treaty, Ottawa lost interest in treaty making even though much of British Columbia, Labrador, northern Quebec, and the two territories were not yet included in treaty. Part of the explanation of federal indifference was that signing of Treaty 11 in 1921 coincided with the lowest period of interest in and commitment to First Nations on the part of the Department of Indian Affairs since Confederation. This was the era in which the Indian Act was changed to permit the government to use involuntary enfranchisement to strip status Indians of their distinctive standing as "Indians" in Canadian law. Federal Indian policy in the 1920s was also marred by the campaign that the Department waged against Indian groups, such as the Six Nations in southern Ontario, who resisted the government and sought to establish their own standing in international affairs. Another telling instance of departmental lack of sympathy was the 1927 amendment of the Indian Act, which made it illegal to give or solicit funds for pursuit of a claim, effectively preventing Indian organizations from obtaining legal counsel. A final, ludicrous example was *Re Eskimos*, the litigation between the federal government and the government of Quebec in the 1930s that culminated in a Supreme Court decision that Inuit were Indians.

Compounding the neglect arising from the government's lack of sympathy for Aboriginal people in this period was the assumption that Native people were simply going to die out. This attitude was general in North America, founded on the indubitable fact that the numbers of First Nations and other Native people had been steadily dwindling for decades. The dramatic initial losses to disease that had been a consequence of post-contact interaction in Canada, like everywhere else in the western hemisphere, were aggravated in the late nineteenth century and well into the twentieth by losses attributable to a variety of factors associated with the increasing pressure of settler society. First Nations found themselves crowded onto reserves, often discouraged or prevented from maintaining themselves with foodstuffs obtained by a traditional hunting-fishing-gathering economy, suffering from impoverishment, and, in the case of about one-third of their young people, were herded into unhealthy residential schools where a shocking number of them died. Between the 1880s and the 1920s population loss, especially to tuberculosis, reduced the First Nations population to less than one hundred thousand. By the time the decline was reversed in the 1930s, the view of First Nations as "the vanishing Indian" had firmly taken hold. Even the authority of science supported the idea. Writing in 1932, anthropologist Diamond Jenness famously concluded the historical section of his influential *The Indians of Canada* by saying, "Doubtless all the tribes will disappear."[45] If all the tribes were disappearing, it hardly seemed sensible to incur the expense of making treaty with those who still were not in a treaty relationship with the Crown.

Even when it became obvious by the late 1930s that First Nations were not going to dwindle to nothing, other factors intervened to prevent the government from turning its attention to treaty making. First, the Great Depression of the 1930s was an all-consuming economic and social crisis during which governments were not likely to devote a lot of thought, much less money, to treaties or to the welfare of Indian and Inuit communities, despite the fact that they were among the hardest hit by the crash. After all, among the Canadian public there was little interest in or concern about the well-being of Native peoples, aside from the major Christian churches who continued their ministrations and tried unsuccessfully to persuade government and their fellow citizens to show some compassion. The Depression was soon followed by the

Second World War, during which, of course, the federal government focused externally on fighting the enemy and internally on avoiding the national disunity that had been such a serious problem during the Great War. A short time after peace was concluded in 1945 the country embarked on a massive economic expansion, much of it based on the extraction of natural resources for export to more mature economies, that would last, with dips from time to time, until the 1980s. As well, from the late 1940s Canadians and their government were preoccupied by the Cold War between communists and the supposedly freedom-loving West.

From the mid-1940s onward there was a gentle stirring of human rights awareness that stimulated some concern over the racist assumptions and objectives of Canadian Indian policy. Rarely would this empathy lead to any concerted action on behalf of First Nations who were not in treaty. The first outcome of this interest in human rights was the 1951 amendment of the Indian Act, which removed some of the most interfering aspects of the law without touching the core assimilative aim of the legislation. A parallel bout of human rights awareness in the latter part of the 1960s culminated in the White Paper, which would have eliminated status Indians entirely and transferred responsibility for programs for them to the provinces. Obviously, with the kind of Ottawa mindset that manifested itself in the 1927 and 1951 amendments of the Indian Act or the 1969 White Paper, the First Nations could scarcely expect sympathy for their interests. It was hardly surprising that from the early 1920s until soon after the issuing of the White Paper no effort was made to fashion treaties in those portions of the country, particularly northern Quebec and the two northern territories, where treaties had not been made or an existing treaty was inoperative.

However, in the half-century after 1923 forces were at work that would produce a powerful movement towards treaty making in the 1970s. The first of these was the Canadian economy's reliance upon the extraction of natural resources – fuel, wood, and minerals especially – for its growth. This process had accelerated noticeably during the Great War and the 1920s, slumped in the Depression, revived dramatically owing to wartime demand in the 1940s, and remained the single most important factor in the long period of prosperity that Canada enjoyed until 1982. What was often ignored in this resource boom was that the oil or uranium or gold or forest products often came from lands in which First Nations were still numerically dominant and for which there were no treaties or only treaties that were ineffective. The long battles that the Lubicon Lake Cree had with the governments of Alberta and Canada in the twentieth century were an example of inadequate treaty coverage. The resistance of territorial Dene groups to proposals to build pipelines to transport Arctic oil southward, especially after the so-called Oil Shock created by the Organization of Petroleum Exporting Countries in 1973 increased public demand for secure energy supply, led the government to create two inquiries into whether or not a northern pipeline should be built. To the amazement of most in southern Canada, the first of these inquiries, conducted by British Columbia jurist Thomas Berger, reported that there should be a ten-year delay before pipeline construction began so that the land rights of northerners could be dealt with. Resource-rich Canada was affluent because of energy and commodities that were largely found in Native-controlled territory. And some of those resource-laden lands where Inuit and First Nations lived were not covered by treaties.

The other factor that combined with the natural resources question to precipitate new treaty talks in the 1970s was Aboriginal political organization. As noted previously, between the end of the Great War and the 1960s all the major Native groups organized, often with great difficulty, to defend their rights. In the early years in particular they often faced the hostility of the Department of Indian Affairs. Nonetheless, first at the provincial level, organization proceeded, with the Prairie provinces and Ontario leading the way. By 1961 status and non-status Indians, as well as the Metis, formed a Canada-wide organization, known as the National Indian

Council (NIC). Probably its most publicized achievement was the creation of an Indian Pavilion at Expo 67, the world's fair held in Montreal in 1967, which condemned Canadians for the decades of neglect to which they had subjected Native peoples. After the NIC subdivided in 1968 into a status organization, the National Indian Brotherhood (NIB), and the Canadian Metis Society, the NIB scored a major victory when its ferocious critique of the White Paper persuaded the Trudeau government to abandon the policy statement. The Inuit, too, organized, forming the Inuit Tapirisat of Canada in 1971, mainly under the leadership of the eastern Arctic Inuit. In the western territories Inuit, Dene, and Metis now were also represented by powerful territorial bodies. Similarly, most of the status Indian organizations across the country also had effectively led provincial political associations by the 1970s.

It was Quebec Natives, specifically those who called themselves the James Bay Cree, who brought a dramatic end to the hiatus of treaty making in the 1970s. The issue that sparked renewed activity was a resource question, of course, specifically hydroelectric power generation. Quebec's young Liberal premier Robert Bourassa had been elected in 1970 on a platform of economic renewal that promised to create one hundred thousand new jobs, many of them to result from damming rivers and generating power in the James Bay watershed. The James Bay Cree, led by a dynamic man named Billy Diamond, moved to thwart this project because they had not been consulted, even though a significant portion of their homeland would be flooded to create the headpond for the electric generators. With a group of Quebec Inuit, the Cree went to court and succeeded in 1972 in obtaining an injunction, later reversed, against any more work in the territory they claimed. Negotiations among the Quebec Natives, the province, and the federal government resulted in the James Bay and Northern Quebec Agreement of 1975, and later, in 1984, the Cree-Naskapi Act. The 1975 Agreement, which both governments carefully avoided referring to as a treaty, provided compensation in the form of grants and royalties payable over ten years, control of traditional sites, and recognition that Aboriginal people would continue to enjoy hunting and fishing rights in the region, an area of some 400,000 square miles. The 1984 Act provided the Cree and Innu (or Naskapi) with powers of administration over those lands that had been set aside by the Agreement for their exclusive benefit. Taken together, the 1975 Agreement and 1984 Act, form a treaty, the first negotiated since the early 1920s. A combination of non-Native desire for access to resources and Aboriginal political resistance to exploitation produced this treaty.

While the James Bay talks were proceeding, other events occurred that paved the way for more modern treaties. In 1973 the Supreme Court of Canada ruled in the *Nisga'a* or *Calder* case that Aboriginal title existed at law in lands controlled by Aboriginal groups who had not made treaty. The Nisga'a had been pursuing Crown recognition of their ownership of the Nass River valley since 1887, but opposition, especially from the province, had always prevented them from achieving their goal. Finally, they had launched litigation to try to establish their claim by judicial means, and the Supreme Court rewarded their effort in part in its 1973 ruling. Six of the seven justices found that there was such a thing in law as Aboriginal title in lands that had not been surrendered, although three of the judges also ruled that Nisga'a Aboriginal title to Nass Valley lands had been extinguished by actions of settler society and its government. One judge ruled against the Nisga'a on a legal technicality, thereby producing a 4–3 verdict against the Nisga'a. However, the Court had found that the law recognized Aboriginal title, and it was clear from the ruling that the Aboriginal right they found in 1973 was more expansive than the right of usage that the previous major Aboriginal title case, the *St. Catharines Milling* case of 1889, had discovered. Although the Nisga'a lost at the Supreme Court, they won; and every Aboriginal group occupying traditional territory that was not covered by a treaty accordingly won along with them.

The James Bay confrontation and the *Calder* case together had a major impact on Ottawa. A perplexed Prime Minister Trudeau mused to First Nations leaders, "Perhaps you had more legal rights than we thought you had when we did the white paper."[46] The result of the prime minister's discovery was the federal government's creation in 1974 of the Office of Native Claims (ONC) to deal with First Nations claims on a variety of issues. The ONC was set up to adjudicate specific claims, which were based on an allegation of unfilled legal obligation (often unfulfilled treaty promises), and comprehensive claims. The latter were claims to territory and resources based on an assertion of Aboriginal title by an Aboriginal group that had not entered into a treaty with the Crown concerning their lands. As the Web site of Indian and Northern Affairs Canada (INAC) puts it, the "primary goal" of INAC's Comprehensive Claims Branch "is to negotiate modern treaties which will provide a clear, certain and long-lasting definition of rights to lands and resources for all Canadians."[47]

Although the process established in 1974 and modified several times since has been bedevilled by delays and a growing backlog of claims, some comprehensive claims have been carried through to a conclusion that is effectively a modern treaty. These include the COPE (Committee of Original People's Entitlement) or Inuvialuit Agreement, which was concluded by the Inuit of the western portion of the Northwest Territories in 1984, and a settlement reached with the Council for Yukon Indians in 1990 (Umbrella Final Agreement, 1993). On the other hand, a Metis-Dene settlement in the western Northwest Territories fell apart when the community rejected it in a plebiscite in 1990. Other, smaller claims were settled in the 1990s, the Gwich'in of the Upper Mackenzie Delta in 1992 and the Sahtu Dene and Metis of the Great Bear Lake region in 1994. The reason that these comprehensive claims were all in the northern territories was clear: federal control of the Northwest Territories and Yukon meant that there were no troublesome provincial governments to deal with. Elsewhere the provinces had jurisdiction over Crown lands and natural resources, necessitating provincial co-operation to assemble enough land for transfer to the Aboriginal claimants. As the

Nisga'a had discovered in British Columbia, provinces were not enthusiastic about such transfers.

The most dramatic of the northern comprehensive claims settlements was that of the Tungavik Federation of Nunavut (TFN), whose pact was embodied in legislation in 1993 and implemented in 1999. The Eastern Arctic Inuit represented by TFN had worked quietly and effectively after initiating a comprehensive claim in 1976, and they had made their mark on the political map in a 1982 plebiscite, suggested by them, which produced a high turnout and an overwhelming vote in favour of splitting the Northwest Territories into two new territories. TFN sought the creation of an Inuit-dominated eastern territory, which they proposed to call Nunavut (Our Land). They reached agreement in 1990 in a deal that covered both land and governmental issues. In return for over a billion dollars and retention of almost one-fifth of the enormous land mass involved, they conceded Aboriginal title to the Eastern Arctic. Equally important, in 1999 the new territory of Nunavut was carved out of the N.W.T. Nunavut is officially a "public government" in which every permanent resident has political rights, but, since its population is over 80 per cent Inuit, it is effectively controlled by the Inuit. Moreover, it has jurisdiction over sufficient territory to build the kind of economy its citizens desire. Nunavut is a unique case: a new Aboriginal-controlled territory that resulted from a comprehensive land claim. It is the product of a modern treaty.

The Nisga'a Treaty of 1996, though less distinctive than Nunavut, is also a major breakthrough. For one thing, aside from Treaty 8, it is the first treaty negotiated in British Columbia since the colonial period. The Nisga'a of the Nass Valley struggled for over a century, both in failed attempts to start negotiations and in litigation such as the *Calder* case of 1973, to secure recognition of their ownership of the lands they claimed. The negotiations among the Nisga'a, Canada, and British Columbia were lengthy and complex, and the result, as noted at the outset, has been controversial in some quarters. The Nisga'a received continuing control of a relatively small portion of the Nass Valley, monetary compensation for resource riches extracted from their lands during the long decades when their rights were not recognized or were under negotiation, and a guaranteed share of the fishery, on which they have relied for millennia.

The Nisga'a Treaty provides a window through which to view more clearly some of the debates that swirl around issues such as Aboriginal title and treaty making today. An effort to understand and, if possible, resolve the differences of understanding about the Nisga'a deal is worthwhile, because Canada in the early twenty-first century continues to face Aboriginal title questions. In British Columbia there is still a great deal of territory uncovered by treaty, and at present negotiations are proceeding with fifty First Nations in a process that has been troubled both by First Nations dissatisfaction and the election in 2001 of a provincial Liberal government reluctant to participate in wide-ranging treaty settlements of Aboriginal title claims. The Campbell government conducted an ill-advised referendum in 2002 that aroused strong feelings on both pro- and anti-treaty sides. Valid ballots were returned by only 35 per cent of the electorate, and although the support for the government's position in the responses was overwhelming, the low rate of participation, in combination with the slanted nature of the questions, nullified any legitimacy the consultation might have had. In the aftermath of the referendum, First Nations in B.C. served warning that, if the province did not modify its policies, there were not going to be any treaties for a long time. Early in 2003 the Campbell government announced a change in its attitude to treaty making, and that spring three B.C. First Nations were reported to be close to finalizing their treaties, with the Snuneymuxw voting on an agreement in principle on June 21. In addition to British Columbia, there are portions of northern Quebec where there are no treaties. In all of Atlantic Canada there are only eighteenth-century treaties of peace and friendship, although in 2001,

Newfoundland and the Labrador Inuit signed an agreement in principle with the government of Canada covering part of the central Labrador coast and the northern peninsula, including nickel-rich Voisey's Bay. In the twenty-first century, Canada will likely see many more treaties negotiated, and no doubt some of them will be influenced by the Nisga'a treaty and the controversies that have arisen over it.

The reasons people say they oppose the Nisga'a Treaty, and, by implication, all settlements of Aboriginal title claims, are several and important. Critics complain that in the Nisga'a Treaty Canada *gave* too much territory to the Nisga'a, *granted* them excessive powers of self-government in the territory they retained, and *handed over* to them a "race-based" fishery. However, such views ignore an important reality concerning First Nations lands: the line of interpretation that the Supreme Court of Canada has established over many years. In the case of British Columbia, the Supreme Court pronounced on this matter in the *Delgamuukw* decision of 1997, which expanded the legal notion of Aboriginal title well beyond the *Calder* ruling of 1973: "Aboriginal title encompasses the right to exclusive use and occupation of the land held pursuant to that title for a variety of purposes, which need not be aspects of those aboriginal practices, customs and traditions which are integral to the distinctive aboriginal cultures. The protected uses must not be irreconcilable with the nature of the group's attachment to that land . . . Aboriginal title is a right to the land itself."[48] If Aboriginal title, on which the Nisga'a Treaty and comprehensive claims settlements are based, is "a right to the land itself," then governments who settle Aboriginal title claims in fact *give* claimants nothing. Rather, claimants retain a small portion – in the Nisga'a Treaty about 8 per cent – of their territory, lands that non-Natives have used and enjoyed without paying for the privilege in the past.

Similarly, treaty assurances that the Nisga'a will enjoy about one-quarter of the salmon from the Nass River, on which they have always relied, is merely the retention of the Aboriginal right to gather, specifically in this case, to fish. Treaties from the eighteenth century in Nova Scotia, from Ontario in 1850, from the Prairies in the 1870s, and from the North in the early twentieth century have recognized the continuation of the right to gather the resources of the region covered by treaty. In this respect, the Nisga'a Treaty is simply a variation on the familiar theme of recognizing by treaty continuing rights to gather. Finally, the powers of self-government that the Nisga'a will exercise in the territory they retain do not infringe on the constitutional, political, and legal rights of non-Natives, either in the Nisga'a territory or elsewhere. The Nisga'a Treaty says explicitly that Canada's Charter of Rights and Freedoms, adopted in 1982, will apply to the Nisga'a government in the Nass Valley.

As analysis of the Nisga'a Treaty and the major criticisms levelled against it shows, the most recent treaty in more than three centuries of Canadian treaty making is consistent with principles and practices that had been developed by Aboriginal communities, non-Native politicians, and the courts. Treaty making will continue in Canada because there is still a great deal of land that treaties do not cover, and Aboriginal groups are determined to secure recognition of what they see as their rights. The alternative to making treaty is either settlements by the courts or standoffs that cause inconvenience and harm the interests of both Natives and non-Natives. Judicial settlements, although sometimes necessary, are less preferable than arrangements parties work out themselves, admittedly often with difficulty. If there is neither negotiated settlement nor court ruling on a land issue, then there will be, as Canadians have seen repeatedly since the Oka confrontation of 1990, clashes of angry First Nations groups with resource companies or private businesses. As British Columbia has found out over the years, these disagreements deter investment and economic growth, discouraging the creation of jobs that provide benefits to many sectors of the population.

What are treaties? They are binding agreements between Aboriginal peoples and newcomers, represented by the Crown, that regulate the coexistence of the two groups in the territory we now call Canada. Why are they perceived so differently today by government and Aboriginal organizations? In part the explanation of the differing perceptions of the treaties is found in the varied assumptions and approaches, on both sides largely determined by differing cultural contexts, that the parties brought to negotiation. Aboriginal peoples saw treaties as compacts or covenants, overseen by the Creator, that established a relationship with God and newcomers, and that provided them with support and friendship in the future. Government viewed the agreements as contracts – limited to specified rights and obligations, and restricted to the letter of the government version – that conveyed title to land in return for compensation. Moreover, the federal government has shown itself inclined to shirk implementation when it could get away with it and to apply a legalistic interpretation of the government version of the treaty when Native protests forced Ottawa to honour terms.

Nonetheless, there are common elements in both Aboriginal and governmental views. Treaties concern sharing territory, include an exchange of benefits, and establish a relationship between Crown and Native people. In a country that relies heavily on the extraction and export of natural resources in Aboriginal-occupied regions for its economic well-being, negotiation of the outstanding differences between the parties would seem to be the most logical approach. Perhaps the best advice about future treaty making was offered by the Chief Justice of the Supreme Court in the 1997 *Delgamuukw* decision. Clearly expressing the Court's desire that the parties negotiate a settlement rather than return to the courts for more litigation, Chief Justice Antonio Lamer pointed out "Let us face it; we are all here to stay."[49]

Notes

1 Paul Tennant, *Aboriginal Peoples and Politics: The Indian Land Question in British Columbia, 1849–1989* (Vancouver: University of British Columbia Press 1990), 56–8

2 Hamar Foster, "Honouring the Queen's Flag: A Legal and Historical Perspective on the Nisga'a Treaty," *BC Studies* no. 120, (winter 1998-99): 12-13

3 *Globe and Mail*, February 13, 1996

4 James (Sákéj) Youngblood Henderson, *The Míkmaw Concordat* (Halifax: Fernwood Publishing 1997), espec. 84–105

5 E.E. Rich, ed., *Copy-Book of Letters Outward &c: Begins 29th May, 1680 Ends 5 July 1687* (London: Hudson's Bay Record Society 1948), 9, 13. I am indebted to Professor Arthur J. Ray, who acquainted me with this source. For parallel practices in Northern Ontario and their relevance to Treaty 9 see John S. Long, "'No Basis for Argument': The Signing of Treaty Nine in Northern Ontario, 1905-1906," *Native Studies Review* 5, no. 2 (1989), 19–23.

6 Rich, *Copy-Book*, 36

7 Edward Ahenakew, *Voices of the Plains Cree* ed. Ruth M. Buck, (Toronto: McClelland & Stewart 1973), "Thunderchild's Conclusion," 72

8 This impressive artifact of Iroquois diplomacy has been catalogued in detail in the "covenant chain trilogy" of American historian Francis Jennings: *The Invasion of America: Indians, Colonialism, and the Cant of Conquest* (Chapel Hill, NC: University of North Carolina Press 1975), *The Ambiguous Iroquois Empire: The Covenant Chain Confederation of Indian Tribes with English Colonies from Its Beginnings to the Lancaster Treaty of 1744* (New York: Norton 1984), and *Empire of Fortune: Crowns, Colonies, and Tribes in the Seven Years' War* (New York: Norton 1988); and also in his edited volume *The History and Culture of Iroquois Diplomacy: An Interdisciplinary Guide to the Treaties of the Six Nations and Their League* (Syracuse: Syracuse University Press 1985).

9 J.A. Brandão and William A. Starna, "The Treaties of 1701: A Triumph of Iroquois Diplomacy," *Ethnohistory* 43, no. 2 (spring 1996): 209–44, espec. 228, 232.

10 David L. Schmidt and B.A. Balcom, "The Règlement of 1739: A Note on Micmac Law and Literacy," *Acadiensis* 23, no. 1 (autumn 1993), 110

11 Treaty of Boston (1725) in W.E. Daugherty, *Maritime Indian Treaties in Historical Perspective* (Ottawa: Indian and Northern Affairs Canada [INAC] 1983), Appendix 1, 76. The other pact, known both as Mascarene's Treaty and Treaty No. 239, which emphasized the First Nations' submission and agreement, is *ibid.*, 78–80.

12 Mr. Justice John Turnbull, *Globe and Mail*, November 5, 1997. The ruling was appealed by the province.

13 Treaty of Halifax, 1752, Daugherty, *Maritime Indian Treaties*, 85

14 See Mi'kmaq Treaty, 1760, *ibid.*, 86–7; Treaty with St. Johns and Passamaquoddy Tribes, 1760, *ibid.*, 88–9; and Treaty of 1761 (Miramichi Tribe), *ibid.*, 90–1.

15 Excerpts from Royal Proclamation, Peter A. Cumming and Neil H. Mickenberg, *Native Rights in Canada*, (Toronto: General Publishing 1972; 1st ed. 1970), 291

16 John Borrows, "Wampum at Niagara: The Royal Proclamation, Canadian Legal History, and Self-Government," in Michael Asch, ed., *Aboriginal and Treaty Rights in Canada: Essays on Law, Equity, and Respect for Difference* (Vancouver: University of British Columbia Press 1997), 161–5

17 Quoted in J.R. Miller, *Skyscrapers Hide the Heavens: A History of Indian-White Relations in Canada* 3rd ed. (Toronto: University of Toronto Press 2000; 1989), 123-4

18 Alexander Morris, *The Treaties of Canada with the Indians* (Toronto: Belfords Clarke 1880), 299. See also Arthur J. Ray, Jim Miller, and Frank Tough, *Bounty and Benevolence: A History of Saskatchewan Treaties* (Montreal: McGill-Queen's University Press 2000), 21–31, 15

19 For Robinson, see Ray, Miller, and Tough, *Bounty and Benevolence*, 35–44; and Janet E. Chute, *The Legacy of Shingwaukonse: A Century of Native Leadership* (Toronto: University of Toronto Press 1998), 108–45.

20 Morris, *Treaties*, 303. The full text of the two treaties is found 302–9.

21 R.C. Macleod, *The North-West Mounted Police and Law Enforcement* (Toronto: University of Toronto Press 1976), 3

22 National Archives of Canada (NA), Records of the Department of Public Works, RG 11, vol. 265, report to government 1869, quoted in Royal Commission on Aboriginal Peoples (RCAP), *Final Report. Volume One: Looking Forward, Looking Back* (Ottawa: RCAP 1996), 165

23 Gerald Friesen, *The Canadian Prairies: a History* (Toronto: University of Toronto Press 1984), 137–8

24 House of Commons, *Debates*, May 2, 1870, 1292–3

25 *The Manitoban*, July 1, 1871; Report of the Minister of the Interior for 1876, quoted in Morris, *Treaties*, 171–2; Hugh A. Dempsey, "One Hundred Years of Treaty Seven," Ian A.L. Getty and Donald B. Smith, eds., *One Century Later: Western Canadian Reserve Indians Since Treaty 7* (Vancouver: University of British Columbia Press 1977), 21

26 Morris, *Treaties*, 170–1. Other chiefs named in the message were Kihewin (The Eagle), The Little Hunter, and Kiskion (Short Tail).

27 This and the other quotations from Mistawasis and Ahtahkakoop are from Peter Erasmus, *Buffalo Days and Nights*. Irene Spry, ed., (Calgary: Fifth House 1999; 1st ed. 1976), 246–50

28 Morris, *Treaties*, 272. Crowfoot continued: "I wish them [police] all good, and trust that all our hearts will increase in goodness from this time forward. I am satisfied. I will sign the treaty."

29 Morris, *Treaties*, 208, 225

30 John L. Tobias, "The Treaty Rights Movement in Saskatchewan," F. Laurie Barron and James B. Waldram, eds., *1885 and After: Native Society in Transition*, (Regina: Canadian Plains Research Center 1986), 248

31 Morris, *Treaties*, 240

32 The exception, at least so far as can be inferred from Alexander Morris's account, was the 1874 talks at Qu'Appelle. If this was the case, the most likely reason was that Saulteaux representatives entered the discussions angry at Canada's payment of £300,000 to the Hudson's Bay Company for their rights and interests in Rupert's Land. Saulteaux negotiators tried for more than four days to extract compensation from Canada for the transaction, without success. See *Bounty and Benevolence*, 107–11.

33 Indian Claims Commission, *Landmark*, spring 1999, 1

34 Morris, *Treaties*, 209. The cleric, Rev. John McKay, was Cree.

35 Morris, *Treaties*, 198

36 For an Elder's understanding of the binding nature of the pipe ceremony at Treaty 6 talks, see *The Counselling Speeches of Jim Kâ-Nîpitêhtêw* edited and translated by Freda Ahenakew and H.C. Wolfart, (Winnipeg: University of Manitoba Press 1998), 109-13. On the importance of oral tradition more generally, see Sharon Venne, "Understanding Treaty 6: An Indigenous Perspective," Asch, *Aboriginal and Treaty Rights in Canada*, 173-7.

37 Morris, *Treaties*, 221. See also *ibid.*, 208.

38 Morris, *Treaties*, 204 (non-interference); 211 (also 231) ("put on top"); and 202 (also 237) (permanent)

39 E.B. O'Callaghan, ed., *Documents Relative to the Colonial History of the State of New York*, (Albany: Weed, Parsons & Co., 1855), vol. 9, 966

40 Venne, "Understanding Treaty 6," 193; Lynn Hickey, Richard L. Lightning, and Gordon Lee, "T.A.R.R. Interview with Elders Program," Richard Price, ed., *The Spirit of the Alberta Indian Treaties*, (Edmonton: Pica Press 1987; 1st ed. 1979), 105-6. Interestingly, the oral tradition in Treaty 7, in southern Alberta, is that the treaty had nothing to do with land. Blackfoot Confederacy First Nations recall Treaty 7 as simply a peace treaty. *Ibid.* See also Treaty 7 Elders and Tribal Council, with Walter Hildebrandt, Dorothy First Rider, and Sarah Carter, *The True Spirit and*

Original Intent of Treaty 7, (Montreal: McGill-Queen's University Press 1996), *passim.*

41 Jean Friesen, "Magnificent Gifts: The Treaties of Canada with the Indians of the Northwest, 1869–76," *Transactions of the Royal Society of Canada*, series V, vol. 1, 1986: 41-51

42 Morris, *Treaties*, 211

43 RG 10, vol. 4006, file 241,209-1, John A. Macdonald, Superintendent General of Indian Affairs, to "Your Excellency in Council," January 19, 1887; and minute in Macdonald's hand of March 31, 1887: "no present necessity for dealing with this subject."

44 "Natives exempted from tax in 1899 treaty, family says: Federal government says verbal deal was not a promise," *National Post*, March 20, 2000. In March 2002 the Federal Court of Canada upheld the tax exemption in what was known as the *Benoit* case. It has since been overturned on appeal. For other instances of the clash of oral and documentary accounts see *Bounty and Benevolence*, 201-2; and Fumoleau, *As Long as This Land Shall Last*, 67, 77–9, 90–1, 180, 216–7, 234–5, and 387.

45 Diamond Jenness, *The Indians of Canada* 6th ed. (Ottawa: National Museum of Canada 1963; 1932), 264

46 Trudeau as quoted by Flora MacDonald, M.P., April 11, 1973, House of Commons *Debates*, p 3207

47 http://www.ainc-inac.gcca/ps/clm/ccb_e.html

48 Supreme Court of Canada, *Delgamuukw v. British Columbia*, December 11, 1997

49 *Delgamuukw v. British Columbia*, reasons of Chief Justice Antonio Lamer, paragraph 186

CHAPTER 4

"All This Region Belonged to Him":
Claims

The nervous Mohawk Warriors who waited behind barricades for an attack by Quebec Provincial Police on a fine July morning in 1990 were proof of Canada's failed Indian claims policy. Oka, which its First Nations inhabitants know as Kanesatake, is located on the north shore of the Lake of Two Mountains, just above the confluence of the Ottawa and St. Lawrence rivers in southwestern Quebec. In pre-contact times it was the territory of some of the St. Lawrence Iroquoians who vacated or were driven from the region between the visits of Jacques Cartier in the 1530s and the arrival of Samuel de Champlain in the early years of the following century. Apparently it was used largely as hunting-gathering terrain by First Nations, with no major settlements of Iroquoian horticulturalists in the immediate vicinity prior to the arrival of the French. Nor did the presence of the French in the valley of the St. Lawrence after 1608 lead right away to settlement at Oka.

Oka/Kanesatake developed as a settled community rather than a hunting hinterland thanks to Catholic missionaries in New France. One of the male missionary bodies, Les Messieurs de

Saint-Sulpice, known in English as the Gentlemen of St. Sulpice, or simply Sulpicians, emerged as a major property-holder and evangelical influence on Montreal Island. Among their early religious activities the Sulpicians developed a mission known as La Montagne (The Mountain) to a mixed group of First Nations people from the Nipissing, Algonkin, and Mohawk in the 1670s in what is now downtown Montreal. This mission settlement was typical of a number of the early "reserves" created by French officials in New France. It ministered to refugee groups of First Nations who had been defeated in warfare by other Indians or who were religious refugees whose new-found Catholicism made them suspect, if not unwelcome, in their former homes. The twin European influences of warfare and Christian evangelization created a number of such communities, of which the reserves of Kahnawake, on the South Shore opposite Montreal, and Akwesasne, opposite Cornwall, Ontario, are probably the best known. Kahnawake and Akwesasne were Mohawk communities, but Kanesatake, as noted, began life as a Sulpician mission and refuge for a mixed population of Algonkians – Nipissing and Algonkin, specifically, and Iroquoians – Mohawk.

This community migrated from La Montagne to Lake of Two Mountains in stages. As Montreal slowly grew in the second half of the 1600s, the Sulpician missionaries became increasingly worried that their charges were coming within reach of pernicious European influences from settlers, traders, and liquor merchants. With great difficulty the Sulpicians persuaded the Nipissing-Algonkin-Mohawk group to relocate to the north side of Montreal Island, at an area known as the Sault-au-Récollet, to escape these baleful influences. However, the respite achieved by relocation to Sault-au-Récollet was short-lived, as settlement and the pressure and enticements of the Europeans followed them northward within a couple of decades. Again, the missionaries decided that the best course of action was removal from contact with settlers, and once more with great reluctance the Natives to whom they ministered agreed to relocate away from European settlement. The argument, again, was that the move would be for the Indians' own good. In keeping with French practice, the king "granted" a large estate, or seigneury, on Lake of Two Mountains to the Sulpicians on the condition that the missionaries erect "a church and a fort to be built there of stone at their [Sulpicians'] own cost, for the security of the Indians."[1] The commitment to build a fort recognized that Lake of Two Mountains was on the western outskirts of France's St. Lawrence colony, at a position vulnerable to enemy attack. Nonetheless, the settlement prospered in the early eighteenth century, with seven hundred Native souls in residence in 1743.

In a relatively short time the Native community at Oka became anxious about their title to the lands they occupied on Lake of Two Mountains. The transition from French to British control consequent on the conclusion of the Seven Years' War cast their security into doubt. For one thing, Britain was an officially Protestant country that did not tolerate Catholicism, although the Articles of Capitulation of Montreal (1760) did guarantee the "Indian allies of his most Christian Majesty" the right to remain in their lands and enjoy "liberty of religion."[2] However, since technically the Sulpicians were the seigneurial landholders from the French Crown and Roman Catholicism was not officially tolerated, how much protection this gave the Indians on the Lake of Two Mountains was unclear. Moreover, friction developed between the Indians and their Sulpician missionaries over how they should divide the revenues derived from non-Native settlers who paid to keep their cattle on Oka lands, leading the Sulpicians to state bluntly that their Native charges had no right to the lands. In response, the Indians presented claims to the British authorities in 1781, 1787, and 1795, basing their case on several considerations. First, they maintained, the original grant of land was to them, not the Sulpicians. They once had had a document that confirmed this fact, but they had given it to the Sulpicians for safekeeping and now the missionaries denied all knowledge of it. During the Seven Years' War they had agreed with the British

Indian Superintendent, William Johnson, not to participate in the conflict in return for confirmation that their lands had been granted to them by the king of France. And they had been assured during the American Revolutionary War that if they supported the British they would, in effect, be fighting for their lands and would be confirmed in them. Now they sought this confirmation.[3] Although Britain was unreceptive, its lack of sympathy did not deter the Indians, who continued to lodge petitions asking for confirmation of their title.

In the early decades of the nineteenth century the area around Oka came under pressure from settlement that was typical of most of the colonies of British North America in this period. This process provided a clear example of the way that the onset of the settlement frontier pinched hunter-gatherer peoples. In the early nineteenth century the colonial administration regularly made land grants to settlers in the lower Ottawa River valley without taking into account the customary harvesting rights and activities of the Nipissing and Algonkin with ties to Oka. It was a graphic demonstration of the incompatibility of hunter-gatherers and settlers along the settlement frontier. The Algonkin and Nipissing groups at Oka responded to this settler pressure by registering a claim with the authorities in 1822 to a large tract of land on both sides of the Ottawa River from a point north of the seigneury of Oka to Lake Nipissing, several hundred kilometres to the northwest. Although the Superintendent-General of Indian Affairs enthusiastically supported this petition, British officials rejected it in 1827.[4] At the end of the 1830s, shortly after the Lower Canadian rebellion of 1837–38 that resulted in the suspension of the Lower Canadian legislature and temporary rule by an appointed Special Council, the Sulpicians used their influence to nip the Indian claims in the bud. First, in 1839 the Sulpicians reached a compromise over land usage and access to firewood with the Indians at Lake of Two Mountains, and then in 1840 they got the Council to pass an ordinance to confirm the Sulpicians' title to the Island of Montreal and the lands on the Lake of Two Mountains. This legislative confirmation of title, which was reiterated by the restored Legislative Assembly in 1841, was apparently a reward by the British to the Sulpicians for the latter's efforts to dissuade the local Indians from joining the rebels during the uprising.

Other indicators of the adverse effects of the settlement frontier were also available at Oka in the first half of the nineteenth century. The advance of farming in the region, coupled with the closure of the local Hudson's Bay Company post as a result of the amalgamation of the HBC and the Northwest Company in 1821, meant that those who relied on harvesting the abundance of forest and stream were especially hard hit. The Algonkin-Nipissing claim petition of 1822 explained to Crown officials that they were hard-pressed "in Consequence of the Increase of Population and the Number of New Settlements on the Lands in which [we] were accustomed to hunt and the Game getting Scarcer in Consequence thereof."

The other evidence of how settlement affected hunter-gatherers adversely was the greater decline in living conditions among the Nipissing-Algonkin compared to their Mohawk neighbours. In the late 1820s a military officer observed that the Algonkin and Nipissing gave "an appearance of comparative wealth and advancement in civilization" alongside the Mohawk "wretchedness and inactivity . . ." However, less than fifteen years later, after settlement had taken its toll, things had changed. While the Mohawk were now described as "far from prosperous," the state of the Nipissing and Algonkin had worsened and was now "still more deplorable:" "their hunting grounds on the Ottawa, which were formerly most extensive, abounding with deer, and other animals, yielding the richest furs, and which their ancestors had enjoyed from time immemorial, have been destroyed for the purposes of the chase. A considerable part has been laid out into townships, and either settled or taken possession of by squatters. The operations of the lumber-men have either destroyed or scared away the game throughout a still more extensive region . . ."[5] The response of the Algonkian groups at Oka was to move away to more remote locations in the Upper Ottawa valley, thereby trying to maintain their hunter-gatherer way of life. The agricultural Mohawk remained at Oka, which they called Kanesatake, and soon became embroiled in increasingly bitter conflict from the middle decades of the nineteenth century onward with their clerical landlords.

The unhappy history of the First Nations at Oka illustrated a number of points that help to explain the emergence of Native claims as a major public issue. First, disputes about rights to territory were the product of the settlement era. In contrast to the earlier age of commercial and military relationships, the settlement era led immediately to friction between indigenous peoples and the burgeoning immigrant society over security of territorial tenure and access to the resources of the land. Second, these changes led directly to encroachments on Native lands by incoming settlers whose colonial governments showed little sympathy for the problems that the process of socio-economic change was creating for the indigenous peoples. Third, Native peoples responded to the pressure and threat to their security by articulating claims to the lands they regarded as their own. That the community at Oka petitioned colonial authorities as early as 1781, keeping up its assertion to be the rightful owner of the lands it occupied through the early decades of the nineteenth century, is clear evidence that Native claims are as old as newcomer settlement in this country. Finally, the unhappy story of Oka down to the middle of the nineteenth century also shows that settler society responded to these early Native claims with indifference at best, hostility at worst. Although the occasional British military official expressed concern about the negative impact of settlement on the Indians and urged that their claims, particularly the Algonkin-Nipissing claim of 1822, be granted, the state never took action to shield them from settler depredations or confirm their control of their lands. In fact, the political representatives of settler society used brute governmental power to crush the Native claim and declare newcomer encroachment legal. Squatting on Native lands, dispossession, marginalization, and rejection were the hallmarks of non-Native society's reaction to Native problems and claims in the early settlement period.

From the middle of the nineteenth century until the confrontation in 1990, the Mohawk at Kanesatake tried repeatedly to get Canada to recognize their claim. Petitions, litigation, and occasional confrontations between themselves and their Sulpician landlords produced no solutions. By the twentieth century the overwhelming preponderance of non-Natives in the neighbourhood made their prospects seem dim, a reality that was underlined by the action of the provincial government when it created a nine-hole golf course without consulting the Mohawk in the 1950s. When Canada created a Native claims resolution process in 1974, the Kanesatake people turned to it in an effort to secure justice. However, the process proved legalistic and slow-moving, and the Mohawk of Oka found their claims denied by the late 1980s. When talk arose about expanding the golf course to eighteen holes by encroaching on land, including a reforested area called The Pines, the Mohawk determined that they would not permit further disregard of their territorial rights. That was why there were Mohawk Warriors behind barricades in The Pines in July 1990 when the Quebec Provincial Police (QPP) approached. That is how a QPP officer died in a hail of gunfire.

Although Canadians by 1990 were regularly barraged by news about Indian claims and blockades, the Oka crisis of 1990 still took the country by surprise. Canadians certainly did not realize that many Native claims had deep roots. Claims ranged from Aboriginal title claims such as Nisga'a or Nunavut to more modest cases arising from Crown failure to discharge treaty obligations, to Treaty Land Entitlement, to claims by Metis organizations in the West for recognition and compensation. The variety and complexity of these issues made the claims area a difficult one to comprehend fully, and the mixed results that were produced when political leaders grappled with them contributed to the confusion and bafflement that often dominated public discussion of claims. In the 1990s Canadians often thought that the issue of Native claims was a recent phenomenon, but the Oka case disproved that opinion. An examination of how claims arose, as well as consideration of the efforts that have been made to deal with them, should help us to understand why the Kanesatake Mohawk waited so long and unavailingly for a settlement and why Aboriginal claims are such an important Canadian public-policy issue in the twenty-first century.

In one sense, claims are as old as contact between indigenous and immigrant peoples in this country. From earliest contact, Aboriginal groups have confronted newcomers and insisted that their territorial rights be recognized by the intruders. Around the year 1000, for example, a small colony of would-be Norse settlers on the northern peninsula of Newfoundland was attacked by indigenous people, most likely either Beothuk or Inuit, whom the Norse referred to as *skraelings*. This Native assault on Europeans who were trying to establish a settlement stood in stark contrast with recent interactions between the two groups that focused on trade. In these commercial encounters the Norse found that the local Natives offered no threats, only disappointment when the exhaustion of trade goods forced a halt to trading. Attempts to establish a settlement with families and livestock were apparently a different matter than barter.

The first recorded French contacts after the resumption of European visits to the shores of eastern North America in the early 1500s also revealed that Native peoples were prepared to claim the territory if the newcomers ignored their prior occupancy. A particularly telling example of Native assertiveness occurred on July 24, 1534, at the tip of the Gaspé Peninsula. A party led by French mariner Jacques Cartier, whose ship had by then spent more than a week in the area uneventfully making observations and trading with the local inhabitants,

> had a cross made thirty feet high, which was put together
> in the presence of a number of Indians on the point at the

entrance to this harbour, under the cross-bar of which we fixed a shield with three *fleurs-de-lys* in relief, and above it a wooden board, engraved in large Gothic characters, where was written LONG LIVE THE KING OF FRANCE. We erected this cross on the point in their presence and they watched it being put together and set up.

When we had returned to our ships, the chief, dressed in an old black bear-skin, arrived in a canoe with three of his sons and his brother; but they did not come so close to the ships as they had usually done. And pointing to the cross he [the chief] made us a long harangue, making the sign of the cross with two of his fingers; and then he pointed to the land all around about, as if he wished to say that all this region belonged to him, and that we ought not to have set up this cross without his permission.[6]

Cartier's experience of Native protest at Gaspé in 1534 was revealing. He had encountered no opposition from the Natives he met so long as he was merely cruising the area and trading with them. Indeed, elsewhere he reported that to initiate trade some Mi'kmaq he met "set up a great clamour and made signs to us to come on shore, holding up to us some furs on sticks," and took great pleasure in trading animal furs, often off their backs, for metal goods, mirrors, and cloth products of European manufacture.[7] However, when the French later provided a visible sign of their pretension to claim land at Gaspé harbour, erecting a Christian symbol emblazoned with "long live the King of France," the mood and behaviour of the locals changed sharply. Not even French efforts to dissemble by claiming that the cross was intended merely as an aid to navigation fooled the chief. He recognized an effort to establish some sort of right to the territory of his people, and he swiftly and energetically counterclaimed the land. Like the martial response of the *skraelings* half a millennium earlier, the loud verbal protest of the chief at Gaspé in 1534 demonstrated that claims have been part of the history of Native-newcomer encounter from the start.

In spite of these inauspicious beginnings, the early history of Native-newcomer relations in the northeastern quadrant of North America was not characterized by disputes – claims and counterclaims – over territory. The absence of differences over territory between Natives and newcomers in this first phase of relations is explained by several factors. First, when the French resumed contact with eastern North America in the early seventeenth century after a hiatus caused by internal conditions in Europe, they came by pure chance to a region unoccupied by First Nations. In contrast to Cartier's explorations in the 1530s, when the mariner had encountered not only claims at Gaspé but also large settlements of agricultural Iroquoians at what are now Quebec and Montreal, Samuel de Champlain's efforts at settlement in the St. Lawrence valley in the first decade of the seventeenth century did not come upon First Nations. The agriculturalists Cartier met in the 1530s, people that scholars term vaguely the St. Lawrence Iroquoians, had disappeared for reasons on which the scholars cannot agree. Whether they died out as a result of epidemic diseases brought unwittingly by the European visitors or were driven out by another First Nation for economic reasons is not clear. But what is certain is that they were no longer in residence when Champlain established Quebec in 1608. The French experience in their other New France settlement region, Acadia – along the Bay of Fundy in what later would become known as Nova Scotia – was somewhat different but had the same result so far as Native-newcomer relations were concerned. The Acadians established themselves in farming communities created in part by diking and reclaiming land from the sea. This form of occupancy meant that their use of lands did not impinge on indigenous use and enjoyment. In other words, it was fortuitous that French settlement did not threaten any established territorial rights, and accordingly did not precipitate any Native claims in the first phase of relations.

A second factor that helps to explain the relative absence of disputes over territory in the New France period was the tiny size of European settlement. Because the newcomers along the St. Lawrence and in Acadia were so few they left but a small "footprint" on Native lands. In the early decades of the seventeenth century the French Crown attempted to pursue its colonial expansion in North America through monopolies it bestowed on French trading companies. Although the king regularly required the monopolist to carry and plant in Canada agricultural settlers as a condition of granting a monopoly of trade, trading companies just as regularly evaded these obligations, bringing as few permanent settlers to New France as they could get away with. By the time the Crown took over the administration of New France directly, making it a crown colony in 1663, the settled population numbered only a few hundred. In spite of persistent French efforts to promote immigration and settlement, the colony of New France remained small. When the French lost control of the region to the British a century after it had been made a colony, the population in Acadia and on the St. Lawrence still only amounted to approximately sixty thousand. The significance of these low population figures, especially in light of the fact that French settlement remained restricted to Acadia and river valleys in the interior where no First Nations were established, was that there was little reason for conflict over territory between Natives and newcomers.

The final factor explaining the relative absence of claims, a factor that also accounts for the slow population increase in New France, was the commercial character of the colony. French agricultural settlement remained small, in spite of the desire of the Crown to foster population growth, because New France's economy was primarily based on fishing and fur trading. In the earliest period of contact much of the presence by fishers and those who harvested whales for meat and oil took the form of annual voyages to the prime fishing grounds, such as the Grand Banks, or whaling waters in the Strait of Belle Isle and the mouth of the Saguenay River. One dramatic indication of the way in which a preoccupation with the fishery discouraged permanent settlement was found in Newfoundland, which was a centre of fishing activity by both French and English. Settlement in the English regions of the giant island was officially forbidden by the English Crown, which saw promotion of the fishery as a means to maintain a large fishing fleet that served as a training ground for crews for the Royal Navy. The same was largely true of the French region of Newfoundland, along the Strait of Belle Isle side of the Great Northern Peninsula. In the English areas, it is recorded, the presence of European fishers promoted conflict between Native and newcomer, but not claims. The English, unlike the French who used salt to cure their catch aboard ship, landed to dry their cod on drying racks, or "flakes." At these sites, which the English fishers left erected from season to season, local Beothuk often helped themselves to tools and other items that the visitors left behind. Such "pilfering," as the English fishers interpreted Beothuk behaviour, touched off violent reprisals on occasion, attacks to which the Beothuk responded by withdrawing into the interior of Newfoundland and away from the intruders and their muskets. One way or another, the presence of fishers did not provoke Native claims in response to newcomer pretensions.

What was true of the fishery was as true or truer of the fur trade in New France. Fur traders had little interest in promoting agricultural settlement, largely because a growing settled population would get in the way of pursuing the fur trade. An expanding agricultural society would drive off game and lead eventually to conflicts with indigenous peoples. Fur traders depended overwhelmingly on local First Nations to locate, capture, and skin furs for trade. For their part, local Innu, Algonkin, Huron, and other First Nations looked to French fur traders as suppliers of marvellous items such as knives, kettles, manufactured cloth, trinkets, and, unfortunately, brandy. The dominance of the fur trade discouraged the growth of agriculture and accounted for relatively harmonious relations between Natives and newcomers in the first, commercial phase of relations. Such a setting, though it could be the site of violence, did not lead settlers to try to take over large tracts of lands for economic practices that got in the way of Native gathering activities. The commercial character of New France accounts for its lack of settlement, its small population, and, consequently, its absence of Native claims in response to newcomer usurpation of indigenous lands.

The dominance of commerce in New France was repeated in all the other regions of the country, with similar consequences. Throughout Canada, the fur trade prevailed, discouraging disputes over territory. When the Hudson's Bay Company began operating in the western interior following receipt of its charter from the king in 1670, the Company's overseers in London instructed their representatives on James Bay to ensure that they obtained the agreement of the indigenous people to the Europeans' presence and commercial activities. Since HBC traders for a century restricted their operations to posts at the mouths of rivers draining into James Bay, there were few occasions for territorial disputes with the Dene, Cree, and Assiniboine of the interior. Even after the Bay began to establish inland posts from the 1770s on in response to increasing competition from Montreal-based merchants, there was no conflict. In fact, it was not until the western fur trade spun off a settlement venture, the Selkirk Settlement in Red River, early in the nineteenth century, that there were signs of indigenous protests against outsider presence and Native assertions of their control of the land and its resources. The clash between the Selkirk Settlement and the Metis at Seven Oaks in 1816 occurred significantly as the commercial frontier between Aboriginal peoples and outsiders was beginning to be challenged by the encroachment of the settlement frontier. There was a revealing echo of this confrontation between settlement and commerce – and, again, it led to forceful assertions of First Nations' claim to the land – in the Treaty 4 talks at Fort Qu'Appelle in 1874. The Saulteaux leaders who demanded the money that Canada had paid to the Hudson's Bay Company for Rupert's Land were asserting their claim to the land.

A similar pattern played itself out in British Columbia from first European contact in the 1770s onward. Here, too, first on

Vancouver Island and along the coast, and later at inland posts as well, the initial form of interaction between Natives and new-comers was the commerce in furs. Whether the interactions occurred in the maritime or land-based phase of the Pacific fur trade, the exchanges did not provoke Natives to assert their ownership of the land. It was only in the middle decades of the nineteenth century, as the Hudson's Bay Company began to shift its emphasis from fur commerce alone to fur trading and resource extraction, that Europeans' activities stimulated Native assertions. Specifically, the HBC began to harvest the forest and mineral resources of Vancouver Island in particular, taking long, straight trees for ships' spars and masts, as well as mining coal for a multi-tude of uses. It was these activities that evoked angry responses by Native peoples who rejected European pretensions. The most dra-matic Native protest occurred in 1846 at Fort Rupert, near the northern tip of Vancouver Island, when a Kwagiulth band first tried to warn off Scots coal miners, and then staked their claim to coal-bearing lands with a string of severed Scots' heads on pikes arranged on the beach.[8] The advent of the mining frontier in British Columbia in the middle of the nineteenth century had an impact on Native-newcomer relations similar to the arrival of the settlement or agricultural frontier in the first half of the nineteenth century in southern Ontario. In all cases where the fur-trade frontier was supplanted by settlement or mining the result was assertions of territorial rights by First Nations. The same was true of British Columbia in the Fraser River gold rush of the later 1850s and the Cariboo phase of the early 1860s. Here, too, treaties were a means of making peace, as in informal arrange-ments that American miners made with some Coast Salish along the Fraser. As well, indigenous groups asserted ownership force-fully, for example in the so-called Chilcotin Massacre of miners by Chilcotin warriors in the early 1860s, when such agreements for sharing territory did not emerge.

The explanation of why the era of commerce in peltries did not provoke claims while the onset of agriculture and mining did is straightforward. Though the fur trade could have its conflicts, as the clashes between the Hudson's Bay Company and the Nor'Westers in the western interior in the early years of the nineteenth century showed, it required co-operation between European and Native. Newcomers needed Native skill and labour to gather the furs and prepare them for market, while Aboriginal peoples strongly desired the trade goods that the newcomers exchanged for furs. Furthermore, as noted above, the fur trade enterprise left a small "footprint" and the activities of European traders did not jeopardize Aboriginal peoples' reliance on harvesting the products, both fauna and flora, of the woodlands. In contrast, would-be farmers or miners cut down the trees to make arable land or destroyed land with mining. The Fraser Gold Rush in British Columbia, in which Euro-American miners disrupted the Salish fishing at selected spots along the river with their camps and their panning operations at river's edge, was an especially sharp example of the incompatibility of mineral extraction and hunting-gathering-fishing.

Far from provoking First Nations' assertion of proprietorship, the fur trade fostered the sharing of territory and much else. One scholar terms the phenomenon "the middle ground" because it was in fur trade country that Europeans and indigenous North Americans met and mixed.[9] The formation of the Métis and country born in the fur trade of the western interior was a clear example of the dynamic of the fur trade that drew different groups together. Whether it was in the trading posts of the upper Great Lakes or in parkland and forest north of the prairies, trader and Native met, formed families, and created a new people. A key element in this process was the emergence of "homeguards," sometimes referred to as the "homeguard Cree," the First Nations who gravitated to and settled around the Europeans' trading posts to avail themselves of the economic opportunities that these outposts represented. Toby Morantz and Daniel Francis, writing of HBC activities in northwestern Quebec, have demonstrated that these clusters of homeguards entered a relationship of economic mutual dependence – symbiosis, to give it a biological label. At certain seasons, the helpful homeguards would provision the post with fowl, fish, and game. Conversely, towards the end of winter – always the hungriest season for hunter-gatherers – the homeguards might be dependent on HBC oatmeal for survival.[10] In such an environment of economic co-operation and mutual dependence, when the foreign fur trader did not fundamentally disrupt indigenous ways of relating to the land, there was little need for assertions of ownership by First Nations.

The initial, commercial phase of Native-newcomer interaction was generally co-operative. With the exception of the Beothuk of Newfoundland, who followed a strategy of withdrawing from contact with the strangers when "harvesting" the goods of the English cod-drying racks led to conflict, and the Chilcotin of interior British Columbia who steadfastly refused to participate in the land-based fur trade, First Nations generally co-operated with commercially minded newcomers.

The same generalization, albeit it with an important twist, applied to the second phase of Native-newcomer relations, the era of diplomacy and alliance. In this period in eastern North America, an epoch that lasted from approximately 1700 until 1817, the dominant European states, France and Britain, along with their North American colonies, were locked in a contest for mastery of the continent. In that engagement their military strategists recognized that securing the armed support of First Nations would be vital to their success. Native North Americans were conversant with the terrain, knew the transportation routes, and were effective forest fighters. That being the case, both British and French bent their efforts to securing the support of the Iroquois and their allies or Algonkian peoples to the north of Iroquoia, the homeland of the Iroquois south of Lake Ontario. If Native diplomatic and military aid could not be obtained by negotiation, then Native neutrality was the newcomers' second most favoured result.

For their part, First Nations in the northeastern part of the continent during this long struggle followed strategies that were founded upon the pursuit of their claim to the territories they occupied. As was noted in the case of the Iroquois League in the Great Peace of Montreal in 1701, First Nations pursued diplomatic strategies that enhanced security in their homelands. In the case of the Iroquois Confederacy, this strategic imperative resulted in 1701 in securing peace agreements that would let them remain neutral in the inevitable showdown between Britain and France. First Nations, almost all Algonkian in culture and economy, in more northerly regions perceived their advantage to lie in alliance with the more commercial society, New France, than with the increasingly agricultural and densely populated Thirteen Colonies of Britain to the south. The consequence of these territorial considerations was that in the Seven Years' War, the final phase of the fight between France and Britain, the northerly Algonkian peoples supported France, while major parts of the Iroquois Confederacy allied themselves with Britain and its colonies. This was especially the case in the colony of New York, where close ties between Britain's major Indian Department official, William Johnson, and the Mohawk prevailed.

After Britain wrested control of eastern North America, First Nations' diplomatic and military behaviour continued to focus on protection of their lands. First, the takeover by the British, whom many First Nations regarded as a more agriculturally inclined people than the French, provoked a wide-ranging war of resistance south of the lower Great Lakes led by Pontiac, a powerful diplomat and military leader of the Ottawa. Pontiac's call to arms expressed First Nations' strategic thinking: "And as for these English, – these dogs dressed in red, who have come to rob you of your hunting grounds, and drive away the game, – you must lift the hatchet against them. Wipe them from the face of the earth, and thus you will win my favour back again, and once more be happy and prosperous. The children of your great father, the King of France, are not like the English.'[11] At the heart of Pontiac's cause was his conviction that the lands from which he and his allies sought to drive "these dogs dressed in red" belonged to the First

Nations, a position he maintained even when negotiating peace at the end of his war in 1765.

This First Nations' claim and the strategy of resisting the expansion of the Anglo-American farmers remained in place for half a century after Pontiac's war. Those nations that resisted the American colonies when they rebelled successfully against British rule in 1775 based their decision on an assessment that the Thirteen Colonies, which were increasingly an expansionist agricultural presence in Aboriginal lands, posed a greater threat to First Nations' security of land tenure than did the British colonies of Quebec and Nova Scotia. The more northerly colonies, now under British rule, had not yet developed agricultural settlements to the same degree as the Thirteen Colonies. At the same time – a point that underlines the fact that First Nations took their decisions during the century of warfare based on calculations of their own advantage – some First Nations sought to remain neutral or even, in a few cases such as the Oneida and Tuscarora, who had close ties to Protestant missionaries from the Thirteen Colonies, to support the rebels. In the long period of uneasy relations following American victory in the Revolution, western First Nations in particular fought resistance actions against the Americans down to the Natives' defeat in 1794. In one victory over the Americans in 1791 they made their feelings about American agricultural expansion into their lands graphically clear: they stuffed handfuls of dirt into the mouths of the American soldiers they had slain.[12] The final phase of this struggle to retain control of their lands against encroaching agriculture came in the War of 1812, when the great Shawnee leader Tecumseh followed a defensive strategy by fighting alongside the British and Canadians against the Americans. Tecumseh's brother, the prophet Tenskwatawa (The Open Door), spoke in terms reminiscent of Pontiac's summons to arms when he denounced the Americans as "the children of the Evil Spirit," and charged, "They are unjust – they have taken away your lands, which were not made for them."[13]

As the continuity from Iroquois strategy in the Great Peace of 1701 through Pontiac to Tecumseh revealed, during the long struggle for control of the eastern half of the continent between 1701 and 1817 many First Nations claimed and fought for their territories in the face of colonial expansion. In general, nations that were associated with the French in fur trade relationships perceived New France as little or no threat to their grip on the territories that sustained them, while increasingly through the eighteenth century they viewed the American colonies, with their greater reliance on agriculture, as a menace to their lands. For the most part, they responded accordingly, supporting the northerly, more commercial society against the more southerly, increasingly agricultural community in the struggle for mastery. The behaviour of the nations that followed Pontiac in the 1762–65 resistance, the eleven years of intermittent warfare following American victory in 1783, and Tenskwatawa and Tecumseh's alliance of western Nations against the American republic in the War of 1812 showed a common pattern. These First Nations diplomatically and militarily maintained a claim to their territories against the pretensions of an encroaching American population. That this century-long strategy of resistance to agricultural expansion consistently failed was, indeed, ominous for security of First Nations' land tenure. Unlike the fur trade period, the century of military struggle had provoked First Nations' claim to land. In the earlier commercial period the question of who controlled the land did not arise because the newcomers were too few and their reasons for being on First Nations' land were compatible with Native interests. In the second stage, the phase dominated by diplomacy and warfare, many First Nations organized to resist the expansion of those Europeans whose land use threatened them. When the First Nations strategy failed again in 1812–14, they had every reason to worry about what would come next.

What came next, of course, was the long darkness of the age of settlement. The onset of the settlement frontier brought with it encroachments on Native lands and disruption of Native peoples' customary way of life. What also has to be noted about the arrival of this blight is that it is dated differently in different parts of the country. In Newfoundland, land of the Beothuk, it began late in the eighteenth century when Britain lifted its prohibition on permanent settlement, and it reached a destructive crescendo early in the nineteenth century. In the Maritime region, in Nova Scotia in particular, the process became noticeable in the later decades of the 1700s, especially after 1784 when the arrival of large numbers of United Empire Loyalists caused a dramatic expansion of settlement and the creation of a number of new towns. In the central colonies, in what are now southern Quebec and Ontario, the onset of the settlement frontier to the detriment of First Nations occurred primarily in the early nineteenth century, especially during the heavy British immigration that followed the cessation of the War of 1812. In Quebec, there had been an earlier influx of Loyalists in the 1780s, but they had gone mainly to a new area known as the Eastern Townships, from which the Aboriginal people were almost completely absent. Most First Nations in Quebec were located either in the far north, in Precambrian Shield country that was inhospitable to agriculture and in which they would continue largely undisturbed until resource industries began to invade their terrain late in the nineteenth century, or in small enclaves or reserves associated with Roman Catholic missions at various points on the St. Lawrence.

In the future Ontario, the invasion of First Nations' lands by agricultural settlers was dramatic and deadly in the first half of the nineteenth century. Representatives of the British Crown, largely following the dictates of the Royal Proclamation of 1763, made treaties with the local Ojibwa to pave the way for non-Native settlers. The Crown kept up this treaty making in Ontario through three rounds lasting until the 1850s: to accommodate the Loyalists after 1783; to provide for refugees after the War of 1812; and to make room for hordes of British immigrants who arrived from 1820 on. While the earlier phases of this recurrent settlement process in southern Ontario had disturbed local First Nations relatively little, the post-1820 wave of farmers-in-the-making was another matter.

Indeed, throughout those parts of British North America that had large amounts of arable land, the early nineteenth century was a menace to First Nations' territorial security. In Nova Scotia and New Brunswick, the latter created in 1784 as a consequence of the Loyalist influx, the settlement era led to the steady encroachment by settlers on First Nations' lands and the gradual dispossession of the original occupiers. Since land treaties had never been negotiated in the Maritimes, what reserves the Mi'kmaq and Maliseet had as the settlement era dawned were vulnerable to settler rapacity. Colonial governments, which were rudimentary and weak, never summoned the will or the means to put an end to the incremental dispossession that Maritime First Nations suffered. In spite of frequent protests by Christian missionaries and occasional government inquiries and calls for defensive action, the colonial state in Nova Scotia and New Brunswick stood by as the First Nations of the region were shoved to the margins of the economy, eking out an uncomfortable subsistence with some gathering, gardening, handicrafts, and alms from the missionaries. A parallel process was observable in southern Ontario in the 1830s, where experimental reserves established in the Orillia–Georgian Bay corridor were subject to encroachment and invasion by neighbouring non-Native farmers. Also in the same colony, the Methodist Ojibwa preacher and chief, Kahkewaquonaby (Sacred Feathers), also known as Peter Jones, struggled for decades merely to secure state recognition of his community's title to their lands. As was usually the case in colonial British North America, his efforts were unavailing. In the oppressive situations that developed in the early settlement era in the Maritimes and southern Ontario, First

Nations entered "claims" by protesting and being supported by some Christian missionaries, but their land claims never succeeded in the face of colonial indifference, if not hostility.

As revealing as the futile claims of First Nations' leaders in Ontario and the Maritimes in the early settlement era are, they pale as examples of the destructiveness of the settlement era alongside the experience of Oka. The desperate straits in which the Mohawk on the Lake of Two Mountains found themselves were all too typical of the adverse effects that the advancing settlement frontier had on First Nations in the nineteenth century. Even more unfortunate than this impact was the fact that settler society seemed to learn little from these experiences.

Treaty making, the other principal artifact of Native-newcomer relations during the creation of a settler society, also sparked Native protests and claims. Indeed, as previously noted, such events as the armed resistance of the Metis to the Selkirk settlers at Seven Oaks in 1816 were merely a spectacular example of the process. Seven Oaks was closely associated with the making of the Selkirk Treaty in 1817. As treaty making expanded in Ontario and the western interior throughout the nineteenth century, the same process of Native claim or protest and state response could be observed. When entrepreneurs and the colonial state ignored the interests of Anicinabe and Metis near Sault Ste. Marie in the late 1840s by authorizing prospecting and mining on Native lands, Chief Shingwaukonse and his mixed-blood allies staged a resistance that forced negotiation of the Robinson treaties of 1850. In parallel fashion, Saulteaux, Assiniboine, Cree, and Blackfoot protests and petitions in the region from the Lake of the Woods to southern Alberta between 1869 and 1875 brought First Nations' insistence that the lands they occupied were theirs forcefully home to the fledgling Canadian state. Statements such as Chief Sweet Grass's 1871 letter to the effect that "We heard our lands were sold and we did not like it; . . . it is our property, and no one has a right to sell them" and the angry stance of the Saulteaux at Fort

Qu'Appelle in 1874 over the compensation that Canada had paid to the Hudson's Bay Company for Rupert's Land showed that First Nations were prepared to stake their claims to land in the face of newcomer encroachment. It was largely because First Nations advanced these claims that the first wave of modern treaty making occurred between 1850 and 1877. The result was that control over and use of a territory stretching from present-day Sault Ste. Marie to the foothills of the Rockies was settled peacefully and quickly.

Native claims continued to be associated with treaty making because the Dominion of Canada continued to show the same insensitivity to First Nations' land rights and lack of concern for First Nations' welfare that had been obvious at Sault Ste. Marie, Oka, and in the West. Unless and until lands controlled by First Nations were desired by resource entrepreneurs based in southern Canada, Ottawa remained indifferent to communications from Native groups about their territorial rights and their resentment of non-Natives' incursions on their lands. Even where treaties eventually were made, the government of Canada stuck to its policy of denying claims when groups came forward to argue that somehow they had been overlooked or left out of the treaty. Modern Canadian history has at least two major examples of this sort of phenomenon: the Teme-Augama Anishnabai claim in Northern Ontario and the Lubicon Lake Cree claim in northern Alberta. Both illustrate the policy of denying territorial claims that has dominated Canadian policy for so long.

The Teme-Augama Anishnabai, or Deep Water People, an Ojibwa group associated with Bear Island in the Temagami region, were missed when the Robinson-Huron treaty was negotiated in 1850. The most likely explanation for the oversight was that the treaty was negotiated at the southern edge of the territory covered by Robinson-Huron, and the Teme-Augama Anishnabai lived in and harvested lands far to the northeast. In keeping with its policy of denial and neglect, the Department of Indian Affairs showed no interest in extending services to them so long as they were subsisting by their traditional harvesting methods. However, by the beginning of the twentieth century, forestry and recreational activities began to invade the Temagami region as southern entrepreneurs sought unspoiled forests to exploit and southern residents yearned for rustic alternatives to the urban problems of summer heat and humidity.[14] When the local Ojibwa population began to protest this incursion on their land and exploitation of its resources, the federal government continued indifferent, encouraged in its stance by the Ontario provincial government, which, like most provincial ministries, treated its constitutional jurisdiction as a mandate to assist the entrepreneurial class. The confrontation – First Nation assertion of ownership and governmental denial – continued through the first two-thirds of the twentieth century. The band's tactics shifted after the election of a dynamic leader, Gary Potts, in 1972. Under his leadership they went to court in 1973 and succeeded temporarily in getting a caution placed on all Crown lands in 110 townships. This action angered the pulp companies and their local workers in centres such as Kapuskasing and worried recreational users on the forests and lakes, needless to say. Eventually the First Nation's legal case was rejected in the courts, and repeated efforts to negotiate a settlement through the remainder of the twentieth century failed. The Temagami claim stands unresolved in the early years of the twenty-first century, and Gary Potts, like Joseph Gosnell, faces the prospect of going grey in pursuit of justice.

The Temagami and Lubicon Lake claims had some resemblances. The Cree of the Lubicon Lake area had not been included in Treaty 8 (1899–1900), and, like the Teme-Augama Anishnabai, were handled on an out-of-sight-out-of-mind basis by government for the next forty years. This malign neglect was not all that worrisome to the Lubicon Lake Cree so long as their lands remained largely unaffected by settlement or resource development. Since the region was not suitable for agriculture, they were safe from the homesteader who would drive off the game and disrupt their harvesting economy. However, the district in which they resided was rich in petroleum reserves, and by the 1940s the Lubicon Lake area was being disrupted by oil exploration.[15] The Lubicon Lake Cree responded in the now-familiar way, by objecting to the invasion and expressing interest in entering treaty and obtaining a reserve that would be exempt from oil-company activity. Although initially both provincial and federal governments favoured responding positively, for a variety of reasons the reserve was never created. Moreover, in keeping with its policy of unmaking Indians wherever possible, Indian Affairs officials in the late 1940s reduced the number of people who were eligible for a share of reserve land by arbitrarily declaring hundreds of Lubicon Lake Cree not to be members of the community. The hidden logic in such apparently bizarre behaviour was that, since treaty entitlement to reserves was calculated on a per capita (or per family of five) basis, the fewer the Lubicon the smaller their future reserve. Such tactics exacerbated relations and prevented the implementation of the plan to create a reserve. The oil and gas boom that struck Alberta in the 1970s simply raised the stakes and made resolution of the claim more difficult. As with the Temagami band, the Lubicon Lake Cree benefited from energetic leadership when Bernard Ominayak became chief in 1984. In spite of legal action, face-to-face negotiations, and even a Lubicon-inspired boycott of the 1988 Winter Olympics in Calgary, no solution was achieved. Like the Teme-Augama Anishnabai, the Lubicon Lake Cree are still without resolution of their claim today. Bernard Ominayak, like Gary Potts, still works and hopes for a just conclusion.

The inability of First Nations such as the Teme-Augama Anishnabai and Lubicon Lake Cree to satisfactorily resolve their territorial claims was a product of Indian Affairs' indifference and hostility that was so visible by 1920, and which lasted for a good fifty years after that. In 1927 the government of Canada made it more difficult for bands to pursue claims by amending the Indian Act to outlaw soliciting or giving money for support of an Indian claim. As though ignoring First Nations unless their lands were coveted was not bad enough, or using the Indian Act to make pursuit of claims difficult, the federal government added to the troubled relationship between itself and First Nations the animosity resulting from decades of failed DIA policies. For its own part, government was increasingly beset by doubt about the efficacy and morality of its racially motivated programs such as residential schools, interference with governance, and denial of basic freedoms such as raising money to pursue a claim. This questioning of policy led to minor modifications in the 1951 Indian Act revision but otherwise the old ways persisted until at least the 1970s. At the same time, Aboriginal communities were beginning to organize politically. As a growing number of them, although still a relatively small minority in their communities, became educated in Euro-Canadian motives and sensitized to Euro-Canadian political practices, these organizations became more assertive. Certainly, the blatant injustice that included Ottawa's consistent ignoring of land claims helped to energize the movement for political organization by irritating Native communities about the treatment they received.

These twin processes of growing irritation and increasing politicization were visible in the history of the Oka claim. The dispute between the Indians of Kanesatake and the Sulpicians on the Lake of Two Mountains simply went from bad to worse from the 1840s onward. The two parties continued to bicker over control, mainly in disputes over the Natives' development of a trade in firewood for nearby communities. The Sulpicians claimed that the Mohawk had the right to cut wood for their own use but not for sale; the Indians ignored them. This economic dispute – simply a product of the quarrel over ownership – was exacerbated by the conversion of most of the Mohawk who remained at Kanesatake to Protestantism in the 1860s and early 1870s. This denominational overlay led to inflammatory events such as a court-ordered dismantling of the Methodist chapel and the destruction of the Catholic church by an unexplained early morning fire in 1877. Chief Joseph Onasakenrat, a former Sulpician protegé who converted to Methodism, was arrested when he challenged the priests' ownership of the disputed lands. The partially denominational dispute of Oka spread dangerously, as a Protestant Defence Association was formed in Montreal and Roman Catholic Quebec lined up in support of the Sulpicians. The federal government tried to cool the situation by two different policies throughout the late nineteenth century and early twentieth century. First, it sponsored the relocation away from Oka of some of the Natives, a program that resulted in removing the few remaining Algonkians, in effect leaving Kanesatake a Mohawk community. As well, Ottawa encouraged and ultimately bankrolled a reference of the dispute to the courts, a policy that culminated in a decision in 1911 by the Judicial Committee of the Privy Council, the highest court in the British Empire, in favour of the Sulpicians. The Mohawk refused to accept this decision as legitimate, but were forced to watch in frustration as parcels of the lands they considered theirs were handed to various interests, including an increasing number of non-Native residential dwellers.

The Oka dispute serves as a barometer of Native claims in general. Up until the 1940s the experience of the Mohawk at Kanesatake had been virtually identical to that of the Lubicon Lake Cree in Alberta or the Teme-Augama Anishnabai in Northern Ontario. Their assertions about their territory were ignored while its resources were harvested by outsiders. However, after the Second World War the terrain of Native claims began to shift, noticeably first in the work of the Joint Parliamentary Committee on the Indian Act that heard from First Nations between 1946 and 1948. The Joint Parliamentary Committee, which contained both Members of Parliament and Senators, was set up to advise on how the Indian Act should be amended. Its creation recognized both that the Indian Act was decrepit, discredited, and ineffectual, and that the racist assumptions on which it was based were out of step with modern times and values. Senators and MPs, with the advice and criticism of First Nations' representatives, were searching for a consensus on legislation that would not offend against current moral and ideological values, which were becoming more culturally pluralistic and morally relative, and might prove more effective in dealing with First Nations.

What the Joint Parliamentary Committee got in its hearings between 1946 and 1948 was a large volume of criticism, advice, and demands. Many First Nations were outspoken in their denunciations of the DIA's interference in their affairs, disregard for their treaty rights, continuing commitment to a segregated schooling system that did not work, and unresponsiveness to their land claims. A forceful example was Kahnawake hereditary chief Matthew Lazare, whose brief to the Committee in 1947 had as its first point "We demand the restoration of our primordial rights, the respection [sic] and fulfilment of treaty obligations, the recognition as a sovereign nation." His submission summarized the Indian Act as "the most bureaucratic and dictatorial system ever imposed on mankind."[16] One spokesman for the Kanesatake Mohawk denounced the legal chicanery of a century earlier by which the Sulpicians had secured a declaratory statute upholding their title with the bitter words, "Since 1841 we have been slaves." Others explained the background of the Oka dispute and demanded that their lands be restored as a reserve.[17] The Joint Parliamentary Committee could not have missed the fact that the Kanesatake Mohawk had a long-standing grievance and claim. A large number of other submissions – much larger than Indian Affairs had anticipated – complained about the inadequate and offensive educational arrangements to which their children were subjected. The government's attitude towards the land claims might be inferred from the fact that the topic was not listed in the eight items that the Joint Committee was instructed to consider. However, the pent-up grievances over unaddressed claims, strengthened by the knowledge among Indian Affairs personnel and Native groups alike that the United States Bureau of Indian Affairs had created a claims commission in 1946 to address land claims in the republic, ensured that claims and resolution processes for dealing with claims would appear in the Joint Committee's deliberations and recommendations. In fact, "The establishment of a Claims Commission" was a prominent recommendation from the Joint Committee.

However, the tactics of evasion and delay with which Indian Affairs had for so long deflected demands for redress from Indian communities ensured that a decisive Indian claims resolution body would not be created, and that the land claims of Aboriginal groups would continue to fester through the 1950s and 1960s. Again, the experience of the Kanesatake Mohawk illustrates what departmental neglect and evasion meant to those with land claims. On top of all their other problems created by the intrusion of non-Native residents in the area, in 1959 the Town of Oka got a private member's bill through the Quebec legislature to create a nine-hole golf course. This scheme involved the conversion of some "common lands" that the Mohawk had used for woodcutting and cattle grazing to non-Native recreational use. The measure authorizing a golf course carried effortlessly because of the fact that the Town of Oka and the disputed lands were in a constituency represented in the provincial legislature by the premier of Quebec. No one bothered to alert the Kanesatake people to the pending changes. When they learned of the development, they noted "What was once reserved for Indian use and profit is now reserved for golf." "We also consider the building of the clubhouse directly adjacent to our graveyard a desecration and an insult to our sensibilities."[18] However, without an effective mechanism for dealing with their land grievances, and in the face of unsympathetic provincial and federal governments, the Kanesatake Mohawk could do nothing about this further attack on their land base.

Other Mohawk groups in Quebec suffered similar insensitivities in the middle of the twentieth century. Particularly noteworthy was the case of Kahnawake, the Mohawk reserve on the south shore of the St. Lawrence River opposite Montreal that had begun as a Jesuit refuge for convert Iroquoians. By the 1950s Kahnawake was the home of a vibrant Mohawk community in which religious traditionalists and Catholic Mohawk frequently found themselves at loggerheads. There were also profound differences on the reserve between those who favoured traditional, hereditary Iroquois government and those who supported a chief and council elected under the Indian Act. In the 1950s Kahnawake experienced the type of high-handed treatment by government with which their kin at Kanesatake were all too familiar. Within a couple of years they saw the area of their reserve, which was already crowded, reduced by flooding attendant on the creation of the St. Lawrence Seaway and by construction of the Mercier Bridge designed to convey commuters to and from the office towers of downtown Montreal.

The government would be forced to change its insensitive ways before very much longer. Ottawa already lifted the ban on raising or giving money for pursuit of a claim in 1951. As well, the combination of judicial action in the *Calder* or *Nisga'a* decision and First Nations' assertiveness in the form of the successful application of the James Bay Cree in 1972 for a temporary injunction to halt work on the mammoth James Bay hydroelectric power project pushed the government of Canada to set up mechanisms for addressing land-related claims. In addition to setting up a comprehensive claims resolution process to deal with claims based on assertions of Aboriginal title, which would lead eventually to modern-day treaties, the creation of an Office of Native Claims in 1974 also provided a method of dealing with what the government called specific claims. Unlike comprehensive or Aboriginal title claims, specific claims were more limited in their scope. The key concept in the government's notion of specific claims was "lawful obligation" – the idea that the Crown still owed an Aboriginal group something because an obligation that the government had incurred to the group had not been discharged. Specific claims did not have to be claims for lands. Specific claims could arise from any undischarged Crown obligation, such as, for example, the promise in some of the western treaties to provide ammunition and twine (the latter for fishing nets) to the First Nations signatories. If, as often happened, the Department of

Indian Affairs neglected to give ammunition and twine to a band that was entitled to it under treaty, that band had a specific claim because the Crown had not fulfilled its "lawful obligation," created by the treaty in this case, to the band. Although specific claims were not necessarily about lands, in fact a large proportion of those advanced after 1974 would be.

The Office of Native Claims (ONC) that was established in 1974 was assigned several tasks in relation to claims. The ONC was empowered to advance funds to a band to help it to carry out the research that often was needed to substantiate a claim. Once the First Nation had researched and written up its claim, it submitted it to the ONC, which considered the case and recommended to government on the claim's validity. If the ONC believed that the specific claim had merit, it recommended to government that Canada accept the claim for negotiation. If a claim passed this hurdle and was subjected to negotiation, the Office of Native Claims represented the Crown or government side in the talks. If, and when, negotiations of a claim led to an agreement, the ONC was charged with implementing and monitoring compliance with the claims settlement. Finally, it was the responsibility of the Office of Native Claims periodically to review the operation of comprehensive and specific claims resolution procedures and make recommendations to the government on changes to policy.

Whatever government thought of the process it set up for resolving specific claims, First Nations found it frustrating. In part the problem with the specific claims resolution mechanism was that the Office of Native Claims took a legalistic and arbitrary approach to cases advanced by First Nations. For example, the ONC flatly refused to consider any claim based on events that occurred prior to Confederation in 1867. Hence, a group like the Chippewas of Sarnia, who alleged that their treaty had been breached by Indian Department actions in 1853, simply were unable to make their case to the ONC. Government representatives fell back on positions and arguments that were well engrained in Canadian law but hardly seemed fair as approaches to Native claims. For example, for a long time ONC would not entertain First Nations' research based on oral history, even though the events that often were at the heart of a claim occurred at a time when the First Nation claimant was not yet literate in a European language and did not keep records of the sort that Euro-Canadian society relied upon. Another example was the doctrine of laches, or the defence that a legal action was barred by the passage of time, on which government sometimes relied. The fairness of such technical defences against claims emanating from groups that for decades had been handicapped by poverty, inadequate education, and oppressive Indian Act provisions such as the 1927 amendment prohibiting the raising or giving of money for pursuit of a claim was hard to detect. In 1982 the federal government announced that it would no longer use statutory limitations or the common law doctrine of laches to thwart claims negotiated by the ONC, although it did reserve the right to invoke these defences if a claimant took the Crown to court.[19]

More generally, claimants found the claims resolution process frustrating because it stacked the cards against them. If, as was usually the case, they needed to borrow funds to research a claim, they had to persuade the Office of Native Claims to provide the resources. Later, if they were successful, the money borrowed would be a first charge on any settlement. Once their research was completed, they had to submit their claim to the same ONC for a decision on acceptance. Usually, as the Kanesatake Mohawk found, a specific claim would be rejected without explanation. In their case, having tried unsuccessfully to make a comprehensive claim to a large portion of southwestern Quebec in concert with the Mohawk of Akwesasne and of Kahnawake, in 1977 they filed a specific claim. Then they waited. And waited. And, finally, almost a decade later, in October 1986 the Office of Native Claims rejected the specific claim, saying only that "the Oka Band has not demonstrated any outstanding lawful obligation on the part of the Federal Crown."[20] If, unlike the Kanesatake Mohawk, a claimant was successful in persuading the Office of Native Claims that its specific claim should be accepted for negotiation, it then faced ONC officials across the negotiating table. If the negotiations proved successful and an agreement was reached, the successful claimant would have to rely again on the ONC to implement the claim resolution agreement. The entire process was one-sided, tilted against the Native party.

Moreover, the process was dreadfully slow. When First Nations obtained their advances for research and completed their case, they found that it took an inordinate amount of time for the Office of Native Claims to adjudicate their contentions and advise government on whether or not the claim should be accepted for negotiation. Then, naturally, negotiation itself took time, while government tried to balance its competing responsibilities to the claimant, to whom it owed a fiduciary responsibility, and to the Canadian taxpayers, who would have to foot the bill for whatever negotiated settlement might be reached. Negotiations that dragged on might lead to turnover in negotiators on either side of the table, something that caused still more delays. In a 2002 interview the Director of Negotiations for Specific Claims acknowledged that First Nations complained about turnover.[21] One consequence of the slow pace of dealing with specific claims was the fact that by December 1981 the ONC could report that only twelve specific claims had been resolved, while 250 still awaited resolution.[22] Another sign that the specific claims resolution process was not working expeditiously was the fact that by the early 1980s an increasing number of claimants were going to court, choosing litigation over negotiation, rather than waiting on the Office of Native Claims.[23] Again the experience of the Kanesatake Mohawk was instructive: their specific claim, filed in June 1977, languished in the ONC until October 1986, when it was dismissed with a bland statement that they had not demonstrated there was any outstanding lawful obligation that the government needed to discharge. A review of the claims mechanism by government in 1981 led to minor tinkering with the process

but no major overhaul. And, unfortunately, there was no noticeable improvement in the rate of handling specific claims. In the
mid-1980s the government abolished the ONC, replacing it with a
Specific Claims Branch and a Comprehensive Claims Branch. The
restructuring changed neither government attitudes nor results.
By 1990 there were no fewer than 371 specific claims lined up for
Ottawa's attention, and new claims were being filed at a rate of
fifty a year as claimant bands brought their research to maturity.[24]

The frustrating and unfair nature of the tardy process was clearly
demonstrated in what happened to the Lucky Man band in
Saskatchewan. In 1879 Plains Cree chief Lucky Man adhered to
Treaty 6 because his followers, some 470 in all, were starving.
Although they got fed as a result of taking treaty, they did not get
the reserve to which they were entitled by the agreement. While
Lucky Man waited for Indian Affairs to act on its commitments,
his band swelled to 754 who were paid annuities in 1880 and 802
in 1881. The chief requested a reserve first in the Battleford area
of west-central Saskatchewan, and then in the Cypress Hills in the
southwest. The Department of Indian Affairs pushed him and
other leaders north out of the Cypress Hills in 1882 as part of an
effort to get Indians away from the relatively game-rich region,
the better to control them through hunger. When Lucky Man
returned to the region, he was threatened with arrest, escorted
back to the Battleford region, and refused recognition as a chief.
In 1883 he received annuities, not as chief but as a regular member
of the band. Through 1884 Lucky Man became involved with a
political-diplomatic movement headed by Mistahimusqua (Big
Bear) that aimed at pressuring the DIA to revise the treaties in the
Indians' favour, and in 1885 the two of them, along with a number
of other innocent chiefs, got swept up in the chaos that ensued
when the Métis under Louis Riel rebelled. In 1886 Lucky Man
and his followers were sharing a cramped reserve in the Battleford
area with Chief Little Pine and his band. The following year,
which Indian Affairs much later insisted was the critical date for
determining the size of the Lucky Man band for calculating the

size of its reserve, only seven individuals were deemed to be entitled to receive annuities. It would take no less than 110 years for
the Lucky Man leadership to get a separate reserve established
for themselves, and, when they did in 1989, Indian Affairs calculated their reserve land entitlement based on sixty members – 410
less than when they had entered treaty. The tragedy of the Lucky
Man case was that such injustices, often compounded by bureaucratic resistance, were all too common.

In 1985 the Supreme Court added to the potential burden of
the claims resolution process with its *Guerin* or Musqueam ruling,
a landmark decision that provided judicial recognition for a new
form of lawful obligation. Hitherto the overwhelming majority
of specific claims had dealt with failures to implement treaty
promises, such as providing the requisite amount of land or the
annual allocations of ammunition and twine that some treaties
contained, or improper taking of reserve lands by doubtful surrenders after the reserves were laid out. The *Guerin* case was different in origin and character. The Musqueam band in Vancouver
sued the government for the Crown's failure to discharge its duty
as a trustee in a matter involving lease of reserve land to a golf
course. The band for some time had doubted that the lease contained terms that were favourable to it, but Indian Affairs stymied
their efforts to find out by refusing access to a copy of the lease.
When the Musqueam finally did get to the bottom of the arrangements, they found that the golf club had been permitted to lease
their lands at rates far below the prevailing market. Their suit
alleged that the government, by permitting this arrangement,
had failed to discharge its legal duty to them. Their case rested
on the law of trusteeship, which placed heavy legal obligations on
those who looked after the affairs of minors. Since in Canadian
law, specifically under the Indian Act, "Indians" were minors and
the Crown was their trustee, the law of trusteeship applied to
their case. When the Supreme Court upheld a lower court ruling
that agreed with this interpretation and awarded the Musqueam
band ten million dollars in compensation, the decision effectively

created a new category of "lawful obligation" on which claimants could rest a specific claim.

As with so much else in Canadian Indian policy, the Oka crisis of 1990 appeared to have broken the log-jam in the claims area. It was not that the generations of frustration, exacerbated certainly by the Mohawk's futile resort to the comprehensive claims and specific claims resolution mechanisms, provoked the violence that broke out in July 1990, although those frustrations had steeled the people of Kanesatake to resist any further incursions on their lands. What brought about the clash in The Pines near Kanesatake was the ill-advised attempt by the Town of Oka and its golf course to expand the nine holes it had to an eighteen-hole golf course by incorporating lands that the Mohawk considered sensitive. Their graveyard was at the edge of land abutting the existing golf course, and the proposed expansion would necessitate levelling some of the woods alongside the course. The Pines was to some extent a buffer between one end of Kanesatake and the non-Native world, and the wooded area had great symbolic value to the Mohawk. When the promoters of golf course expansion ignored Mohawk protests and their occupation of The Pines by obtaining a court injunction ordering them to stand aside, the stage was set for trouble. It broke out when the Quebec Provincial Police moved into the woods early one summer morning, resulting in the death by gunshot of a policeman and an eleven-week standoff between Indians, Kanesatake Mohawk supplemented by volunteers from across Canada, and the state – first in the form of police and later the Canadian army. The Oka confrontation, coming only weeks after the failure of the Meech Lake Accord, aroused the ire of Quebec, and threatened relations between First Nations and governments, not just in Quebec but across the country.

The Mulroney government responded to the Oka crisis in a series of steps that included giving attention to the flawed claims resolution process. One major response was the creation of the Royal Commission on Aboriginal Peoples, which eventually reported in November 1996 and was largely ignored by the Liberal government by then in office. However, in 1991 the Canadian government also took steps to mollify First Nations' anger by removing some of the irritating features of the claims process. Its arbitrary limit on the number of comprehensive claims it would negotiate at any one time was raised, and its equally arbitrary refusal to consider specific claims originating in the pre-Confederation period was also removed. What appeared to be a significant concession was the creation of an Indian Claims Commission (ICC). This, as noted earlier, had been called for during the work of the Joint Parliamentary Committee on the Indian Act in the late 1940s, but not implemented. The government indicated in the mid-1960s that it would finally set up a body similar to the American one, but in the White Paper of 1969 reneged on the promise, high-handedly dismissing the idea: "Consideration of the questions raised at the consultations and the review of Indian policy have raised serious doubts as to whether a Claim Commission as proposed to Parliament in 1965 is the right way to deal with the grievances of Indians put forward as claims."[25] All the government did was appoint Dr. Lloyd Barber, later president of the University of Regina, to be a commissioner of claims charged with recommending ways to resolve claims. If 1969, when the governing Liberals were riding high, was not the right time to proceed with a meaningful claims commission then 1991, when the Mulroney government was reeling from the setbacks it had suffered in constitutional reform and Indian policy, apparently was.

Although well-intentioned in its creation and assiduous in its efforts, the Indian Claims Commission proved to be merely another failure in the long history of Native claims. Created to act as a type of appeal body for those whose specific claims had been rejected, the ICC soon evolved a series of procedures that gave such appellants a thorough and sympathetic hearing. Composed almost equally of Native and non-Native commissioners, a minority of whom had legal training, it heard cases put forward by claimants in their entirety, not acting narrowly as an appeal court might have by considering only points of law. Moreover, it proved itself ahead of the Canadian courts by hearing and weighing oral history evidence from claimants. The Commission also engaged in considerable research in the cases it heard, using its own staff. The ICC established a track record of compiling reports on individual specific claims that were models of thoroughness and careful consideration.

The ICC's role in revealing the abusive treatment of some First Nations by Indian Affairs that gave rise to claims came out clearly in the case of the Kahkewistahaw band.[26] Kahkewistahaw (He Who Flies Around) was a Plains Cree chief, son of one of the chiefs who signed the 1817 Selkirk Treaty, and a noted warrior and medicine man. In 1874 he led his followers into Treaty 4 at Fort Qu'Appelle. Although his community were Plains hunter-gatherers, they settled down on a reserve on the south side of the Qu'Appelle Valley in what is now Saskatchewan and began to learn farming. Although the post-treaty years were difficult ones for prairie farmers, thanks both to lengthy periods of adverse weather and misguided policies of the Department of Indian Affairs, the Kahkewistahaw band began to make their way in growing crops and then in raising cattle. There was no doubt, too, of Kahkewistahaw's commitment to peaceful coexistence with the queen's white-skinned children: in 1885 he was instrumental in persuading his followers not to participate in the Northwest Rebellion. On the other hand, negative developments in the early reserve period were population decline as a result of changed diet and disease, and the growing desire of the settler population to get its hands on parts of the Qu'Appelle reserves, including Kahkewistahaw.

Between 1885 and 1907 there were no fewer than six instances when local settlers expressed the desire to acquire large portions of the reserve. In part their cupidity was fuelled by the rapid growth in settler population, especially after 1896, but it was also justified in their own minds by the decline of the Kahkewistahaw population. To each of the entreaties to surrender land, Kahkewistahaw and his followers responded emphatically in the negative. Memorably, in 1902 the aged and blind chief responded to Indian Commissioner David Laird, who had been a Crown signatory of the 1874 treaty: "When we made the treaty at Qu'Appelle you told me to choose our land for myself and now you come to speak to me here. We were told to take this land and we are going to keep it. Did I not tell you a long time ago that you would come some time, that you would come and ask me to sell you this land back again, but I told you at that time, No." Unfortunately for the band, the settler pressure continued and Indian Affairs inclined increasingly to the homesteaders' side. After the band lost its most effective leaders with the death of Kahkewistahaw and two leading councillors, local Indian Affairs officials, with the blessing of the department in Ottawa, returned to the attack. At a meeting in late January 1907, the time selected apparently because the band would be most hard-pressed in the depth of winter, Commissioner William Graham made a renewed request for a surrender and offered a significant amount of cash in the form of per capita payments to the male band members entitled by the Indian Act to vote on the issue. Although the vote against surrender was fourteen to five, for reasons that are disputed another meeting was held a week later at which a majority voted to accede to Graham's request. As a result Kahkewistahaw lost more than 70 per cent of their lands, giving up mainly good, arable land and retaining fields that were not suitable for growing cereal crops or hay for cattle.

When it dealt with a claim based on these events in the 1990s, the Indian Claims Commission blasted the government for the conduct of its Indian Affairs representatives in 1907. The ICC found that the Kahkewistahaw band had a legitimate claim because, although the 1907 surrender was technically valid, the behaviour of Indian Affairs officials then had amounted to the abdication of the department's obligation as trustee under the Indian Act to act in the best interests of the Indians. Specifically, Commissioner Graham's behaviour in setting up the surrender meeting so as to put maximum pressure on the band to give up the land tainted the proceedings. In this case "the evidence indicates not only that Canada failed in its duty to protect the Band from sharp and predatory practices in dealing with reserve lands but that Canada itself initiated the 'tainted dealings.'" The 1907 surrender, the Indian Claims Commission concluded "marked the moral low ebb in the relationship between the aboriginal and non-aboriginal Canadians on the western prairies. For all Canadians, there can be only shame in those events and in the application of that policy to the Kahkewistahaw First Nation." The Commission found that Kahkewistahaw had a valid claim, and recommended that the band and Canada enter into negotiations to set compensation for the surrender. In 2002 negotiations resulted in a settlement of the claim.

There was only one problem with all of this: the Commission was purely an advisory body, and most claimants did not enjoy the success that the Kahkewistahaw band did. Unlike its American counterpart, the ICC was a commission of inquiry with statutory powers only to advise government on what its inquiries found. Unfortunately, government appeared to ignore its findings, which often included clear calls for quick and generous actions to redress specific claims in which First Nations had been wronged. The government often did not respond to the ICC reports and recommendations, or responded only after long delay. The resulting frustration and disappointment jeopardized the ICC, with the commissioners threatening to resign as a group in 1997. Apparently they were dissuaded from carrying out their threat, but their anomalous status – having powers to inquire and recommend, but not implement – did not change. As of December 31, 2002, the last date for which figures are available, there were 525 claims under review, with another 114 under negotiation (ninety-eight "in Active Negotiations," and another sixteen "in Inactive Negotiations.")[27]

In June 2002 the Minister of Indian Affairs, Robert Nault, introduced legislation to change the Indian Claims Commission as part of a new package of Indian Affairs statutes, a package that returned to Parliament in 2003. The measure would create an independent claims-resolution commission with an annual budget of $75 million, with authority to settle claims up to a maximum value of $10 million. While the change to decision-making powers from an advisory function represented progress, the financial limitations imposed on the new body revealed that it would not be able to make much of a dent on the more than five hundred claims that were still unresolved. After deducting administrative costs, the new claims adjudicating body would have sufficient funds to resolve up to seven claims at the maximum allowed per claim, or more if the claims were smaller. Since many of the claims in the past were for much larger amounts than $10 million – the Kahkewistahaw band, for example, settled their claim for $94.6 million – it was obvious that the federal government still intended to force many claimants to litigate their cases in court rather than settle them through the new claims-resolution body. In November 2003, in the last days of Jean Chrétien's prime ministership, a claims commission bill passed through Parliament. However, the modest amount the measure allocates for relatively small claims settlements means it will not solve the claims problem.

It would be misleading to leave the impression that there has been no progress at all on the specific claims front. As was noted with comprehensive claims, there have been some accomplishments, however small they are in relation to the job that needs to be done. In the specific claims area, there have been advances, such as the minority of specific claims that swim upriver through the government-mandated mechanisms to solution, or the judicial recognition of a lawful obligation in the form of the Crown's fiduciary responsibility in the *Guerin* decision. Sometimes negotiation works, too – if you are patient enough. The case of Treaty Land Entitlement (TLE) in Saskatchewan is one of those exceptional cases. Treaty Land Entitlement refers to cases where bands did not get all the land to which they were entitled by the formula in the treaty they signed in the 1870s or the early part of the twentieth century. For example, if a band signed Treaty 4 in 1874, it was entitled to a reserve whose area was to be calculated on the formula of "one square mile for each family of five." The expectation was that a reserve would be laid out that would provide 128 acres for each man, woman, and child, 128 being the figure that resulted when one square mile, or 640 acres, was divided by five. However, many things could have prevented a band in Treaty 4 from getting its full entitlement of reserve land. The government officials might have surveyed the population when many were away hunting or visiting relatives in another community, or the officials might simply have made a mistake. The result of such oversights, unintentional or otherwise, was that many Prairie bands had reserves that were smaller than they were entitled to by treaty. Or, perhaps like the Lucky Man Cree band, they had never got a reserve. Such issues had festered for many decades before governments were willing to grapple with them.

Beginning with the Trudeau government (1968–79, 1980–84) in Ottawa and the NDP government of Alan Blakeney (1971–82) in Regina, Canada and Saskatchewan struggled for close to twenty years before success was reached on TLE. By the late 1970s they had agreed on a formula for settling the problem, but it was never implemented. There was resistance to the settlement plan in some quarters in Saskatchewan for a variety of reasons. Rural municipalities feared that land awarded to claimant First Nations and converted to reserve status would have the effect of lowering the rural councils' tax revenues, because reserves were exempt from taxation. Livestock producers in some locales worried that part of the land that would be taken to satisfy bands' entitlement under TLE would be community pastures on which they depended to graze cattle. Would such lands be available to them on as favourable terms once they formed part of an Indian reserve? The election in 1982 of a provincial Conservative government that relied heavily on rural votes for success effectively created a roadblock to resolution. Two years later, the election of a federal Conservative government headed by Brian Mulroney, who worked closely with

Grant Devine, the new Saskatchewan premier, ensured that negative opinions from Regina would have a hearing in Ottawa. First Nations kept up the pressure, however, and the return of an NDP government under Roy Romanow in 1991 changed the complexion of negotiations, while the Oka crisis made the Mulroney government eager to find solutions to Native issues to which it could point at election time. Modifications were made to make TLE more palatable to rural Saskatchewan residents. Governments would provide one-time compensation to rural councils that stood to lose tax revenue, and the principle of "willing seller, willing buyer" was introduced to remove any fear of compulsion or expropriation of non-Native or Crown lands. Finally, and significantly on the eve of the 1992 federal election, Canada and Saskatchewan signed a Treaty Land Entitlement agreement to settle the issue.

TLE has been an enormous success in Saskatchewan. Twenty-five First Nations in the province qualified for more than $450 million to meet their entitlement, and four more bands joined later, raising the entitlement package to $539 million. The agreement required that bands use most of the funds to acquire lands on the "willing seller, willing buyer" basis to convert to reserve status. However, once their quota of entitlement lands was met, bands could use the surplus for economic development projects. Since the settlement coincided with a downturn in the rural economy, it has proven relatively easy for entitlement bands to acquire land from willing sellers, and often at reasonable prices. Hence, the rural backlash against TLE that long had been a factor in preventing settlement proved not to be an issue. However, TLE bands showed interest in properties aside from farmlands. Since Saskatchewan had already pioneered the creation of urban reserves prior to the TLE settlement by setting up seventeen of these enclaves in no fewer than nine municipalities, and since the urban reserves provided excellent economic development opportunities because of the tax-exemption provisions that reserve lands and residents on reserves enjoyed, it was an obvious choice for some bands to fulfill their entitlement in urban settings. To date this has usually taken the form of purchasing buildings and land in a town or city and seeking their conversion to reserve status. Thus far, there has been little opposition to the process. In other words, TLE in Saskatchewan, although uncomfortably long in creation, has proven to be a major success and a spectacular exception to the rule of disappointing results in the claims area.

At the present time, the broad front of Native claims in Canada is not as encouraging as Treaty Land Entitlement in Saskatchewan is. The accomplishments of the claims-resolution process established in 1974 and augmented by creation of the Indian Claims Commission in the early 1990s have been modest. The future of the claims-resolution agency heralded in the Liberal government's 2002–3 legislative package is uncertain, and, even if it works as it is intended to, it will still leave a large body of claims to be resolved elsewhere.

Major claims that were being handled by direct negotiation also remain unresolved and a source of potential unrest and disturbance. The Mohawk at Kanesatake have settled into an uneasy truce with the Town of Oka and the Province of Quebec, while the federal government continues ineffectually to try to complete a land assembly program that will provide the Indians with a compact territory of their own. Presumably, once that is accomplished, Kanesatake will be established as a reserve, a status it has never enjoyed in spite of repeated demands over a long period by the Mohawk that it be done. The Teme-Augama Anishnabai and Lubicon Lake Cree claims are also unresolved. Governments come and governments go; the Lubicon and their lawyers persist and try to get the governments to negotiate a settlement without success. The political will has never existed in Edmonton or at Queen's Park in Toronto, apparently, to make resolution possible. And there are also major Metis claims, with at least one of long standing, unsettled. The Manitoba Metis Federation launched litigation more than twenty years ago alleging that the Crown owed it compensation for lands that were promised to the Metis of Manitoba in the Manitoba Act but for the most part not granted because of fraud and chicanery by representatives of the Crown. Both claimant and Crown carried out massive historical research in the 1980s, at equally massive cost to the federal treasury, but the case never got to trial on its merits. Early in February 2002 the case was adjourned indefinitely in the Court of Queen's Bench in Winnipeg.[28] A similar court case initiated by the Metis Nation of Saskatchewan to a large portion of west-central Saskatchewan in 1994 has barely entered the research stage and is years from a hearing. The fact that the Metis acquired status as an Aboriginal people in the 1982 refashioning of the Constitution means that Metis claims are a ticking time bomb in the volatile and incendiary claims area. The growing frustration of First Nations with both comprehensive and specific claims, and of Metis at the snail's pace of the claims resolution process is a constant invitation to confrontation, usually in the form of roadblocks and occupations, and, possibly, conflict.

What is to be done? This history should make clear that the problem lies not with the Native claimants but with governments and the general population. Responsibility for the mess in the claims area lies not at the door of First Nations and Metis because it is they, especially First Nations, who have been seeking redress for many years. The First Nations at Oka, more particularly the Mohawk who call their settlement Kanesatake, have been pursuing their claim to the lands that they occupy since they first petitioned the Crown in 1781. Since then they have repeatedly reminded the Crown of their case and their problems, withstood attempts to eliminate the community by having all its members relocate, participated in a major court case that went all the way to the Judicial Committee of the Privy Council, articulated their grievances and demands to a joint parliamentary committee, and availed themselves of both the comprehensive and specific claims resolution processes. Finally, they took up defensive positions in the spring of 1990 and attempted to repel what they regarded as an "invasion" of their lands by Provincial Police in July of the same year. To this day, in spite of federal government insistence that it wishes to resolve the problems at Kanesatake, the Mohawk still await the consolidation of their properties into one compact tract and its conversion to reserve status.

While other Native claimants cannot point to more than two centuries of waiting as the Kanesatake Mohawk can, other groups certainly have been both persistent and patient in attempting to obtain redress of their claims. The Teme-Augama Anishnabai began their efforts to be included in treaty at the end of the nineteenth century, the Lubicon Lake Cree in the 1940s. Neither has been successful, and one wonders if, like the Nisga'a who struggled for over a century until their "canoe arrived," they have decades yet to wait. The Metis Nation of Saskatchewan might well be wondering what lies in store for the land claim lawsuit it launched in 1994. The Saskatchewan Metis are only in the early stages of carrying out the historical research that will be needed to sustain their allegations.

While each of the many protracted claims has its unique qualities that help to explain why so much time has passed and so little progress been achieved, underlying all of them are some common elements that have to be addressed if Canada is ever to improve its record on Native claims. Governments at two levels over literally centuries have lacked the sympathy and political will to address the claims in ways that are acceptable to the claimants. British Crown officials denied the Oka claim for almost sixty years before allowing an appointed council to thwart the claimants by passing declaratory legislation that upheld the Sulpicians' title. In that and other cases, most notably Temagami and Lubicon, federal and provincial governments could never unite on a solution that was acceptable to the claimants. Behind governmental indifference and will is the brute fact that the general population also has not seen the merits of many of these cases. In the absence of public support and desire for resolution, governments do not act. There are always some non-Native interest groups – pulp and paper mill workers in Kapuskasing, Ontario, or oil company executives and petroleum patch roughnecks in northern Alberta – who loudly oppose any move to grant the claim. Until Canadians and their governments change their attitudes, resolution of Native claims will continue to elude the country.

Two sorts of options are open to governments to change the climate for dealing with these claims. The federal government either can delegate resolution to an independent third party with decision-making powers, or it can devote more resources to negotiating claims and providing compensation. The first option was implemented in November 2003 when a claims commission bill passed. There will still remain, however, a significant number of claims in excess of $10 million that that commission cannot handle, and there is every reason to expect that the proposed new claims commission will not make appreciable inroads on the backlog of claims that have already been lodged. The second option is for the federal cabinet to allocate greater resources to tackling claims, both to provide the larger workforce that will be required to deal with more claims more quickly, and also to pay the necessary compensation. Since Confederation, and most visibly since the creation of the Office of Native Claims in 1974, the federal cabinet has been unwilling to take such a step, primarily because support for doing so has not existed among the politically active public.

The obvious question is, Why should Canadians rouse themselves about the claims issue and urge their government to inject more energy and resources into the resolution process? There are at least three reasons. First and most fundamental is the fact that resolving Native claims more expeditiously and effectively is the right thing to do. Just as Canadians, in particular the government of British Columbia, no longer deny the existence of Aboriginal title, they can recognize that changing their attitudes towards the resolution of specific claims will put them on the right side of history. Native claimants, as our history since at least 1781 shows, are not going to give up and go away. Over time the moral and political strength of their case has grown. It will continue to increase and win adherents. Second, there are serious costs to not settling Native claims. Just as in the case of comprehensive claims, where the costs of not settling in terms of foregone investment and development have been acknowledged in British Columbia, failure to settle specific claims is expensive. At a minimum the failure to resolve them retards the development of Native societies, making them more likely candidates for financial assistance from government. In the extreme, as in the eleven-week standoff at Oka in 1990, failure to redress claims can result in crisis, enormous expense to the public treasury, and an international black eye for Canada. Finally, it is wise to settle claims soon because it will never be cheaper to do so than it is now. Delays increase costs by multiplying the expense of research and legal counsel, both of which can be considerable. And delayed settlements are more costly than timely ones because there are now several precedents from comprehensive claims settlements that require compensation to the claimants for the loss of their resources on or under their lands prior to settlement. Native claims should be addressed and settled soon because doing so is the least expensive approach, because it is costly not to settle, and because settling is the right thing to do.

Notes

1 Indian and Northern Affairs Canada (INAC), Claims and Historical Research Centre, "Materials Relating to the History of Land Dispute at Kanesatake (Oka)," document K-59, title of concession, April 27, 1717 (translation).

2 A. Shortt and A.G. Doughty, eds., Article XL of Capitulation of Montreal 1760, *Documents Relating to the Constitutional History of Canada, 1759-1791* (Ottawa: King's Printers 1918), 33

3 Great Library, Osgoode Hall, Toronto, "Privy Council vol. 32" containing "Factums and support documents for Angus Corinthe et al v. The Ecclesiastics of the Seminary of St. Sulpice of Montreal," vol. 1, speech of several Indian chiefs to Col. Campbell, February 7, 1781, 93-6; speech by Principal Chiefs to Sir John Johnson, February 8, 1787, 99-102; and letter of Indians to Joseph Chew, August 7, 1795, 132-4

4 National Archives of Canada [NA], RG 10 Records of the Department of Indian Affairs, Series A3 (Administrative Record of the Military 1677–1857), vol. 492, 30248-51, claim petition to Lord Dalhousie of Algonkin and Nipissing chiefs of Lake of Two Mountains, July 22, 1822; "Documents Relating," G.M. Mathieson's "Blue Book," RG 10, vol. 10,024, John Johnson to Colonel Darling, April 1823; Darling to Oka Indians in council at Caughnawaga, October 5, 1827; and Report of a Committee of the Executive Council, June 13, 1837

5 *Journals of the Legislature of the Province of Canada, 1844-45,* Appendix EEE, Section II, Part 3. See also the testimony of James Hughes, Superintendent, Indian Department, January 16, 1843, in Report on the Affairs of the Indians of Canada, *Journals of the Legislative Assembly of the Province of Canada, 1847,* Appendix T

6 Cartier's Narrative of 1534, H.P. Biggar, *The Voyages of Jacques Cartier* (Ottawa: King's Printer 1924), 54-5

7 *Ibid.,* 53

8 J.D. Belshaw, "Mining Technique and Social Division on Vancouver Island, 1848–1900," *British Journal of Canadian Studies* 1 (1986): 53-4

9 Richard White, *The Middle Ground: Indians, Empires, and Republics in the Great Lakes Region, 1650-1815* (Cambridge: Cambridge University Press 1991)

10 Daniel Francis and Toby Morantz, *Partners in Furs: A History of the Fur Trade in Eastern James Bay 1600-1870* (Montreal and Kingston: McGill-Queen's University Press 1983), 84–93

11 C.J. Jaenen, *Friend and Foe: Aspects of French-Amerindian Cultural Contact in the Seventeenth and Eighteenth Centuries* (New York: Columbia University Press 1976), 7

12 White, *The Middle Ground,* 454

13 Quoted in John Sugden, *Tecumseh: A Life* (New York: Henry Holt 1997), 23

14 This account is based on Bruce Hodgins and Jamie Benedickson, *The Temagami Experience: Recreation, Resources, and Aboriginal Rights in the Northern Ontario Wilderness* (Toronto: University of Toronto Press 1989), which covers the Temagami claim down to the late 1980s.

15 This account is based on John Goddard, *The Last Stand of the Lubicon Cree* (Vancouver: Douglas & McIntyre 1991), which covers events to 1990.

16 Canada. Parliament. *Special Joint Committee . . . [on] the Indian Act: Minutes of Proceedings and Evidence,* Session 1947, June 12, 1947, 1707

17 *Ibid.* 1735 (James Montour re "slaves"), 1788–94 (1944 brief to minister), 1830–1 (George Cree), 1832–3 (James Montour, second appearance), and Lewis Gabriel (1838–40)

18 Canada. Parliament. Joint Committee of Senate and House of Commons on Indian Affairs, *Minutes of Proceedings and Evidence*, No. 1 (Ottawa: Queen's Printer 1961), 14–15, 23–5, 319

19 Canada. Indian Affairs and Northern Development. *Outstanding Business: A Native Claims Policy* (Ottawa: Minister of Supply and Services 1982), 20–1

20 Indian and Northern Affairs press release, "An Overview of the Oka Issue," 3; and Bill McKnight to Grand Chief Hugh Nicholas, October 14, 1986, and R.M. Connelly, Specific Claims Branch, to Chief Nicholas, May 10, 1984. Photocopies of the McKnight and Connelly letters were obtained by an application under the *Access to Information Act* and are in the author's possession.

21 Interview with David Millette, Hull (Gatineau), QC, March 14, 2002

22 Canada, Indian and Northern Affairs, *Outstanding Business: A Native Claims Policy*, 13. This total included twelve claims settled for cash payments of $2.3 million; seventeen claims rejected by ONC; five claims suspended by the claimants; seventy-three claims in negotiation; eighty under review by government; twelve claims filed in court; and fifty others "referred for administrative remedy (e.g. return of surrendered but unsold land)."

23 Daniels, *Claims*, 227

24 Canada, Indian and Northern Affairs Canada, *Transition*, Special Edition, Feb. 1991

25 Canada, Department of Indian Affairs and Northern Development, *Statement of the Government of Canada on Indian Policy* (Ottawa: Indian Affairs 1969), 11

26 This account follows Indian Claims Commission, *Inquiry Into the 1907 Reserve Land Surrender Claim of the Kahkewistahaw First Nation* (Ottawa: Indian Claims Commission 1997).

27 INAC Web site, www.ainc-inac.gc.ca/ps/clm/nms_e.html, "National Mini Summary." The distinction between active and inactive negotiations is not explained. The Web site also reported that 246 claims had been settled, eighty rejected "(No Lawful Obligation found)," and sixty-five were in "Active Litigation."

28 *Globe and Mail*, February 8, 2002

CHAPTER 5

"Left Hanging in the Middle":

Assimilation

A s Ochankuhage recalled the event, "We youngsters were playing tag nearby when someone called me. I stood still and hesitated to approach my elders until my grandfather, Panapin, called me by name.

"As I stood before them, one of the elders pointed to the tatoo I had on my left cheek beneath the eye and said to my grandfather:

"'Panapin, mark that tatoo on your grandson's cheek. You are fortunate indeed to have that mark of identification on your grandson's face. One of the redcoats at Fort Walsh told me that when the westward migration of the whitemen begins in earnest, they will come in swarms like the grasshoppers in flight. They will occupy all of our buffalo country and will build centres like the anthills. When these things have come to pass . . . the Redcoats told me that we would not be able to identify our own people!'

"'And, furthermore,' he continued, 'our children and grand-children will be taught the magic art of writing. Just think for a moment what that means. Without the aid of a spoken word our children will transmit their thoughts on a piece of paper, and that talking paper may be carried to distant parts of the country and convey your thoughts to your friends. Why even the medicine men of our tribe cannot perform some such miracles!'"

Although Ochankuhage "stood spellbound and listened in awe" to these predictions, he was to find from bitter personal experience that the impact of the coming of Euro-Canadians to the Canadian West was far different than the Elder's prediction.[1] "In 1886, at the age of twelve years, I was lassoed, roped and taken to the Government School at Lebret," he further recalled. "Six months after I enrolled, I discovered to my chagrin that I had lost my name and an English name had been tagged on me in exchange." Why did Ochankuhage, "Path Maker" in Assiniboine, become Dan Kennedy? An interpreter told him that "the Principal remarked that there were no letters in the alphabet to spell this little heathen's name and no civilized tongue could pronounce it. As we are going to civilize him, so we will give him a civilized name." Equally unsettling was the grooming to which he was subjected on entering the Catholic school. "In keeping with the promise to civilize the little pagan they went to work and cut off my braids, which, incidentally, according to Assiniboine traditional custom, was a token of mourning – the closer the relative, the closer the cut. After my haircut I wondered in silence if my mother had died, as they had cut my hair close to the scalp."[2] Ochankuhage, or Dan Kennedy, actually thrived in the school, excelling academically and earning the approval and gifts of one of the most highly placed officials in the Indian Affairs bureaucracy. And yet, after graduation from residential school, the young man became an extremely energetic opponent of government policies that sought to control and culturally change First Nations. He advised his band on how they might resist legislation that sought to curb their summer spiritual ceremonies, and, in general, worked against the federal government's assimilative campaign, of which residential schools such as the one he had attended, were a part.

Ochankuhage was only one target of attempted assimilation in a long and depressing history of the policy. Almost from earliest contact between Europeans and North American indigenous people, the newcomers have tried to alter the culture and behaviour of the Native population. Unlike the short-lived Norse attempt to colonize Newfoundland around the year 1000, the French, British, and others who have come to what is now Canada have found elements of First Nations' behaviour and beliefs in need of modification. During various periods of post-contact history the pressure for change has varied. In the French colonial period there was less effort at cultural redefining than there was in the British colonial era; an intense campaign to change Aboriginal peoples for most of the first post-Confederation century gave way by the 1960s to a more subtle approach to the old assimilative game. With equal consistency, the indigenous peoples of Canada have for the most part rejected efforts to change their beliefs and practices. While some individuals and groups have voluntarily adopted European ways – in technologically oriented matters especially – for the most part they have resisted assimilative campaigns directed their way. The problem overall has been that the assimilative effort, even when it failed, still caused damage. It frequently left its Aboriginal targets confused or doubtful about the identity and worth of their culture and themselves, and the resulting dysfunction contributed greatly to the disproportionate representation of Aboriginal people among the powerless, the socially alienated, and the incarcerated. In other words, Europeans' lengthy, misguided, and unsuccessful effort to assimilate Aboriginal peoples to non-Native ways over the past four hundred years has ended up hurting all elements of Canadian society.

Even though the sixteenth-century voyages of Jacques Cartier did not lead to permanent French settlement in eastern North America, they did provide early evidence of the European desire to meddle in the cultural practices of the indigenous population. After only a few days' mingling with Mi'kmaq in the Bay of Chaleur region in the summer of 1534, Cartier observed that the Natives "would be easy to convert to our holy faith."[3] The explorer's expression of interest in evangelizing the First Nations was hardly surprising, for missionary work among the indigenous population was always a high priority for the French Crown that authorized the voyages of Cartier and later explorers. Especially in the seventeenth century, the era in which permanent French settlement took root along the St. Lawrence River and the Bay of Fundy, the French were intensely interested in all aspects of religion, including its export to people in other lands who did not share their Christian faith. For Catholic Europe the 1600s were in many ways a Century of Faith, as a newly revitalized Roman Catholic church responded to the challenge of the Protestant Reformation with internal reform and zeal for conversions, both at home and abroad. The seventeenth-century commitment to the expansion of the Christian religion fuelled a great deal of the European power's efforts to establish a presence in the northern half of North America. Given that emphasis in French society on the propagation of their religion, a desire to evangelize the First Nations in Canada was hardly surprising.

Although France's program of cultural change in North America took primarily a religious bent, it did not always extend to aggressive efforts to interfere with other aspects of the indigenous peoples' culture. For one thing, contact between First Nations and French missionaries in the small settlements on the banks of the St. Lawrence and its tributaries was infrequent, usually once a year when distant Indians brought furs to trade. The other major area of contact was in the Native-controlled hinterland, where the French were outnumbered by the Algonkin or Huron to whom they were ministering. In these settings, the missionary could only combat Aboriginal ways by trying to outwit and defeat his professional rival, the shaman, by providing more efficacious cures or other feats, or privately rail in his journal about the ungodly ways of the Indians. Missionaries at most contact points in New France found their opportunity to alter Aboriginal society and behaviour non-existent.

Moreover, for the most part the French state, which exerted direct control over New France's development in 1663, had little interest in changing many aspects of Native society. In the seventeenth century the French were interested in North America mainly for its furs; in the eighteenth century, the era of a long contest with Britain for control of the continent, they added diplomatic and strategic motives to their reasons for dealing with Indians. After 1700 French planners were interested in the First Nations of the northern part of North America for their potential military strength in times of uneasy peace with their British neighbours and in their actual fighting ability when peace gave way, as it frequently did between 1700 and 1760, to shooting wars along the border of New France and the northerly Thirteen Colonies. Whether the French were interested in the Natives for their ability to supply furs or for their diplomatic and military talents, the newcomers had little reason to believe that changing Native society would advance their interests. It was skills inherent in First Nations society – talent in transportation, hunting, provisioning, diplomacy, and fighting – that made them so valuable as commercial partners and comrades in arms. The contrasting attitudes of missionaries and administrators to dealing with the Indians was perhaps symbolized best by the late-seventeenth-century quarrel between the Jesuits and Governor Frontenac over the use of brandy in the fur trade. The missionaries opposed its use because they saw how it could debauch some First Nations; the Governor was indifferent to such concerns because he focused on Indians in their roles as fur traders and allies.

Given the numerical dominance of First Nations and the relative indifference of the state to changing them, New France in some areas saw a blending of Aboriginal and European practices into distinctly North American patterns of behaviour. This coming together of Aboriginal and European ways was visible in the economic, social, and military life of the colony. The fur trade, for example, induced Frenchmen to emulate Indian ways, for the indigenous methods of hunting, fur-gathering, travelling, and provisioning oneself were obviously the most sensible, far superior to trying to carry out those tasks in the European fashion. The symbol of the way in which the fur trade encouraged hybridization of Native and newcomer was the coureur de bois, literally "woods runner," though in reality the term applied, sometimes disapprovingly, to the young French men who went into the interior, traded and often lived with the Indians, and adopted most of their techniques to survive. Socially, as censorious observers from France often noted, the Aboriginal influence was most visible in the tiny settlements of the colony where the French woman or *Canadienne* adopted the short skirt of the Indian woman to replace the longer garment that was common in France.

In the military theatre, the Europeans quickly adapted to the Indians' style of forest warfare, with lightning raids by small parties replacing the large set-piece battles between opposing lines of infantry that constituted the European style of fighting. Indeed, one military historian has suggested that by the end of the French colonial period military strategists, having been heavily influenced by Indian practice, followed policies that conserved manpower, for example, rather than deploying troops without regard to potential loss of life: "Constant contact with Indian allies in wartime and the success of their tactics resulted in Canadians adopting not only Indian methods of fighting but also their attitudes towards war, such as the idea that victory involved inflicting losses on the enemy without incurring any and that the campaigning season was over when a victory, however insubstantial, had been achieved and honour gratified."[4] This was a North American, and Aboriginal, way of conducting hostilities.

European borrowing or admiration of Indian ways did not, however, mean that the French newcomers regarded Natives as their cultural equals. On the contrary, Europeans viewed Native society as deficient in many ways, although they inclined to view these defects as culturally rather than racially grounded. The logical consequence of that assumption was that the newcomers believed that they could and should modify those aspects of Native society that they found most repugnant. In this regard the principal target of European efforts, as had been implied in Jacques

Cartier's observation before French settlement began, was the replacement of the Natives' animistic spirituality, which Christians termed "paganism," with "our holy faith." Consequently, French missionaries, both male and female, ministered to First Nations wherever they could in New France. Female religious, priests, and non-ordained "brothers" in New France provided a range of social services, emphasizing especially schooling and health care, that were always accompanied by a vigorously expressed message about the superiority of the Roman Catholic faith.

A particularly revealing area of French missionary work was the series of residential schools that various orders created in succession, only to see them fail. First the Récollets and then the Jesuits experimented with small schools to which they attracted some reluctant students in the 1620s and 1630s, but the children either fled at the first opportunity or languished miserably unhappy in the institutions if they could not get away. The priests complained that Indians believed "that they ought by right of birth, to enjoy the liberty of Wild ass colts, rendering no homage to anyone whomsoever, except when they like."[5] By the late 1630s, as the Jesuits were giving up on residential schools, the first order of female religious, the Ursulines, arrived and took some Indian girls into their school. Like male clerical colleagues before them, the Ursulines found that their Native charges were desolate separated from their families and friends, and this experiment, too, soon dwindled. The next phase of French experimentation with residential schooling for Native children resulted from the assertion of direct French rule in 1663, when New France for the first time became a royal colony. French planners concluded that New France could be improved socially by sponsoring more immigration of French settlers and adopting a policy to "Frenchify" the Indians through a more aggressive schooling policy. The aim, said Colbert, the French minister in charge, was to school Indian children in the French, Catholic way so that Indians and French would come to "form only one people and one blood."[6] France and its governor, Frontenac after 1672, coerced the Jesuits and Sulpicians to take more Indian children into their schools, but the results under royal patronage were no different than they had been earlier when the missionaries operated on their own initiative. By the 1680s these renewed efforts at residential schooling were also a failure, and no other religious groups in the history of New France were any more successful than these religious pioneers had been between the 1620s and the 1680s.

The fundamental problem with residential school efforts in New France was that the Natives who were the targets of them wanted no part of what they offered, and that powerful forces on the French side could see little purpose to them. Native society certainly thought, especially when it came to child-rearing and preparing children for successful lives as adults, that it had little to learn from the French. French society seemed to them rigid, ungenerous, and, when it came to dealing with children, down-right cruel. Aboriginal society used little direct discipline in the rearing of children, relying instead on devices such as gossip, ridicule, and shame to curb anti-social behaviour and to shape the younger generation to fit into adult society. Some Indians referred to French mothers as "porcupines" because of what seemed to the Natives cruel French methods of dealing with their children. So far as French fur traders, soldiers, and, eventually, administrators were concerned, it also was apparent that "Frenchifying" Indian society was not needed to make Natives valuable to the newcomers. After all, First Nations already were adept in carrying out those tasks in which the French were most interested. In short, neither Native proclivities nor newcomer priorities necessitated a fundamental alteration of Aboriginal society in the New France era.

What areas of cultural change were visible at the end of the French period were quite restricted. New France had seen some spectacular instances of individual conversion, of which the Mohawk Kateri Tekakwitha was probably the most prominent. She was typical of a small number of Indian women and men who were persuaded that the Christian message was the truth and should replace Aboriginal spiritual outlook and practices. She was famous during her lifetime for her piety and strict religious observances. Kateri Tekakwitha exemplified another factor in the cultural change that took place among a minority of First Nations in New France: she was a resident of the mission settlement that had developed at Kahnawake near Montreal, dying there in 1680. For a variety of reasons New France produced a number of reserves at which Indians who were to a greater or lesser degree converts to Christianity established themselves. Some, like Sillery near Quebec, were the result of missionary initiative, as the Jesuits in this case attempted to establish a sedentary mission near French settlements at which they could propagate their faith. Yet others, like Kanesatake or Oka, were essentially refuges established under missionary administration to which a variety of First Nations repaired after converting to Catholicism in their home settlements or being defeated by First Nation enemies in inter-tribal war. Even in the hothouse atmosphere that prevailed in such reserves it seems clear that complete conversion and cultural change did not occur. Today such southern reserves as Kahnawake and Kanesatake are the sites of strongly opposed religious groups supporting either Christianity or traditional Aboriginal beliefs, and, while it is obvious that there has been considerable adaptation to Euro-Canadian ways, it is equally clear that the residents of these reserves consider themselves proudly Indian.

For the great majority of First Nations people in the area that once was New France, the degree of cultural change is far less than the modest amount in the southern reserves. Most Indians who traded or otherwise dealt with the French in the New France period lived in small communities in Precambrian Shield country remote from the region of settlement along the St. Lawrence and other rivers. Until hydroelectric development and mining ventures began to penetrate northern regions in the late nineteenth century, the residents of Quebec's north had little contact with newcomers. In the twentieth century greater pressure came their way as a result both of greater Euro-Canadian economic penetration and the increased presence of state agencies such as schools and other social services. However, as the response of the James Bay Cree in the early 1970s to the proposed James Bay hydro-electric power project indicated, these northern residents felt detached and different from southern society, as well as determined to preserve as much of their homeland's resource-gathering economy as they could. The resistance of northern First Nations in Quebec to the James Bay hydro juggernaut showed very clearly how northerners remained distinct and apart from the society that had evolved from New France. In short, at the end of the French colonial day in the 1760s there was little evidence of profound cultural change, let alone cultural assimilation of the First Nations.

The British North American phase of Native-newcomer relations brought a heavier emphasis on promoting cultural change by the newcomers. It was not because the dominant newcomers now were British rather than French that relations changed. Contrary to some popular mythology, there has not been much to choose between British and French when it came to their attitudes towards and treatment of Aboriginal people. Rather than ethnicity, the primary explanation for the increased interest during the British era in effecting cultural change lies in the shifting economic patterns of European occupancy and use of northeastern North America. Unlike the New France period, during which newcomers were primarily interested in dealing with First Nations to secure furs or obtain military alliance, during the British North American era (from 1763 to 1867) the motive that predominated among newcomers was the establishment of a settlement frontier. The difference between Native-newcomer relations along a commercial or military frontier and relations between the same two parties in an era of heavy immigration and settlement is that in the latter the strangers were not dependent upon the indigenous population for furs or alliance. The immigrants tended to regard the indigenous population as an obstacle to accomplishing the economic objectives that now brought the newcomers to North American shores. In other words, the altered nature of newcomer motives for their presence among Aboriginal people changed their relationship to Natives and their attitudes towards them. Native peoples went, in the eyes of strangers, from being valued commercial partners and allies to obstacles to economic development.

In such a changed atmosphere newcomers' treatment of Aboriginal people shifted. One of the most dramatic changes occurred in newcomer attitudes towards Native peoples. As indigenous peoples' utility to immigrants declined, their image deteriorated, too. Newcomers tended to regard Natives as useless at best, and barriers to "progress" at worst. In the case of the Imperial government, this shift in attitude was compounded by the fact that Britain began to resent its financial outlays for Indian policy now that the First Nations of North America were no longer militarily useful to them. The two changed sets of attitudes – of settlers and of officials – led to a greatly strengthened desire to effect cultural change in Native peoples. While Europeans during the French era had always shown some interest in modifying Aboriginal religious belief and practice, for example, now British and Anglo-American planners began to gravitate towards programs designed to bring about extensive changes in Native society. In other words, in the era of the settlement frontier, when Aboriginal people were no longer perceived as valuable partners and increasingly were viewed as irrelevancies or obstacles, settler attitudes and government policy both moved towards aggressive assimilation.

Assimilation is a wide-ranging ideology and policy that seeks to eradicate a people's identity and cultural practices in favour of another group's ways of doing things. Sometimes referred to as cultural replacement, assimilation contains two major thrusts or emphases. First, the assimilator aims to stamp out those aspects of the target group's attitudes and practices that are viewed as objectionable, and, second, the proponent of change seeks to implant its outlooks and customs. Such an approach is dramatically different from what occurred in the earlier phase of Native-newcomer relations, the era of commercial or commercial-military relations between indigenous and immigrant groups. However, in the earlier phase these adaptations and borrowings were voluntary and did not disrupt the way of life of the groups that chose to adapt to the ways of the other. Assimilation is different from voluntary adaptation because it seeks to impose extensive cultural change on an unwilling recipient. Such an aggressive approach to cultural change occurs when one group, the assimilative party, becomes numerically and politically dominant, and, as noted, when factors emerge to suggest that there is some gain, either material or in power, to bringing about change. All these factors emerged, of course, in the era of the settlement frontier. Native people were less valued as traders when the fur trade declined and as allies when military conflict in eastern North America ceased after the War of 1812. The population balance changed with heavy immigration, first Anglo-American to Atlantic Canada and Ontario, and later British immigration from 1820 onward. These economic, military, and social changes set the stage for an assimilative assault on First Nations by a newly dominant British society by the late years of the eighteenth century.

A harbinger of the changed Native-newcomer relationship and what it meant for First Nations emerged in colonial New Brunswick after 1787. New Brunswick typified the conditions required for an assimilative regime, because its population balance shifted against the indigenous Mi'kmaq and Maliseet after Loyalists fleeing defeat in the American Revolutionary War began to enter the territory in the early 1780s. Next, the New England Company, a non-denominational Protestant missionary organization centred in Britain, shifted its operations from the Thirteen Colonies to New Brunswick after American victory made the presence of British organizations uncomfortable. Through the 1790s until 1804, and then again from 1807 until the 1820s, the New England Company operated what it termed an "Indian College" in Sussex Vale, not far from present-day Saint John. The theory behind the institution was that the missionaries would teach Native children a basic academic education in the school at which they boarded and, when the children were old enough, place them with local farm families as apprentices. The apprentice children, according to the theory, would learn the skills they would need to live with Europeans, and the host families would receive relatively generous grants from the New England Company.[7]

The actual operation of the Sussex Vale experiment revealed a pattern in assimilative initiatives that would be repeated over and over again in Canadian history. First, Native families initially proved very reluctant to surrender their children to the missionaries. Over time, however, as the economic position of First Nations in New Brunswick worsened as a result of the increasing pressure of non-Native settlement, Indian families gradually acquiesced in providing some children for the Indian College. Second, neither the academic instruction in school nor the vocational training through apprenticeship worked very well, and the Native children did not acquire skills that they would need as adults. Finally, the apprenticeship system often was a system of exploitation rather than instruction. Because of local demand for labour, children were often bound out as apprentices at younger ages than official New England Company policy decreed. Moreover, they were frequently denied a reasonable level of care and support in spite of the generous financial assistance that their colonial hosts received from the missionaries. Worst of all, there was a widespread pattern of exploitation of apprentices, as they were often overworked, physically mistreated, and, in at least a minority of cases, sexually abused. These were all attributes with which Canadian history would become familiar during later phases of the residential schooling story. So, too, was the fact that the New England Company appeared to learn little from the disaster it wrought at Sussex Vale. Although the missionaries eventually closed the Indian College because of the mistreatment of the students and the poor academic and vocational results, the Company merely shifted its operations to other parts of British North America. In the 1820s and 1830s the New England Company would open new boarding schools at Red River and Upper Canada. The failure to learn from their mistakes was a hallmark of assimilators in general, and of residential school promoters in particular.

These later experiments in residential schooling coincided with a cresting of assimilative activity throughout British North America from the Maritimes to the future Manitoba. The increasingly coercive campaign for assimilation of First Nations that became so obvious by the 1820s was fuelled by several forces. One, already noted, was the continuing demographic pressure created by immigration from Britain and settlement. Upper Canada, the future Ontario, was the principal recipient of this immigration, its population increasing tenfold between the end of the War of 1812 and the census of 1851. A second factor was the growing dominance of Great Britain in world affairs, as the high noon of British imperial expansion approached in the decades after the conclusion of the Napoleonic Wars. Imperial expansion was accompanied by renewed overseas efforts by British Christian missionary and humanitarian bodies to export Christianity and British culture and institutions along with British woollens and other manufactures to new overseas possessions and dependencies. The tendency of increased British power and prestige to encourage efforts to foist British ways and values on dominated groups was encouraged in turn by the development of an ideology known as scientific racism.

Scientific racism, as the name suggests, was a body of thought that advanced racist ideas with the supposed support of scientific discovery. Holders of these beliefs, like others before them, believed that there was a hierarchy of racial groups in the world, with some considered more virtuous, progressive, and successful than others principally because of the racial differences. This much was not new, especially among the British who traditionally viewed peoples beyond their tight little island as inferior to themselves. What were new in the nineteenth century were British world dominance and an ideology that purported to show that science backed up with evidence what hitherto prejudice and ignorance alone had maintained: the British (and Anglo-Americans) were the most advanced, highly developed, and, therefore, superior people in the world. Scientific racism was a mélange of theories that included new fields of investigation such as phrenology, which consisted of reading the contours of the human head, and newly emerging cultural anthropology. When British, and more generally European, investigators began reading people's heads or observing non-European societies, they simply and largely unconsciously assumed that European features and ways of doing things were the norm, and all others were in some fashion deviations. Such matters as the shape and capacity of people's crania were, it was argued, evidence for greater brainpower on the part of Europeans. Out of such dubious materials early social scientists fashioned theories about different societies that supported notions of racial inferiority and superiority, all of it presented as science.

Later in the nineteenth century, after the development of Charles Darwin's evolutionary theories, this rudimentary scientific racism would be refashioned into an even more powerful and virulent ideology. Darwin argued that through a process that he labelled "natural selection," species over time adapted to greater or lesser degrees. Those that took advantage of physical characteristics to thrive did best, while those that were not so fortunate in their colouring or other features weakened and fell by the wayside. The process would lead to the "survival of the fittest," by which Darwin and his followers meant simply that in the great competition for preferment that was nature, those best suited fared best. There was no moral element to the Darwinian analysis; Darwin argued that natural selection produced the survival of the "fittest," not the superior. However, in the latter half of the nineteenth century social scientists, especially in Great Britain and the United States, modified the theory to change "fittest" to "best," applied it to human communities, on which Darwin had not pronounced, and in the process produced a virulent strain of racism known as social Darwinism. According to this theory, those societies – such as the countries of western Europe and, increasingly towards the end of the nineteenth century, the United States – that were powerful, rich, and dominant had reached their positions through a natural competition, resulting in the survival and pre-eminence of the "best" among nations. Such perversions of Darwinian thought were used to justify imperial expansion and dominance of non-Caucasian peoples internationally, and at home to justify discriminatory policies directed at African Americans in the United States and First Nations in Canada. The nineteenth century produced spurious science that justified domination of one racial group by another. Such theories also united with Christian evangelism and humanitarianism more generally to buttress programs that aimed at the assimilation of Native peoples in British North America.

Upper Canada became the laboratory for the implementation of this "science" as assimilative policy in the half-century between the end of the War of 1812 and Confederation. Anglican missionaries had been active in a couple of centres among First Nations since the 1780s. After 1815 both the Anglican and Methodist evangelists ministered to a variety of Native groups just as those Aboriginal peoples began to feel the effects of a combination of their own irrelevance to Europeans' developmental ambitions, population loss to disease, increasing settler intolerance, and incipient racism. To this poisonous mixture was added the influence of the state, initially in the form of the British military and Indian Department. The signature by Britain and the United States of the Rush-Bagot Convention in 1817, which demilitarized the Great Lakes and effectively ushered in an enduring peace between the U.S. and BNA, raised in pointed form the question of future relations between the Imperial government and First Nations in central British North America. In the past the rationale for a close relationship between Crown and Indians had been the dependence of the former on the latter's fighting skills, but now the prospect of lasting peace undermined the official justification for Imperial support of First Nations. In that regard, the continuing costs of giving annual presents, both an emblem and preserver of the Crown-Indian alliance for decades, became an issue and cause of resentment in official British circles.

The Imperial response to the uncertainty about its Native policy that was created by changing circumstances in North America was to commence a search for a revised policy, a quest that would end up by transferring responsibility for Indian policy to the settlers themselves. The first phase of this search for a Native policy that suited the altered North American situation was a number of inquiries in the 1820s by British military officials into how policy should be revised. In 1830 Sir George Murray, secretary of state for war and the colonies, observed that "the course which has hitherto been taken in dealing with these people, has had reference to the advantages which might be derived from their friendship in times of war." Since these were no longer "times of war," that policy would no longer do. Instead, a "settled purpose of gradually reclaiming them from a state of barbarism, and introducing amongst them the industrious and peaceful habits of civilized life" made more sense. To that same end another British military official had already proposed a program of encouraging cultural and economic change to the lieutenant-governor of Upper Canada:

> the most effectual means of ameliorating the condition of the Indians, of promoting their religious improvement and education, and of eventually relieving His Majesty's Government from the expense of the Indian department, are, – 1st. To collect the Indians in considerable numbers, and to settle them in villages, with due portion of land for their cultivation and support.
>
> 2d. To make such provision for their religious improvement, education and instruction in husbandry, as circumstances may from time to time require.
>
> 3d. To afford them such assistance in building their houses, rations, and in procuring such seed and agricultural implements as may be necessary, commuting where practicable, a portion of their presents for the latter.[8]

The proposal captured both the humanitarian reasons for shifting policy, helping the hard-pressed Indians to survive difficult circumstances, and the economic, saving the British treasury money. It was no coincidence that Britain in 1830 transferred administration of Indian affairs from the War department to civilian officials.

The emerging policy to promote what officials styled "civilization" among First Nations in Upper Canada was first implemented in what was known as the Coldwater-Narrows experiment between 1830 and 1837. Land was cleared in a tract between Orillia (The Narrows) and Georgian Bay on which Indians were encouraged to settle in relatively compact settlements. The Indian Department and co-operating missionaries provided instruction in both elementary schooling and agricultural methods. All the elements of the policy described as "the most effectual means" of helping both Indians and the treasury were put in place. Unfortunately, however, the policy proved a failure and was abandoned by 1837. The local Ojibwa, the recipients of the tutelage at Coldwater-Narrows, resisted giving up completely at least some hunting and fishing as they prepared to make the transition towards sedentary agriculture. The Indian Department exacerbated the situation by its impatience, failing to understand that the evolution it was trying to foster among hunter-gatherers was one that in Europe had taken millennia to accomplish. And, finally, the Coldwater-Narrows experiment was bedevilled by denominational infighting between Methodist and Catholic missionaries, and by the encroachment on lands set aside for Ojibwa farming by Euro-Canadian squatters. By 1837 this first attempt at fostering "civilization" was abandoned.

In spite of the inauspicious beginning at Coldwater-Narrows, the so-called civilization program remained the central thrust of British policy towards First Nations in Upper Canada until Confederation. In the 1840s, following the recommendations of yet another commission of inquiry into Indian affairs, the Indian Department and missionaries resurrected many of the elements of the failed 1830s policy, now with a significant addition. At a conference of bureaucrats, missionaries, and First Nations chiefs at Orillia in 1846, the Department proposed that Indians relocate to more compact settlements and urged the chiefs to accept "manual labour schools" for their children. These institutions were a contemporary version of residential school, at which Indian boarders would spend half the day in academic instruction and half in work in fields, barns, kitchens, sewing rooms and the like. The theory behind these schools was that they would teach Indian children Christianity, rudimentary learning, and vocationally useful skills, all the while costing their operators a minimal amount because of the child labour that the half-day system guaranteed. At the Orillia Conference Native leaders rejected the proposal to relocate, seeing the idea as likely to result in their losing yet more land, but they agreed to support the creation of manual labour schools, going so far as to promise that they would donate one-quarter of their annuities for twenty-five years for the maintenance of the schools. First Nations' support for residential schools, probably a surprising phenomenon to modern Canadians, resulted from the fact that the chiefs in general wanted their children to have access to Euro-Canadian schooling so as to learn how to deal with the newcomers and their economy more effectively, and that Indian missionaries like Ojibwa Peter Jones and John Sunday were enthusiastic proponents of residential schooling. Men like Jones, an ordained Methodist minister and a chief, expected residential schooling to produce graduates like himself, biculturally educated adults who could function effectively in both Native and newcomer worlds. Other chiefs had more worldly reasons for favouring schooling. Chief Shawahnahness of St. Clair River told Peter Jones in 1833 that, while he rejected Christianity, "we agree to send our children to school that they may learn to read, put words on paper, and count, so that the white traders might not cheat them."[9]

The novel education program of the 1840s was augmented in the 1850s by a legislative program of civic assimilation in the future Ontario. The colonial legislature in that decade introduced definitions of Indian status and provided a mechanism by which adult

Indians might jettison that status, the process of enfranchisement, in statutes passed in 1850–51 and 1857. The enfranchisement program was premised on an assumption that as Indian youths were educated in residential schools they would lose their attachment to their own community and Aboriginal identity – this assimilative outcome was, after all, one of the major purposes Euro-Canadians had for creating such schools – and want to become like other people around them. Schooling, status, and enfranchisement were part of a policy continuum that contemplated Aboriginal society becoming Euro-Canadian over time, as Indians were educated to want to cease being Indians and to prepare for an examination for entry into Euro-Canadian citizenship. It was an integrated policy of social and civic assimilation, with schools expected to alter identity and social ties, and enfranchisement to obliterate separate Indian status. In theory, then, the colonial state had developed a neat program of assimilation in the 1840s and 1850s. Great Britain capped the process in 1860 by transferring jurisdiction over Indian affairs from London to the various colonial governments, thereby effectively abandoning their former allies and trading partners to settler societies that showed little appreciation for Indians.

For their part, when Indians were exposed to the full assimilative blast of these programs, they organized to resist them. The Rev. Peter Jones and the early history of manual labour schools in southern Ontario is a good example of the process. As noted, Jones was an enthusiastic promoter of these institutions, believing that they would equip his people to coexist successfully with the now numerically dominant Europeans. He even expected to be made the principal of the residential school that the Methodists were to operate at Munceytown. However, ill health prevented Jones from taking over Mount Elgin when it opened in 1850, and he and his associates watched in dismay as the school, run by non-Native Methodist missionaries, became an oppressive operation that cared poorly for their young charges in a material sense and subjected them to a barrage of assimilative religious and secular learning. Jones personally turned against residential schooling, none of his sons attending the new schools, and the First Nations of southern Ontario more generally also resisted the engines of assimilation by a form of passive resistance, withholding their children from the schools. By the end of the 1850s colonial legislators recognized (after still another inquiry into Indian policy revealed Native opposition) that the nascent residential school policy was a failure. Nonetheless, these schools would continue to exist in Ontario, and after Confederation they would spread to other parts of the country.

The pre-Confederation experiences of Natives in other colonies of British North America were different in kind, but no better in result than those of Ojibwa and other First Nations in Ontario. The Maritime record was typified by a gradual process of dispossession of First Nations, as settlers steadily encroached on their lands and the colonial and imperial states did nothing effective to prevent the exploitation or help deal with its impact. For the most part, what little assistance First Nations received in the Maritime colonies came from the voluntary efforts of Christian denominations moved by the Natives' appalling economic conditions. There was almost no state policy development like Ontario's, not even in the politically advanced colony of Nova Scotia. The lack of government policy focused on Native peoples was something the Maritime colonies shared with Britain's western possessions. The region that would evolve into the Prairie provinces, part of the Hudson's Bay Company territory known as Rupert's Land until 1870, was neither much beset by settlers nor afflicted with institutions of government prior to Confederation. There was missionary presence and even a short-lived residential school at Red River in the 1820s, but nothing like Upper Canada's extensive network of missionary enterprises developed in the early West. The Red River boarding school did train some Native men in Christianity and academic learning, and one of them, the Rev. Henry Budd, would go on to operate a small boarding school for a time. Like Peter Jones in Upper Canada, Budd was an advocate of schooling, not assimilation. Although the rudimentary settlement of Red River did not manifest the fully developed First Nations policy that pre-Confederation Ontario produced, it was the site of noticeable racism directed by newly arrived Europeans at both First Nations and Métis by the 1830s. This development did not bode well for the future of relations in the prairie West.

In the westernmost colonies of Great Britain in North America, in what would become British Columbia, the pattern was reminiscent of Red River down to the 1850s. The early Europeans were fur traders, who gave way in time to missionaries and miners. Roman Catholic, Anglican, and Methodist missionaries introduced their versions of residential schools by the 1860s, but their efforts did not have a large impact on First Nations. So long as Natives enjoyed numerical dominance in British Columbia – which they did until the 1880s – they did not experience the worst effects of assimilationist efforts by church or state. However, the fact that B.C.'s colonial legislature in the 1850s was sufficiently hostile to First Nations to oppose treaty making did not augur well for relations in the Pacific province either.

By Confederation British North America was well advanced on a path of racial intolerance towards Native peoples and an effort to change them culturally. Whether the various colonies had a developed legislative program of assimilation like Ontario's or not, they all had shown their lack of sympathy for Native peoples in a variety of ways. The process had been capped by transfer of Indian Affairs to colonial jurisdiction in 1860, consigning the victims effectively to the oversight of the victimizers. These developments were ominous for First Nations in the new Dominion of Canada.

Once Canada had completed the transcontinental expansion of the Dominion and made treaties with the First Nations of the western interior by the late 1870s, the federal government turned to formulating a series of initiatives for Indian peoples. As these policies unfolded over the next quarter century, the aggressively assimilative nature of state plans for Native peoples in pre-Confederation Ontario emerged clearly. Post-Confederation Canada usually stuck to the paths that had been blazed in pre-1867 Ontario when it came to Indian policy, in large part because that had been the only British North American colony that had developed much policy and also because many of the leading politicians who decided upon programs in the federal cabinet came from Ontario. As in Upper Canada, when Canada turned after the union of the colonies to formulating a plan to deal with First Nations, especially in the newly acquired West, the country's leaders almost instinctively looked to Christian missionaries to carry out many of those policies.

There were many reasons why a state-church partnership in Indian policy emerged in Canada in the 1880s and beyond. In the first place, the political leaders fashioning policy, like the great majority of Canadians of the time, were themselves Christians who looked to the church and its clergy for direction in many areas of life. Canada was a thoroughly Christian country, most of whose citizens automatically thought of Christian organizations when they considered what to do in areas such as health care, child care, and education. For many non-Native Canadians in the 1880s, most social services came from voluntary denominational organizations. In the twentieth century Canada would develop secular institutions and agencies for the delivery of social programs, but in the immediate post-Confederation decades the churches were still major players in charitable work and social policy. This was especially the case in programs dealing with Native peoples for the simple reason that missionaries had been active in this work for decades. If a government wanted to get services for First Nations communities up and running quickly, it made sense to look to people who had experience in dealing with Natives to deliver them. Finally, government thought of Christian missionary bodies when it pondered Indian policy because it knew that the churches would bring to the task both zeal and economy. Missionaries were enthusiastic about dealing with Native peoples, and they had learned to do so relatively cheaply. As the man whom the federal government appointed to recommend an educational policy for western First Nations put it in 1879, "The advantage of calling in the aid of religion is, that there is a chance of getting an enthusiastic person, with, therefore, a motive power beyond anything pecuniary remuneration could supply. The work requires not only the energy but the patience of an enthusiast."[10] Missionaries were experienced, zealous, and efficient.

So far as the missionaries themselves were concerned, they readily accepted the government's invitation to enter into an informal partnership for delivering assimilative programs to First Nations. First and most fundamental was the fact that close and continuing contact with Native communities would permit them to pursue their primary objective, Christianization of Native peoples. To Christians, First Nations who had an animistic spiritual outlook on the world and followed spiritual practices that lacked – to Christian observers at least – a systematic theology were "pagans." By that term missionaries meant either that Native people lacked religion entirely or subscribed to a mistaken belief. At its most censorious this Christian perception regarded First Nations' spiritual practices as devil worship. Given the missionaries' background and their view of Native societies' spiritual state, it was hardly surprising that the churches were anxious to rescue Natives fallen into error, superstition, or worse by teaching them about Christianity and inducing them to adopt Christian beliefs and ways. The other major motivator for missionaries when it came to serving Native communities was Christian compassion for people who were suffering materially as well as spiritually. Everywhere that the settlement frontier had established itself and spread in Canada, Native peoples had been dispossessed of their lands, seen the game on which they depended for sustenance depleted, and seen their means of subsistence attacked if not destroyed. Christian missionaries recognized these material consequences of the settler presence and were motivated to try to assist Native communities in dealing with these problems. Whenever missionaries are criticized for misguided and sometimes harmful activities in Native society, it might be recalled that the missionaries, for all their deficiencies, at least cared about the welfare of Native peoples. The same could hardly be said of Canadian society in general, and of Canadian politicians in particular.

Missionaries' zeal for proselytization and concern for Native welfare created ambivalent attitudes in their ranks. Because missionaries believed that Native people could overcome their material problems by modifying their way of life and learning to earn a living as Euro-Canadians did, the evangelists in many respects were proponents of Native adaptation to non-Native ways. These attitudes emerged most clearly in missionary support for assimilative schooling and for adoption of farming, ranching, or other European economic practices. To this degree nineteenth-century missionaries were pro-assimilation. On the other hand, missionaries, unlike distant bureaucrats, often lived in close proximity to Native communities for long periods of time in order to carry out their work. They learned close-up what problems Natives faced, and in the process often developed some degree of sympathy for Aboriginal communities beset by disruptive and bewildering change. Most missionaries down to the twentieth century also ministered to Native communities in the Native language simply because that was the most efficient way to communicate with the indigenous people. Christian missionaries spent many months learning an Indian language, and the most adept missionaries also translated scriptures and hymns into Native languages. Methodist missionary James Evans even developed a Cree syllabary, or system for rendering the oral language in written form, while serving at Norway House, Manitoba, in the middle of the nineteenth century. Other churches produced accomplished linguists, such as the Roman Catholic missionary priest A.G. Morice and the Anglican bishop William C. Bompas, as well. Until well into the twentieth century their comfort with Native languages made missionaries unenthusiastic proponents of the government's policies of discouraging Native languages in government-supported schools. Their lukewarm attachment to the thorough-going assimilative program that Ottawa favoured was reflected in their uneasy attitude towards language suppression. Even in the mid- and late-twentieth century, Catholic and Anglican missionaries in the Far North continued to employ First Nations' languages in their evangelical work.

The ambivalence of many missionaries about ruthless assimilation, a feature of the evangelical presence not well understood in Canada generally, is a reminder that the evangelists' attitudes and contributions were more complex, more mixed than they usually get credit for in the twenty-first century. Revelations of the abuses perpetrated in missionary settings – above all in the residential schools that the churches ran on behalf of the federal government – have left the Canadian public with a simplistic, almost totally negative perception of missionaries and their work among Native people. This misperception about missionaries does these people a grave disservice. As noted, they were an honourable minority in Canadian society in caring about the welfare, both material and spiritual, of Native peoples. Moreover, most Christian missionaries who toiled among Native people were decent, hard-working individuals who neither meant nor did harm to Indian children in residential schools or Natives more generally in missions and hospitals. The heinous crimes of a minority have unfairly coloured Canadians' view of the historic role of Christian missions to Native peoples. Missionaries did better in their own day, and they deserve better now.

Who were the Christian missionaries who for their own reasons became partners with the federal government in delivering programs to Native peoples? Particularly in northern and western Canada, Roman Catholic and Anglican missionaries predominated numerically. Among the Catholics the primary evangelical body was the Oblates of Mary Immaculate, or Oblates, although the Society of Jesus (Jesuits) continued their historic role of providing missions and assistance in Quebec and Northern Ontario. With both these churches, but more so in the case of the Catholics, a great deal of the missionary effort – possibly the majority with the Catholics – was provided by female religious. Sisters who took vows of celibacy, poverty, and service staffed the majority of positions in Catholic schools, hospitals, and orphanages. In some of the institutions, particularly a minority of the residential schools such as the Roman Catholic institutions in North Vancouver and Spanish, Ontario, the Catholic female religious ran the institutions. Anglicans, and the Protestant churches that were the major players in Native missions until the middle of the twentieth century, the Methodists and Presbyterians,[11] also relied on a volunteer army of Christian women who raised money for missions in their home communities and often opted to work in the mission field themselves. If government viewed missionaries as providing "a motive power beyond anything pecuniary remuneration could supply" when it came to delivering social programs to Native peoples, the unwaged or ill-paid labour of female missionaries was a large part of the explanation.

From the 1880s until the 1950s the four Christian denominations operated most of the institutions that the federal government used to carry out social policy directed at Aboriginal people. In the latter half of the twentieth century the Catholics, Anglicans, United Church, and Presbyterians were joined by a variety of smaller denominations in running missions and schools. After the Second World War, Baptists, Mennonites, and, especially from the late decades of the twentieth century, Pentecostalists and a smattering of small fundamentalist churches also contributed to the mission field. Whatever the missionary denomination, the activities of the evangelists concentrated on churches and missions, schools, hospitals, and orphanages. The degree to which these activities were funded by the federal government depended on two considerations: how central to government policy the particular social program was; and how little Ottawa could get away with contributing. Generally speaking, the Department of Indian Affairs was most willing to assist with the cost of First Nations' and Inuit schooling, whether day or residential schools, although here, too, Ottawa consistently attempted to restrict and reduce its outlay, regularly trying from the 1890s onward to shift a greater share of the financial burden of Native social policy to the churches or the Natives themselves. Support for hospitals (and later sanatoria) that catered to Indian and Inuit patients was always grudging, with the federal government consistently resisting demands from the missionary churches that more be done to provide health care for Natives. In the Far North in the first half of the twentieth century the Oblates and Anglicans fought a running battle with Ottawa for more health care funding, often with little or belated success. The government's resistance to greater expenditure on Native social programs reflected political reluctance to spend taxpayers' dollars on a segment of Canadian society about which most voters cared little. First Nations, of course, did not have the federal vote until 1960.

However, from the 1880s onward the government of Canada did become involved in a series of social programs and campaigns aimed at First Nations in particular in which the missionary churches participated as partners. The reason that the start date was the early 1880s was simple. By this time Confederation was completed from coast to coast, treaties were made in the West, and major infrastructure initiatives such as railways linking the Maritimes and Ontario or the western transcontinental were launched. Also significant was the fact that the federal government had established the infrastructure of Indian policy, too, with passage of the Indian Act (1876) and creation of a separate Department of Indian Affairs (DIA) in 1880. The era that began in the early 1880s lasted formally until the 1950s, although some of the programs that were instituted in this period continued on after 1950. What many of the DIA policies shared was a strong emphasis on promoting assimilation of First Nations, and, as time passed and the policies proved unsuccessful, a tendency to resort to greater coercion in carrying out the policies.

Chronologically, the first of the government's assimilative programs was residential schooling, an ill-starred initiative that simultaneously revealed the state's predilection for enforced cultural change, Native resistance, and the failure of the policy. As has previously been explained, Canada was not without experience with European schooling for Native peoples, and not unaware that such initiatives were often rejected by the First Nations at whom they were targeted. Residential schools had been tried in New France, New Brunswick, Red River, and Upper Canada. In all those prior efforts, First Nations, some of whom in the nineteenth century expressed a keen interest in obtaining schooling for their young, had resisted the assimilative aspects of what schooling was provided. The abortive experiment with the Mount Elgin school in southern Ontario had shown the shortcomings of using schools run by missionaries for assimilative purposes as recently as the 1850s. Indian communities who at the Orillia Conference of 1846 had pledged one-quarter of their annuities for twenty-five years to support manual labour schools very quickly turned against the institutions once they realized that the schools would mistreat their children physically and wound them spiritually. When the Department of Indian Affairs turned to fashioning an educational policy for First Nations these failures were overlooked.

Although the DIA's decision to favour residential schooling was surprising in light of experience in Upper Canada, in reality it was virtually inevitable given the tenor of the times. Not only was residential schooling a historically proven failure, it violated educational promises in most of the numbered treaties negotiated between 1871 and 1877. In Treaties 1 through 6 "Her Majesty agrees to maintain a school on each reserve hereby made, whenever the Indians of the reserve should desire it," although in the final numbered treaty, the Blackfoot Treaty of 1877 "Her Majesty agrees to pay the salary of such teachers to instruct the children of said Indians as to her Government of Canada may seem advisable, when said Indians are settled on their reserves and shall desire teachers."[12] The shift in commitment from providing "a school on each reserve" to paying "the salary of such teachers," as well as the later inclusion of a clause that said the educational promises would be implemented when doing so "seem[ed] advisable" to the government were a harbinger of what treaty implementation in general, and honouring schooling promises in particular, would mean for First Nations. Indeed, several Plains chiefs reiterated requests for the creation of schools when they met with Governor General Lorne during his tour of the prairies in 1881.

The reasons why Ottawa decided soon after making treaties to use off-reserve residential schools, in violation of commitments in at least six of the treaties, are clear and revealing. First, missionaries and bureaucrats alike were disillusioned with the day schools that existed in Indian communities, arguing that erratic attendance and a continuing influence from home and community that worked to preserve Aboriginal identity and culture rendered the day schools largely useless. In part because of the influence of contemporary American examples, particularly the large residential school in Carlisle, Pennsylvania, planners believed that boarding institutions would be more effective pedagogically than day schools because they would guarantee regular attendance and bar the cultural influence of community and home. Besides the American examples, there were also Canadian precedents that the new Department of Indian Affairs claimed were encouraging. The DIA report for 1880 pointed out that there were no fewer than twelve boarding schools already operating in Ontario, Manitoba, the North-West Territories, and British Columbia under missionary auspices, and argued that their results were "sufficiently satisfactory to prove the superiority of such establishments over ordinary day schools."[13]

By the time Ottawa was ready to announce a new educational policy in 1883, Indian Affairs had come out firmly in favour of residential institutions run by Christian missionaries for both pedagogical and assimilative reasons. Cabinet minister Sir Hector Langevin argued that the new "industrial schools," as the government styled them, should be located away from Indian reserves. "If these schools are to succeed, we must not place them too near the bands; in order to educate the children properly we must separate them from their families. Some people may say that this is hard, but if we want to civilize them, we must do that."[14] The new phase of residential schooling that Ottawa initiated in western Canada in 1883 was clearly as much cultural as pedagogical in purpose from the beginning.

Although federal policy gave pride of place to off-reserve industrial schools for several decades after 1883, these institutions were always a minority of schools provided for status Indians by the federal government and Christian churches. Throughout the history of Ottawa-directed Indian schooling down to the 1970s, more Indian children attended – or, at least, were enrolled in – day schools on reserves than were lodged in residential schools. Moreover, the numerous small boarding schools that predated the industrial school policy of 1883 continued to exist, and in some regions were augmented. Industrial schooling, which began with three institutions in present-day Saskatchewan and Alberta, expanded in the West and British Columbia in the 1880s and 1890s, but by the early twentieth century government was becoming disillusioned with their high cost and meagre pedagogical results. In 1923 the federal government amalgamated industrial and boarding schools into a single category, residential schools, and operated them in tandem with the churches until 1969, when the decision was taken to phase them out. Residential schools of all types were most common in the prairie West, British Columbia, and the northern Territories. They were relatively sparse in eastern Canada, all of Atlantic Canada having only one, and that one created well into the twentieth century. The reason for the small number of residential schools in the East was consistent with their assimilative purpose: eastern Indians, who had been in contact with Euro-Canadians for a long time, were deemed sufficiently adjusted or acculturated from that exposure, and accordingly not as much in need of the cultural change that formed the core of residential schooling's purpose.

Wherever they were located, residential schools all operated approximately in the same way and with much the same results. The Department of Indian Affairs authorized the creation of the schools, established the maximum number of students for which it would pay grants, and regularly negotiated the amount of its per capita subsidy. The churches staffed the schools, supplemented the government's always insufficient funding, and operated the institutions from day to day. Nominally, Ottawa exercised oversight through inspectors, but their visits were infrequent and their influence minimal. Until the second half of the 1950s residential schools operated on the half-day system, like the manual labour schools authorized in Upper Canada before Confederation. Students spent half their time in class and half in work around the school. The half-day system multiplied the barriers to effective teaching, with children who frequently spoke only their Aboriginal mother tongue receiving instruction for only half the time that non-Native children did in public schools from teachers who rarely had training in cross-cultural pedagogy or Indian languages. The latter deficiency was not considered a problem by government, for official policy discouraged the use of Indian languages. This enforced unilingualism discomfited some missionaries, particularly in the late nineteenth and early twentieth centuries, and it never was effectively enforced among Dene children and Inuit students in the North, but it was totally consistent with the assimilative purpose of residential schooling.

In residential schools Native children were subjected to a barrage of Christian, Euro-Canadian teachings that denigrated Native ways. Besides discountenancing the use of Indian languages, the missionaries who taught in the classrooms and oversaw the dormitories and playgrounds also discouraged students' identification with Aboriginal culture by means of a variety of tactics, stretching from the students' recreation to their worship. In the playground there was a strong emphasis on British or Euro-Canadian games, cricket and English football enjoying support for a time in some prairie schools, and such activities as brass bands, Cubs, Brownies, Scouts, Girl Guides, and Canadian Girls in Training being vigorously promoted by staff. In the classroom teachers and students followed a curriculum almost identical to that in non–Native schools of the province in which they were located. In chapel missionary supervisors and clergy usually delivered a religious message with both negative and positive aspects: anything Aboriginal was bad; and everything Christian was good. The aggressively assimilative quality of residential schools' religious instruction was epitomized by a graphic catechetical device that Catholic schools throughout the West employed. Known as Lacombe's Ladder after the famous Oblate, Albert Lacombe, who adapted it from European and American models, this device for teaching religion depicted parallel columns, known respectively as the Way of Good and the Way of Evil. The former led to Purgatory and Paradise, and the latter to Hell. What many students remembered most about Lacombe's Ladder, as a former student in Saskatchewan explained, was that most of the people on the road to Hell were Native: "If you participated in your rituals and things like that, that's where you were going to end up," he recalled. On the other hand, "you were an angel if you followed the priest or nun walking with a cross. . . . You went to heaven if you were white."[15] The assimilative aim of residential schools could not have been clearer than it was in the alternatives for Eternity presented to students in Lacombe's Ladder.

As corrosive as the residential schooling experience was for Indian and Inuit children between the 1880s and 1970s, these schools were only one part of a broad program of attempted assimilation that Indian Affairs promoted. The year after Canada's modern residential schooling policy was introduced with the creation of three western industrial schools, the Indian Act was amended to target cultural practices of North West Coast First Nations. The Potlatch, a sharing ritual used to mark important transitions in the lives of Coast people of high status, offended missionaries and some Indian agents because it involved the giving away of vast quantities of material goods by the host of the Potlatch. A particularly famous gathering, Dan Cranmer's Potlatch in 1922 involved, among other things, the giving of twenty-four canoes, three pool tables, four gas–powered boats, jewellery, clothing, blankets, four hundred sacks of flour, sewing machines, musical instruments, gramophones, and an undisclosed amount of money.[16] The Potlatch also entailed a great deal of feasting and dancing, some of the latter involving real or simulated biting of animals and humans. All these features, particularly the anti-capitalist redistribution of property, offended many Euro-Canadians, as well as some Christian converts among Coastal First Nations who joined in a demand for its eradication. Missionaries in particular recognized that the Potlatch system was a cultural glue that embodied and perpetuated many of the Aboriginal values – such as gaining prestige and status by giving away property rather than by accumulating it – that would have to be dissolved if thorough conversion and cultural change of North West Coast peoples were to be accomplished. Accordingly, in 1884 Parliament acquiesced to demands from missionaries and some convert Indians to eradicate it. It banned the "Potlach" or "Tamanawa" dance in the wide-ranging amendment of the Indian Act of that year.

When the wording of the Potlatch ban proved deficient and unenforceable, Indian Affairs returned to the attack in 1895. On the recommendation of the DIA, Parliament amended the Indian Act to make the law more effective:

> Every Indian or other person who engages in, or assists in celebrating or encourages either directly or indirectly another to celebrate, any Indian festival, dance or other ceremony of which the giving away or paying or giving back of money, goods, or articles of any sort forms a part, or is a feature, whether such gift of money, goods or articles takes place before, at, or after the celebration of the same, and every Indian or other person who engages or assists in any celebration or dance of which the wounding or mutilation of the dead or living body of any human being or animal forms a part, or is a feature, is guilty of an indictable offence.[17]

By specifying the individual acts that were banned rather than just outlawing the "Potlach," Indian Affairs intended to make the legislation easier to enforce.

However, the 1895 modification also brought within the ban a series of Plains summer ceremonials such as the Sun Dance, the Thirst Dance, and other celebrations. These spiritual rituals usually involved redistribution of property as the hosts of the festivities gave presents to their guests. The Sun Dance sometimes also included what missionaries regarded as "wounding or mutilation," for young men who participated often slit the skin on their breast or shoulders, passed a skewer through the flesh and tethered themselves by a cord to the Sun Dance pole, and then danced and strained against the cord until the skin tore in an act of sacrifice. As with the Potlatch and dances of the North West Coast that involved biting, the prairie dances also appalled many Euro-Canadians because of these practices. Moreover, many officials disapproved of the giving away of property, and regretted that the days–long summer rituals took reserve farmers away from their crops during the critical growing period. Like the Potlatch, Prairie dances typified values that in many ways were the antithesis of what Euro-Canadians cherished. For parallel reasons these Plains observances had to go. They were prohibited by a portion of the 1895 Indian Act that remained on the books until 1951. Of course, the ban delivered the message that non-Native society considered these Aboriginal ways unacceptable and encouraged First Nations to drop them.

As astonishing and interfering as the ban on Potlatching and prairie dancing was, it was by no means the end of the program of attempted control and assimilation that the Department of Indian Affairs fashioned in the 1880s and 1890s. Particularly in relation to the First Nations of the prairie West, Ottawa became more invasive and intimidating in this period, especially after the Northwest Rebellion of 1885. In addition to the attack on spiritual ceremonies such as the Sun Dance, Indian Affairs also tried to regulate prairie reserve residents' mobility and economic freedom, while working strenuously to change their way of relating to the land and to farming. Indian Affairs attempted to control movement off-reserve in the West after 1885 by means of a wholly extra-legal pass system that required an Indian who wished to leave the reserve to obtain a pass authorizing absence from the agent. Although the pass policy had no basis either in statute or cabinet order, although it clearly violated treaty guarantees as to freedom to hunt and gather, and although the mounted police by the early 1890s were declining to enforce it because it aggravated their relations with Indians, Indian Affairs still favoured its enforcement. Its other weapons for controlling mobility were a general law against vagrancy or the Indian Act prohibition on trespass on reserves by non-residents, measures which the DIA could insist police use to inhibit movement by people the Department wished to control.

In the economic realm the attack on prairie Aboriginal spirituality in the 1895 amendment of the Indian Act was paralleled by the permit policy, severalty, and "peasant farming." The permit system required reserve producers to obtain a permit from the Indian agent before taking produce to town for sale, ostensibly to protect the producer from exploitation by ruthless townspeople. Cynics thought the permit system was just another way to try to control Indians. Severalty, a direct imitation of the American Dawes Act of 1887, was a policy introduced in 1888 to encourage reserves to allow the subdivision of communally held property into individual plots. The intention was to encourage economic individualism, a clear example of attempted assimilation of attitudes about landholding to a capitalist pattern.

The "peasant farming" policy that prevailed on the prairies from 1889 until 1897 was the brainchild of Indian Affairs deputy minister Hayter Reed, who subscribed to the racist social science theories of the time that held that there was an iron rule of evolution that bound societies. They could only succeed if they advanced from savagery to barbarism to subsistence agricultural production to commercial farming. The emergence to full "civilization" required adherence to this sequence; skipping stages would result in inappropriate adjustment to modern, western ways. To force Plains hunter-gatherers to adhere to this iron law of social development, Reed instructed agents and farm instructors to prevent reserve farmers from purchasing mechanized equipment that was becoming available by the 1880s and to require them to sow, reap, and thresh their crops by hand. "Peasant farming," which, mercifully, was axed along with Hayter Reed's deputy ministership by a new Liberal government in 1897, retarded the advance of prairie reserves in agricultural production, removed reserve producers from competition with non-Native farmers for local markets, and both frustrated and insulted Plains nations. Dakota at Oak Lake in Manitoba, for example, were making good progress on becoming successful commercial farmers in the 1880s, until Reed's pet scheme thwarted their ability to use machinery to harvest large crops. They subsided into a morass of inactivity and dependence as a consequence. Like severalty, passes, permits, prohibitions on dancing and Potlatching, and residential schools, the lunatic "peasant farming" policy was part of a widespread campaign of attempted assimilation to which First Nations were subjected from the 1880s onward.

Although this vicious assimilative assault had only limited success in bringing about cultural replacement among First Nations, it had a long-lasting and destructive impact. Its effect was limited because First Nations resisted it by a variety of tactics, many of which they had been using since Euro-Canadians first started to compel them to change in pre-Confederation Ontario. They could use passive resistance: implementation of severalty required band agreement, which was not forthcoming. They could and did evade the assimilators. Some families were absent when it was time to round the children up to send them to the distant residential schools. Many students ran away from residential school at the first opportunity. They defied the attempts to denigrate their culture and change them, as generations of residential school inmates did, in an astonishing variety of ways. They refused to participate in the classroom, either acting up or simply ignoring what the teacher was trying to do. They sabotaged the assimilators' efforts, adulterating food in the kitchen or stealing it from pantry or barn. A girl assigned to the staff dining room at one school tried and found the horseradish that accompanied the roast beef she was serving not to her liking. She spat the mouthful she had sampled back into the condiment container and left the treat for staff to enjoy another day.[18] They fought back, in the most extreme case by acts of carefully calculated arson intended to destroy the school and free them to return home. In the twentieth century, resistance to the campaign of assimilation increasingly took the form of political organization, for most of the First Nations political movements critiqued Indian Affairs' policies, assimilation and otherwise, to which they objected. In the long run political organization would free them from most of the assimilative attack.

In the meantime, however, the assimilative program developed in the 1880s and 1890s harmed Native people emotionally and psychologically, and it left lasting scars on the spirit. The horrific experience of being told and shown daily that the apparently dominant Euro-Canadians had nothing but contempt for Aboriginal ways took its toll, especially upon impressionable young people in residential schools. In many cases the assimilative campaign succeeded only in its negative aspect, undermining or destroying the Native person's confidence in and attachment to Aboriginal identity and culture without replacing it with something positive. A former student of the Anglican Shingwauk school in Sault Ste. Marie told a school reunion in 1991 that when he left the institution he did not know what he was. He thought, he said, he was "a Shingwauk Indian." The contempt and mistreatment that non-Natives directed their way prevented most Native people from embracing their tormentors' beliefs and practices. Certainly some were converted to Christianity, but there is ample evidence that most of the so-called converts incorporated Christian beliefs and observances alongside Aboriginal spiritual observances.

For most of its targets the assimilative campaign, especially down to the 1970s, merely destroyed or weakened the Aboriginal portion of their psyche without replacing it with another. They frequently described themselves as feeling like "people in between," not fitting in with either Native or Euro-Canadian society. John Tootoosis, one of the most respected and most effective First Nations political leaders the prairies ever produced, described their situation – and his – poignantly. Referring to residential schools, one of which he had attended, Tootoosis said: "When an Indian comes out of these places it is like being put between two walls in a room and left hanging in the middle. On one side are all the things he learned from his people and their way of life that was being wiped out, and on the other side are the whiteman's ways which he could never fully understand since he never had the right amount of education and could not be part of it. There he is, hanging, in the middle of two cultures and he is not a whiteman and he is not an Indian."[19] The long-term cost of this suspension to both Native and non-Native society has been enormous.

By the 1940s the non-Native consensus in support of the program of assimilation was breaking down. By then it was obvious that the Department of Indian Affairs' assimilative programs, such as residential schooling for example, simply did not work. These schools neither educated students effectively nor, as John Tootoosis's observation indicates, turned them into brown-skinned Euro-Canadians. Most of the Christian churches involved in residential schooling, recognizing the ineffectiveness and inappropriateness of the institutions, wanted out of them. For its part, the federal government watched uneasily as First Nations' birth rate began to climb rapidly by the 1940s, knowing that the larger the number of First Nations children, the greater the government's financial liability to build and operate more schools strictly for Indian children. These practical considerations on the part of government were reinforced by new ideological and intellectual patterns as well. The Second World War had revealed in Nazism the implications of state policy based on racist assumptions about one people's inferiority. As an Alberta Member of Parliament put it in 1947, "the Canadian people as a whole are interested in the problem of the Indians; they have become aware that the country has been negligent in the matter of looking after the Indians and they are anxious to remedy our shortcomings. Parliament and the country is [sic] 'human rights' conscious."[20]

If the country was "human rights conscious," it was because of the influence of the social sciences as well as the recent world war. By the late 1940s social sciences such as anthropology were moving away from earlier racist theories about a hierarchy of human societies and their evolution from one stage of "development" or "progress" to a higher one, theories that frequently had underwritten and justified the kinds of discriminatory policy that the Indian Affairs department and churches had foisted on Native people. Anthropology was abandoning the concept of race entirely, preferring the idea of culture, and instead of a hierarchy of societies, anthropologists now perceived human communities as roughly similar in worth. Cultural relativism replaced racism as the intellectual foundation of social sciences by the middle of the twentieth century.

Equally important in undermining the foundations of Canadian Indian policy were the growing number of First Nations political organizations that were formed throughout the first half of the twentieth century. By the 1940s strong provincial First Nations organizations had been established in Ontario and the western provinces, although the emergence of an enduring and effective national body would have to wait until the 1960s. These new organizations voiced First Nations' opposition to DIA policy in everything from treaties to inadequate schooling. Their new-found articulateness and effectiveness were revealed between 1946 and 1948 in the hearings of a parliamentary committee appointed to look into the Indian Act and recommend changes that would modernize it. The various First Nations provincial political organizations joined individual bands in criticizing government policy, including a wide-ranging attack on segregated Indian education in general and residential schooling in particular. Their criticism of DIA educational policy was well rounded and devastating: not only were residential schools offensively assimilative, but they did not manage to educate their students in secular subjects effectively. The hearings and records of the joint parliamentary committee, which also revealed missionary doubts about the morality and efficacy of the programs in which they were partners with government, amounted to a devastating critique of Indian Affairs policy.

The aftermath of the hearings on the Indian Act revealed the tenacity of the Indian Affairs bureaucracy and the hold that racist attitudes and attachment to assimilation had on policy planners. In spite of the momentum that had built up to abandon many of the policies, little of substance in fact changed for a long time. For example, because of strong Roman Catholic, principally Oblate, opposition, the residential schools were not immediately dismantled. The residential schooling policy would last until 1969, when the federal government finally insisted on phasing the schools out, and some of the individual institutions would continue to operate until the 1980s. So far as the Indian Act itself was concerned, the denouement to the drama of the joint parliamentary committee's hearings, the revised Indian Act of 1951, illustrated both the resistance of the bureaucracy to change and the officials' ability to get their way. The 1951 amendment did make some changes, repealing coercive or intrusive clauses such as those banning giveaways and sacrificial dancing, as well as the 1927 prohibition on giving or soliciting money for pursuit of a claim, the 1933 provision for involuntary enfranchisement, and a number of powers the minister of Indian Affairs had taken in various amendments to allow him and his officials to interfere in bands' internal political affairs. What did not change, however, was the underlying assumption and objective of assimilation of First Nations. That remained in the Act after 1951 as continuing clauses dealing with enfranchisement (now voluntary as it had been in 1857, 1869, or 1876) demonstrated. Historian John Tobias summarized the 1951 changes, "The new act definitely differs from the Indian Acts between 1880 and 1951, but only because it returned to the philosophy of the original Indian Act: civilization was to be encouraged but not directed or forced on the Indian people. . . . Speedy assimilation was not repudiated as the goal of Canada's Indian policy — what was repudiated was the earlier means to achieve it."[21] Enfranchisement, the principal symbol and core policy of Indian Affairs' assimilative goal would remain on the books until 1985.

Many signs remained after 1951 that Indian Affairs had merely poured the old assimilative wine into new bottles. Integrated schooling, a policy towards which the DIA had begun to inch in the late 1940s and which it pursued energetically in the 1950s, was a good illustration. Integrated schooling both responded to the new ideological fashions and met practical department objectives. If First Nations children were taught alongside non-Native children in publicly supported schools rather than in segregated schools, whether day schools on reserves or residential schools, there would no longer be grounds for criticizing the Department for sponsoring racist schools that kept Native children apart from non-Natives. Moreover, if they were enrolled in public schools, Indian Affairs would no longer have to allocate funds to build new residential schools especially for the burgeoning First Nations youth population, or to pay for teachers, supervisors, accommodation, food, clothing, and so on of the students and staff, and equipment for or upkeep of the schools. Of course, in the integrated classrooms Indian children would be a minority, would invariably be taught by non-Native teachers following a provincial curriculum that was not culturally appropriate to First Nations' societies, and would be subjected to a different form of assimilative education.

The integrated schools that accommodated increasing numbers of First Nations students in the 1950s and 1960s were effectively a new form of assimilative schooling. In spite of the good intentions and hard work of many of the non-Natives who supported or worked in integrated schools, the supposedly non-racist schools favoured by Ottawa after revision of the Indian Act were equally assimilative in purpose. As Tobias said of the Act itself, the schools changed the methods but not the objective of policy. And for most First Nations students these ideologically improved schools were as unhappy and unsuccessful a learning experience as the residential schools had been for their parents and grandparents. The federal government did not give up its support of integrated schooling until political pressure from First Nations political leaders forced it to adopt a policy of "Indian control of Indian education" in 1973.

Equally revealing of government's tendency to maintain assimilative policy in the guise of less objectionable programs was the outcome of a renewed search for a viable Indian policy that preoccupied politicians and bureaucrats in the mid to late 1960s. The reason for the search for an effective policy that involved the Pearson (1963–68) and Trudeau governments (1968–79, 1980–84) was similar to the motivation behind the abortive move to revise the Indian Act after the end of the Second World War. Existing policy did not work, and by the 1960s, when decolonization movements around the world and Indian political action in North America were sensitizing people to the plight of non-white peoples, the continuing problems in relations between First Nations and government in Canada were a growing embarrassment. The result of policy bankruptcy and political pressure was a search for a new policy that began under Lester Pearson and continued into the early months of the government of Pierre Elliott Trudeau, who appointed Jean Chrétien as his Minister of Indian Affairs and Northern Development in 1968. Since Trudeau had won the leadership of the Liberal party and then a resounding majority in a general election on a commitment to involve ordinary Canadians in government – "Come Work With Me," his leadership campaign posters had beckoned – and to strive for a "Just Society," expectations were high. Under Pearson the government had initiated a process of consultation with First Nations leaders to develop a new policy. Trudeau and Chrétien, of course, continued the consultation process.

When the result emerged in June 1969 in a statement of federal Indian policy known as the White Paper, there was disillusionment and bitterness.[22] To the consternation of Indian leaders, the government announced that all the problems First Nations faced were the result of their distinct and separate status in Canadian society. They suffered from poverty and unemployment not because they had been systematically dispossessed of their lands and subjected for close to a century to demeaning and discriminatory treatment. It was the "separate legal status of Indians and the policies which have flowed from it [that] have kept Indian people apart from and behind other Canadians," said the White Paper. They had been on "the road of different status, a road which has led to a blind alley of deprivation and frustration." Obviously, the solution was to eradicate their problems by eliminating their special legal status. The White Paper recommended that "the legislative and constitutional bases of discrimination be removed": their distinct status as "Indians" would be eliminated, they would get their services from the provinces as other Canadians did, control of Indians lands would somehow "be transferred to the Indian people," and "the Indian Act [would] be repealed."[23] Then all their troubles would be over.

In spite of the White Paper's honeyed words about ending discrimination and ushering in a just society for First Nations and others, the proposed policy was the bluntest and most threatening assimilative effort the federal government had come up with yet. Ottawa was advocating the elimination of Indian status in law, winding up the treaties through which many First Nations had a special relationship with the Crown and Canadians, and eliminating the government department and legislation that recognized their distinctive status and entitlement. They would become just like other Canadians, as was symbolized by the proposal that they acquire government services through the provinces, and they would be just another chip in the multicultural mosaic that the Trudeau government was soon to proclaim as government policy. The most obvious precedent for the White Paper was not the political philosophy of Pierre Elliott Trudeau, which the bureaucrats and politicians who prepared the White Paper were following, but the Indian termination policy of American president Dwight D. Eisenhower. In 1954 the American government had introduced a new policy that ended the distinctive status and government entitlements of many Native Americans, much in the spirit of ideological progress and economy that had underlain Canada's ill-starred adoption of integration in Indian education. What the White Paper of 1969 would have done, had it been implemented, was eliminate Indians as Indians, much as the U.S. termination policy had attempted, unsuccessfully for the most part, to do after 1954.

Impassioned and united resistance from First Nations political organizations, speaking through powerful provincial bodies such as the Indian Association of Alberta and the young vehicle known as the National Indian Brotherhood (NIB), forced the Trudeau government to renounce the White Paper policy within a year. Concessions such as funding of land claims research, adoption of a policy of "Indian control of Indian education" in 1973, creation of an Office of Native Claims in 1974, core funding for the NIB, and appointment of a Claims Commissioner, Dr. Lloyd Barber, were acts of atonement by a chastened federal government. The one encouraging note in the unsettling affair was that exposure of the brutal assimilative purpose of the White Paper provoked an outcry that militant and effectively led First Nations political organizations used to defeat an objectionable policy. Those developments were new.

Unfortunately, defeating an ill-advised policy did not automatically produce a substitute that was workable, effective, and acceptable. Since 1969–70 Canada has intermittently struggled to develop a better policy. The repeated efforts to remodel the Constitution in a way that would include First Nations and other Aboriginal peoples – the 1982 constitutional package, the offensive Meech Lake Accord of 1987, and the rejected Charlottetown proposal of 1992 that contained constitutional recognition of Aboriginal self-government – are the clearest proof that governments, both Native and national, recognize that there is much unfinished business to deal with. In addition, of course, the influence of Supreme Court decisions on Aboriginal rights has simultaneously encouraged Aboriginal peoples to try to scale new heights and provoked something of a backlash in non-Native society. The slow progress on land claims resolution in general and the constipated treaty-making process in British Columbia in particular contribute to the unsettled and discontented feeling of Canadians about the Aboriginal dossier.

Strange to say, there is ample evidence that Canadians and their governments still have an attachment to attitudes that are fundamentally assimilationist. As noted earlier, the principal assimilative policy, enfranchisement, remained on the books until the adoption of gender equality provisions in the 1982 Charter of Rights and Freedoms forced the government to eliminate the gender discrimination in the Indian Act provision that stripped Indian women who married non-Indians of their status. In the measure that dealt with this, Bill C-31 of 1985, Parliament also removed the concept of enfranchisement from the Indian Act. However, in the process of supposedly eliminating gender discrimination Ottawa introduced new conditions of regaining status – the double grandmother rule, for example – whose purpose clearly is to eliminate status for large numbers of future generations. Legal assimilation lives on in the coils of Bill C-31. Also in the mid-1980s, the Mulroney government undertook a review of federal government program spending that targeted expenditure on Indians, effectively recommending a series of changes that would have re-enacted key elements of the 1969 White Paper. When details of these proposals were leaked to Native organizations and the press, the ensuing outcry forced Mulroney to recant, as Trudeau had in 1970.

The legacy of such events in 1969–70 and 1985 is a poisoned atmosphere in which all discussion of Aboriginal policy must take place. Native leaders, remembering the White Paper especially, are constantly on the lookout for signs that the federal government is attempting surreptitiously to reintroduce elements of the assimilative proposals of 1969. Such thinking underlies much of the suspicion and hostility that greeted Indian and Northern Affairs minister Robert Nault's attempt in 2002–03 to develop new legislation on First Nations' control of their lands and on greater accountability of First Nations to the federal government. Such Aboriginal perceptions are strengthened when a major national newspaper greets the legislation with an approving column titled "A better life for natives – and a whiter one, too" that argues that the only defect in Nault's legislation was that it was not frank about its likely assimilative impact.[24] First Nations political leaders' suspicions are hardly surprising.

Finally, it is clear that at least a portion of non-Native Canadians support the assimilation of Native people as a solution to the problems that they face. The evidence for this is widespread. It emerges frequently in comments made on radio phone-in shows, in televised town-hall meetings, and in letters to the editor arguing that "they have to join the mainstream," referring to the supposed necessity of Aboriginal peoples to make major accommodation to, if not adopt completely, non-Native ways in order to be successful. In December 2001, for example, the *National Post*, having eight months earlier set its editorial writer Jonathan Kay "the task of investigating Canada's aboriginal problem," published the resulting analysis and proposal in a lengthy two-part feature titled, "The case for Native Assimilation."[25] Kay argued that scholars and educators had romanticized Aboriginal knowledge, a mistaken approach: "By conflating the intellectual traditions of aboriginal societies with those of Europe, we have given credence to the idea that new-world cultural practices are compatible with economic advancement." In fact, Kay said in an echo of the assumptions that had underlain residential schools, "peasant farming," and many other misbegotten policies inflicted on Aboriginal peoples over the years, traditional Aboriginal culture is incompatible with "modernity." Gordon Gibson, a former adviser to the British Columbia government and an articulate critic of Indian Affairs policies, attributed Indians' problems in 2001 to other Canadians' treatment of them as different and distinct. After tracing a trail of wrong-headed policies that did harm, Gibson observed, "And always the baleful background music was this: 'You are an Indian. You are different,'" in an echo of the 1969 White Paper.[26] Reiterating the theme that ran through DIA policies from enfranchisement to severalty, he concluded, "When you invest in the individual, it is hard to go wrong. When you empower the collective, error proliferates. It is long past time the Indian people were set free."

Other commentators are more subtle, but do not disagree fundamentally with the notion that Aboriginal people must change and adopt Euro-Canadian ways to survive and succeed. For example, the *Globe and Mail*'s John Stackhouse ended a fourteen-part series that analyzed Native problems and successes in a piece titled, "First step: end the segregation," as though more than half the Native, and about half the status Indian population did not already live off-reserve.[27] Stackhouse praised the changes that Parliament Hill rumours then said Robert Nault was contemplating: "Most aboriginal communities are too small to manage their affairs effectively without some external check on power. To change this, a new age of accountability is needed desperately. It's what Robert Nault, the current Indian Affairs Minister, has been trying to do in his hope to amend the Indian Act with modern concepts of democracy." Truly "modern" Indians understood the need to change: "For this generation, the talk is no longer of assimilation. It is about integration, in which the part contributes to the whole." The message underneath was the same as Jonathan Kay's: true Aboriginal ways did not compute in the modern world. Stackhouse brightened the message by adding a hopeful note: modern, with-it

Aboriginal people understood this, were accommodating Euro-Canadian ways, and were no longer hung up on old-fashioned worries about assimilation.

But is the assimilative impulse dead in twenty-first century Canada? Has it disappeared from public thinking or merely transformed itself into different shapes, different policies? For those in doubt an influential book published in 2000 was instructive. University of Calgary political scientist, public commentator, and now chief of staff to Canadian Alliance leader Stephen Harper, Tom Flanagan, published an uncompromising attack on what he called "the Aboriginal orthodoxy" and a call for more assimilation in *First Nations? Second Thoughts.* This forcefully argued and well-written commentary received enormous press attention, particularly from newspapers in the Southam chain, and won recognition in the form of book prizes from the Donner Foundation and Canadian Political Science Association. The so-called Aboriginal orthodoxy, by which Flanagan meant a supposed consensus among intellectuals and opinion-makers in favour of Aboriginal distinctiveness, was pernicious because it encouraged and justified Indians' withdrawal into their own enclaves, their own governments, and, worst of all, "their own 'aboriginal economies.'" This was self-defeating; it took Aboriginal people in "the wrong direction if the goal is widespread individual independence and prosperity for aboriginal people. Under the policy of withdrawal, the political and professional elites will do well for themselves as they manage the aboriginal enclaves, but the majority will be worse off than ever." Aboriginal people needed "to acquire the skills and attitudes that bring success in a liberal society, political democracy, and market economy. Call it assimilation, call it integration, call it adaptation, call it whatever you want: it has to happen."[28] It was the same message that assimilationist policy planners had advocated in Upper Canada in the 1830s, in Hayter Reed's West in the 1880s, and in Pierre Trudeau's 1960s. To retain Aboriginality was to cling to the past and condemn oneself and one's community to hardship and worse. To embrace the lure of assimilation – individualism, adjustment, "modernity" – was the path to success.

The assimilative theme in Native-newcomer history has always been present, and threatens, obviously, to be with Canadians for some time yet. Although Europeans were not initially strong advocates of thorough-going cultural change because their economic activities did not seem to them to require it and because they valued Aboriginal culture for the knowledge and skills it contributed to fur commerce, diplomacy, and forest warfare, they favoured limited Native adoption of some European values, such as Christianity. When the relationship changed with the decline of the fur trade in eastern Canada and the end of vulnerability to external attacks, and with the onset of the settlement frontier, Euro-Canadian attitudes changed, too. Now leading elements in government favoured cultural replacement, believing that Aboriginal people had to become like them to succeed and to facilitate Euro-Canadian material success. From 1830 onward Indian Department policy consistently promoted assimilation, at some periods more aggressively than others, but always to one degree or another. Just as steadfastly, Aboriginal communities and political leaders resisted assimilative policies, but always at a cost to them materially, socially, and psychologically. The upshot of the last 170 years of attempted assimilation is the lethal legacy Canadians face in the twenty-first century.

The next chapter considers ways in which Canadians might respond.

Notes

1 Ochankuhage (Dan Kennedy), *Recollections of an Assiniboine Chief*, James R. Stevens, ed. (Toronto/Montreal: McClelland & Stewart 1972), 48

2 *Ibid.*, 54

3 Cartier's Narrative of 1534, H.P. Biggar, *The Voyages of Jacques Cartier* (Ottawa: King's Printer 1924), 56

4 Martin L. Nicolai, "A Different Kind of Courage: The French Military and the Canadian Irregular Soldier During the Seven Years' War," *Canadian Historical Review* 70, no. 1 (March 1989), 59

5 R.G. Thwaites, ed., *The Jesuit Relations and Allied Documents* (Cleveland: Burrows Brothers 1897), vol. 6, 243

6 M. Eastman, *Church and State in Early Canada* (Edinburgh: University Press 1915), 117

7 Judith Fingard, "The New England Company and the New Brunswick Indians, 1786-1826: A comment on the Colonial Perversion of British Benevolence," *Acadiensis* 1, 2 (spring 1972): 29–42

8 Sir G. Murray to Sir J. Kempt, January 25, 1830, and Sir J. Kempt to Lt-Gov. J. Colborne, May 16, 1829, in *British Parliamentary Papers* [Irish University Press Series], "Correspondence and Other Papers Relating to Aboriginal Tribes in British Possessions," 1834, no. 617, 88, 40–1

9 Quoted in J.R. Miller, *Shingwauk's Vision: A History of Native Residential Schools* (Toronto: University of Toronto Press 1996), 79

10 National Archives of Canada [NA], MG 26 A, Sir John A. Macdonald Papers, vol. 91, 35428, N.F. Davin, "Report on Industrial Schools for Indians and Half-Breeds," confidential, March 14, 1879, 15

11 Methodists and a majority of Presbyterians joined with Congregationalists in 1925 to form the United Church of Canada, the country's largest Protestant denomination. After church union in 1925 the continuing Presbyterians operated some missions and schools on their own.

12 Alexander Morris, *The Treaties of Canada with the Indians* (Saskatoon: Fifth House 1991; 1st published 1880), 315. The first set of words is from Treaty 1, but the next five treaties contained schooling clauses that were identical or very similar. For the altered educational commitment in Treaty 7 see *ibid.*, 371.

13 Report of the Department of Indian Affairs for 1880, *Canada Sessional Papers (No. 14) 1881*, 8

14 Canada, House of Commons, *Debates*, May 9, 1883, 1377

15 Bill Whitehawk, a former student of St. Philip's school near Keeseekoose Reserve, in Miller, *Shingwauk's Vision* 191. For more detail on the assimilative quality of the residential school experience, see *ibid.*, chapters 6-7.

16 Douglas Cole and Ira Chaikin, *An Iron Hand Upon the People: The Law Against the Potlatch on the Northwest Coast* (Vancouver: Douglas & McIntyre 1990), 119-20

17 *58-59 Vict., c. 35*, sec. 114

18 Miller, *Shingwauk's Vision*, 362

19 Jean Goodwill and Norma Sluman, *John Tootoosis* 2nd ed. (Winnipeg: Pemmican Publications 1984; 1st ed. 1982), 106

20 Canada. Special Joint Committee of the Senate and House of Commons [on] the Indian Act, *Minutes of Proceedings and Evidence* 2 (1947), 1673, June 10, 1947 (J.H. Blackmore)

21 John L. Tobias, "Protection, Civilization, Assimilation: An Outline History of the Indian Act," J.R. Miller, ed. *Sweet Promises: A Reader on Indian-White Relations in Canada* (Toronto: University of Toronto Press 1991), 140

22 The term White Paper was not intentionally racist. In the elaborate policy planning system that Trudeau put in place, a "white paper" was merely a policy proposal on which the government was seeking comment. At another stage of policy development a "green paper" was sometimes used. The White Paper might as easily and accurately been termed a position paper or preliminary policy proposal.

23 Canada. Department of Indian Affairs and Northern Development, *Statement of the Government of Canada on Indian Policy* (Ottawa: Indian Affairs 1969), 5–8

24 Jonathan Kay, "A better life for natives – a whiter one, too," *National Post*, June 19, 2002

25 Jonathan Kay, "The case for Native Assimilation," *National Post*, December 8, 2001

26 Gordon Gibson, "Make individuals the focus of native reform," *National Post*, December 10, 2001

27 John Stackhouse, "First step: end the segregation," *Globe and Mail*, December 15, 2001. The series began in the issue of November 3, 2001.

28 Tom Flanagan, *First Nations? Second Thoughts* (Montreal and Kingston: McGill-Queen's University Press 2000), 195–6

Making Our Way Forward

While the four centuries of interactions between indigenous peoples and immigrants in Canada that produced present-day problems have not been happy ones, they have been instructive. On the whole, the early period of contact, in which commercial ties or a combination of commercial and diplomatic linkages dominated relations between Natives and newcomers, was one of relative harmony between the two peoples. While there certainly were problems in the early fur trade and military alliances – brandy, violence, casualties in battle, and, especially, major losses of life to epidemic disease – over all relations were harmonious. This fruitful first period of interaction gave way between the later decades of the eighteenth century and the middle of the nineteenth century to a new era, the onset of the settlement-mining frontier. This period began at different times in various parts of the country: by the 1780s in Maritime Canada; in the first five decades of the 1800s in the central provinces; by the 1870s on the Plains; and between the 1850s and 1880s in British Columbia. In the North its start can be dated by the Klondike gold rush of the later 1890s in Yukon and by the penetration of military forces and the Canadian state by the 1940s in the Eastern Arctic. Whatever the dating of the onset of the settlement-mining frontier, its consequences were similar across southern Canada. With the exception of British Columbia, where settler opposition prevented widespread treaty making, the settlement era came accompanied by land-related treaties, missionary ministrations, and increasingly intrusive legislation aimed at First Nations. The era of settlement was also a time of attempted coercion and control of Aboriginal peoples by non-Natives acting through their colonial or, later, national governments. The era of coercion, in turn, gave way by the latter half of the twentieth century to a period of confrontation, as Aboriginal peoples organized themselves politically to assert their rights and advance their interests. In the early years of the twenty-first century Canada is still working through the dynamics of confrontation.

The successive phases of Native-newcomer relations in Canada are reflected in the history of the five topics surveyed in the preceding chapters. For example, there was no action by government to attempt to define Aboriginal peoples, and relatively modest attempts by religious authorities to reshape their beliefs, in the initial era dominated by military and commercial considerations. Similarly, efforts to assimilate Native peoples socially, economically, and politically through a variety of legislation, much of it embodied after 1876 in the Indian Act, were, like land treaties, a consequence of the changed relations of the settlement-mining era. To almost all these coercive forays Aboriginal peoples responded with a variety of resistance measures. Sometimes resistance was passive, as in the defeat of voluntary enfranchisement after 1857 or severalty (individual allocation of reserve lands) on the prairies after 1888, where the newcomers' attempts to change Native ways required at least some co-operation by the targets of attempted interference. Because relatively few First Nations males would apply for enfranchisement down to the 1950s the policy was never effective. Similarly, the chiefs and councils of few western reserves asked to have their lands surveyed and allocated as individual plots, effectively frustrating the campaign for individual landholding. Where necessary, as in some First Nations' response to efforts to reshape their governance practices by deposing their leaders or imposing elective institutions on them, Aboriginal resistance was active and assertive. The Mohawk at Akwesasne and the band led by Wahpeemakwa (White Bear) in Saskatchewan vigorously resisted government attempts to impose elections on them. Increasingly through the twentieth century, Aboriginal resistance took the form of political organization and activity. From the 1970s onward especially, all three Aboriginal groups were organized in effective national political bodies that expressed their communities' opinions to governments.

From these patterns in Native-newcomer relations over the last four centuries several conclusions emerge, findings that might help Canadians understand our present conundrum and assist in finding a way out of it. First, relations between indigenous and immigrant societies in this country are better when both parties have an interest in acting in concert with each other. It was not mutual admiration of Natives and newcomers that led to relatively harmonious relations in the fur trade. Rather, the two parties co-operated because each gained something from the alliance. From the relationship European fur traders got a skilled, experienced, and efficient labour force for harvesting furs and bringing them to trading posts, allowing them to achieve their commercial objectives with lower investments in labour than otherwise would have been possible. Native peoples obtained access to European goods, the fruits of a technology that in many areas was more advanced than their own. In the period of alliance European states and their colonial offshoots obtained valuable fighting allies, while First Nations who entered into agreements with the French or British to support each other thought they were pursuing the most efficient way of defending their lands. Unfortunately for the First Nations, European allies proved unreliable once the fighting stopped, often betraying the territorial interests of their Aboriginal partners in the peace talks, and invariably overrunning First Nations' lands with immigrant settlers.

Because the settlement-mining era, unlike the earlier commercial-military period, provided little by way of a foundation of mutual self-interest, relations between immigrants and indigenous peoples quickly cooled, then soured. When newcomers levelled forests to make farms, they jeopardized the livelihood of hunter-gatherer First Nations, and the intruders increasingly found the presence of those First Nations an impediment to the type of economic development they now wished to pursue in North America. Similarly, exploration and mining frequently interfered with First Nations' economic activities, thereby creating friction between Natives and miners. This pattern was observable near Sault Ste. Marie in the late 1840s and on the Fraser River in the 1850s. In such cases, relations between Natives and newcomers quickly deteriorated, with indigenous leaders such as Shingwaukonse in Upper Canada or the Sto:Lo on the Fraser resisting the intruders. The pattern would be repeated nearly half a century later on the Klondike, and later still in the part of northern Alberta that the Lubicon Lake Cree considered their homeland. Like the era when sedentary agriculture was established on a large scale, the onset of the mining frontier brought with it poor relations between Native and newcomer. The reason was simple. The two parties were no longer drawn to co-operate by mutual self-interest; now their interests pitted them against each other.

The product of poorer relations between Native and newcomers has been the successive periods of attempted coercion, indigenous resistance, and political confrontation that have dominated the relationship for more than a century and one-half. The consequences of these unhappy developments have been the thwarting of non-Native initiatives and the demoralization of Aboriginal peoples. Because Native groups invariably resisted attempts to control and change them, policies that developed for those purposes inevitably failed. Enfranchisement, voluntary or involuntary, was not achieved, and by 1985 Canada had to abandon the policy after close to 130 years of frustration. At the same time, decades of being subjected to initiatives from state and church that denigrated their culture and depreciated their identity left psychological scars on Native peoples. Even failed policies of attempted assimilation made their mark, leaving their targets feeling suspended between two worlds, not fitting comfortably into either any more. Many First Nations organizations contend today that the grave problems of substance abuse, family break-down, and over-incarceration that plague their communities are explained largely by that psychological damage. Certainly the legacy of the residential schools, probably the most dramatic example of the policies of attempted control and change of First Nations, seems to support that view.

Next to the residential schools, the biggest symbol of oppression to First Nations is the Indian Act. It is impossible to understand the depth of Indian hostility and distrust without appreciating the baleful role that that statute has played. The incorporation of all previous legislation dealing with First Nations by the Canadian Parliament in 1876 created an overarching policy framework that is still largely in place today. Although the Act has been amended many times since its creation, it still stands as Canada's legislative statement of policy towards First Nations. Few non-Native Canadians know, for example, that no one with Indian status can make a valid will unless the cabinet minister in charge of Indian Affairs approves the document. That extraordinary provision is an artifact of the Act's overall assumption that First Nations people are legal minors, technically wards, whose future the government should plan and whose interests the government should protect. Other sections of the earlier legislation, such as enfranchisement or the prohibition on Indians' consuming alcohol, have been deleted over the past half-century, but the Act still stands, some-times with obsolete provisions still intact. In many ways the Indian Act symbolizes everything in the coercive, confrontational rela-tionship that First Nations detest. A few of them, such as the

Sechelt in British Columbia or some of the Yukon First Nations, have removed themselves from the grip of the Indian Act through their specific self-government agreements, but more than six hundred bands still find themselves in its grasp. Much of the bitterness in relations between the federal government and First Nations today is rooted in the stultifying role that the Indian Act plays in the lives of First Nations communities.

It is difficult to exaggerate the degree to which First Nations have always taken exception to, and continue to be affronted by, the Indian Act. Many chiefs and councils made representations to government against the legislation from its earliest existence well into the twentieth century. During the post-war hearings of the Joint Parliamentary Committee in 1947 a hereditary Mohawk chief from Kahnawake denounced the Indian Act as "the most bureaucratic and dictatorial system ever imposed."[1] And in 2002, during discussion of Robert Nault's first introduction of legislation to replace the governance and financial accountability provisions of the Indian Act, a British Columbia chief pointed to some of its features to illustrate the repressiveness with which the Canadian government had always responded to First Nations' political assertiveness: "The Indian Act amendment [of 1884] prohibited our grandparents from conducting ceremonies, it [the amendment of 1927] prohibited them from hiring lawyers to protect our rights. It even prohibited our grandparents from having gatherings unless an Indian agent allowed it."[2] First Nations' hostility to the Indian Act is long-standing and intense.

As more than one newspaper columnist or editorialist has asked in recent decades, "If the Indian Act is such a deterrent to First Nations' action and progress, why don't their leaders support its abolition?" After all, First Nations leaders responded with fury to the proposal in the White Paper of 1969 that the Act be repealed. The paradoxical stance of Indian leaders towards the Indian Act – loathing it, but opposing its repeal – can be understood only in relation to another bitter product of the coercive relationship in general, and the Indian Act regime in particular. Simply put, some 170 years of bad relations have created so much distrust in the ranks of Native leaders that they are afraid to take a chance on government initiatives that will significantly alter the Indian Act, let alone support its annulment.

When the history of government-Native relations over the past three decades in particular is considered, Aboriginal suspicion and reluctance are understandable. The federal government involved First Nations in consultations in 1968–69, talks that led up to the infamous White Paper of 1969. The National Indian Brotherhood, not surprisingly, concluded that they had been hoodwinked by politicians who sought the termination of their distinctive status as Indians. The suspicion that the White Paper created had not died down much when the Mulroney government's program review of 1985, the results of which were leaked to First Nations leaders, seemed to suggest another attempt to implement aspects of the 1969 policy. Similar dark fears about government intentions have been kept alive by inconsistent policy positions taken by a succession of governments. The Penner Committee in 1983 called for an expansive approach to Aboriginal self-government, but the Mulroney government responded in 1985 with a version of self-government as a delegated municipal-style regime that has had few takers. First ministers could not agree to adopt Aboriginal self-government in principle as a constitutional right in three conferences between 1984 and 1987, but the same politicians quickly assembled a constitutional package that recognized Quebec's distinct status and the right of its government to promote that status. Such events keep Native leaders on the alert.

Recent years have not improved the climate of relations between Aboriginal groups, especially First Nations, and government to any extent. Some First Nations suspect the federal government of seeking to dismantle the Indian Act and implement the White Paper policy stealthily, in stages. Bill C-31 of 1985, which appeared to end the gender discrimination in the Indian Act, turned out to have provisions that would in time do more to unmake "Indians" than anything the government had done between 1869 and 1985. Some First Nations leaders see the federal government's support for groups that fought in the courts for voting rights for off-reserve band members – the Corbiere decision in 1999 that awarded the vote to non-residents – as another attempt to weaken First Nations politically. Such events confirm those who are wary of government motives in their suspicions and make them all the more determined to oppose further government initiatives involving the Indian Act. They neither accept nor are prepared to jettison the legislation.

In May 2003 Matthew Coon Come, chief of the Assembly of First Nations (AFN), provided a dramatic example of First Nations leaders' suspicion of government motives. Writing on the ongoing public debate on public health funding, Coon Come detailed the problems that First Nations have had for many decades getting Indian Affairs to address the dangerously poor water quality found on many reserves. Coon Come summed up: "I have reluctantly concluded that this public health situation is deliberate. I believe it is actually the continuing implementation of the infamous assimilationist 1969 Trudeau white paper by other means – namely through the deliberate maintenance of intolerable social conditions in First Nations' communities." To those who would ask what might be the purpose of such a policy, Coon Come responded, "To drive First Nations citizens away from traditional lands and resources, to offload them onto the cities and into provincial jurisdiction – to complete, by state-imposed duress, the original plan of the cultural extinction of First Nations societies."[3]

It is this legacy of suspicion and fear that explains the recent impasse over Indian Affairs Minister Robert Nault's proposals to amend the Indian Act in the areas of governance and financial accountability. Efforts to negotiate a process for consultation prior to the drafting of legislation broke down, with the Assembly of First Nations demanding a wide-ranging approach that would address their concerns, such as entrenchment of Aboriginal self-government as a section 35 constitutional right, and the government insisting on a more modest approach, apparently in a desire to keep the process manageable. Deterioration in relations between the government and the leadership was soon followed by government cuts to funding for the national organization and by criticisms of AFN leaders leaked by unnamed bureaucrats to national newspapers. By the time Nault introduced his legislation in June 2002, relations had become so bad that a hostile reaction by the AFN and other First Nations leaders was a foregone conclusion. When it was reintroduced in the autumn of 2002 and debated in 2003, relations had degenerated to outright, across-the-board resistance. Even though the actual contents of the measures were relatively innocuous – assuming that they were feasible – the initiative was greeted with howls of outrage, threats to oppose it politically, large demonstrations, and resort to the courts by the Federation of Saskatchewan Indian Nations in an effort to get an injunction to halt parliamentary consideration of the bills. The unhappy situation that prevailed is intelligible only in a context that includes those intense suspicions that First Nations' political leaders hold of government intentions after decades of policy initiatives that have attempted to reduce their political influence with their own community, and after more than a century of assaults under the Indian Act.

The further tragedy of the impasse over Nault's legislation is that Aboriginal voices that support the initiative go unnoticed in the brouhaha between the AFN and government. Among nearly half of status Indians who live in towns and cities there is widespread disenchantment with on-reserve leaders, and a desire for greater accountability and responsiveness to the needs of off-reserve Indians. Similarly, many First Nations women, both on- and off-reserve, support any mechanism that will make the reserve-based chiefs and councils more accountable for their spending and policies. However, in the verbal strife between leaders like Matthew Coon Come and Robert Nault, these other important voices are rarely, if ever, heard.

Relations between government and Aboriginal bodies are, then, poisonous and apparently intractable. While there is relatively little public acrimony between Inuit political leaders and governments, both Metis and First Nations leadership is seething with resentment and frustration. For the Metis the source of their discontent is principally the failure of governments to act on the implied promises that were made when Metis were defined as an Aboriginal people in section 35 of the 1982 constitution. Although that document said that the Metis, along with the Inuit and First Nations, were Aboriginal peoples, and although it insisted that their "aboriginal and treaty rights are hereby recognized and affirmed," the Metis have thus far not been able to advance much in securing meaningful recognition of those rights. There has been essentially no progress on the Metis quest for recognition of self-government rights or land claims, and the federal government has thus far stuck to its historic position that the federal level of government is not responsible for Metis affairs. The dead end has left the Metis with few options but to go to court to secure support for implementation of their twenty-year-old section 35 rights. So far as First Nations are concerned, at the national level relations between them and the Government of Canada have descended to a low point reminiscent of the immediate aftermath of the release of the White Paper in June 1969.

If a survey of four hundred years of Native-newcomer relations helps to explain why matters have come to the apparently intractable position they have in the early twenty-first century, does it provide any guidance in looking for a way forward? Certainly, it would be unwise to expect that lessons from history can serve as predictors of future developments. While an understanding of how things came to be as they are today is helpful for assessing the scope and difficulty of the present problem, it is of limited help for the future. The various factors that influence political developments are so many, and their interplay so unpredictable, that prophecy is foolish. Furthermore, the same history that helps explain the intractability of our present situation also shows that solutions fashioned only by one side invariably fail. Without a process for consultation and negotiation in a co-operative climate, no answer to Canada's twenty-first-century conundrum that has any chance of implementation or success will emerge. If, however, a reading of the past does not provide specific answers, does it offer any help at all in approaching resolution? It does. Given the fact that Canadians, both Native and non-Native, are presented at the moment with three distinct approaches to grappling with the problems in our common relationship, there are insights from the past that allow them to assess the relative merits of the three. Over the past half-century three different ways of casting the issue of relations between Natives and newcomers have emerged in Canada. These can be labelled two-row wampum, assimilation, and Citizens Plus. There are lessons from the history of the Native-newcomer relationship that permit Canadians to evaluate the three options.

"Two-row wampum" is the modern metaphor or shorthand description for a view that sees Natives and non-Natives as co-existing as parallel sovereignties. The kind of self-government favoured by many First Nations chiefs, the Assembly of First Nations, and the Royal Commission on Aboriginal Peoples emphasizes their inherent sovereignty and requires parallel First Nations' governments. The name, "two-row wampum," derives from a seventeenth-century wampum belt that represented sym-bolically the early Dutch-Iroquois relationship as two canoes moving in the same direction. The two paths, one occupied by the Iroquois and the other by the Dutch, representing non-Natives, symbolize the two communities, and the fact that they move in parallel represents the expectation that the two would coexist in friendship, neither interfering with the other. As the Oneida Indian Nation in New York put it on its Web site, "These two rows will symbolize two paths or two vessels, traveling down the same river together, side by side, but in our own boat. Neither of us will make compulsory laws or interfere in the internal affairs of the other. Neither of us will try to steer the other's vessel." The metaphor was adopted in 1996 by the Royal Commission on

Aboriginal Peoples (RCAP) to represent its own approach to self-government recommendations. The Royal Commission proposed a system of parallel sovereign nations, in which sixty to eighty Aboriginal national governments, including one for the Metis nation, with province-like powers would operate alongside existing non-Native government institutions, and in which a new House of First Peoples would take its place alongside the House of Commons and Senate to represent Aboriginal political interests in Parliament.

While the two-row wampum concept has its attractions, as a general approach to addressing the problems in the Native-newcomer relationship it faces major difficulties. The strongest argument in its favour is that it represents the strongly held views of First Nations political leaders about their peoples' proper place in the Canadian political system. It has been the position of the Assembly of First Nations and many provincial First Nations organizations for almost a quarter-century that a two-row wampum, or nation-to-nation, configuration of political representation best suits their situation. First Nations leaders argue, with reason, that historically they possessed political sovereignty, as well as the irrefutable fact that Euro-Canadian political systems that have been imposed on them with greater or lesser thoroughness have been ineffective and caused them harm.

On the other hand, there are also compelling arguments against the two-row wampum approach to the relationship between Natives and newcomers in Canada. The first is that there is little reason to believe that a system of national governments can be fashioned for such a large number of separate communities. While the Royal Commission did not advocate 633 separate Aboriginal national governments, preferring sixty to eighty groups instead, it is highly doubtful that even that many would be sustainable. More particularly, when it is remembered that each of these Aboriginal national governments would represent constituencies of between only five thousand and seven thousand individuals, the problems of feasibility and affordability become obvious. The special case of the Metis is also an obstacle to the implementation of a future relationship based on the two-row wampum approach. The Metis people are so varied across the country and often so intermingled with non-Native citizens in urban centres that it is difficult to see how a Metis national government could be formed and operate. Finally, it seems highly unlikely that there is much support for the two-row wampum approach among non-Natives in Canada. Canadians, like most citizens of western nations, were moving away from heavy reliance on the state to achieve their goals in the 1990s, just as RCAP was embracing the idea of multiplying national governments within Canada. There is also reason to suspect that the parallel sovereignties of the two-row wampum approach to relations between Native and non-Native Canadians make at least non-Natives extremely uncomfortable, suggesting to them a growing apart rather than greater co-operation in the future. It is politically significant that when the federal government in January 1998 issued its formal response to RCAP, known as *Gathering Strength*, it had virtually nothing to say about the Royal Commission's governance recommendations, the part of the report that most clearly embodied two-row wampum thinking.

At the other extreme of options for shaping relations between Natives and newcomers in the future is the assimilative approach. As noted in the previous chapter, assimilative thinking has been prominent among policy makers for almost two centuries now, and there is good reason to suspect that it is still alive and well both in the halls of government and more generally among non-Native Canadians. Newcomers to Canada have always sought to bring about some cultural change among Aboriginal peoples with whom they interacted, in the early centuries in the realm of religious practice and belief particularly. Beginning in the late eighteenth century in Maritime Canada and accelerating in the future Ontario in the 1830s, such thinking underlay Canadian government policy towards First Nations from Confederation onward. When one examines the inner workings of Bill C-31, the 1985 measure designed to deal with gender discrimination in the Indian Act and reads contemporary newspaper columnists and editorials, it is hard to believe that pro-assimilation views have disappeared among non-Native Canadians. Assimilation appeals both to those who think that cultural homogenization is inevitable in a highly technological world dominated by a single superpower and to those who long for a dramatic, comprehensive, and final resolution of the challenges that arise from cultural diversity.

Although the assimilative approach to fashioning a Native-newcomer relationship in the future is seductively attractive to some, its apparent allure is a snare and delusion. The powerful arguments against it are three: it has not worked; attempts to impose it have caused damage; and its intended targets are adamantly opposed to it. The British Indian Department and Canadian Department of Indian Affairs have pursued assimilation for at least 170 years without visible success. It has not mattered how interfering and coercive government was in its attempts. Whether it forbade cultural practices such as the Potlatch and the Sun Dance or attempted to force Euro-Canadian elective institutions on First Nations, the effort never succeeded. A long and consistent record of resistance to attempts to assimilate Natives culturally, economically, and politically demonstrates that the approach will not work. Secondly, the process of trying to impose different cultural, economic, and political values on unreceptive targets merely damages the victims psychologically without leading them to function effectively in non-Native society. If there is any single lesson to be learned from the sorry history of residential schooling for Native youths, surely it is that assimilation not only does not succeed, but that it leaves people damaged from its corrosive effects. Finally, as generations of Aboriginal leaders have made clear, Native peoples have never been, are not now, and will never be interested in replacing their Aboriginal identity with a non-Native one. Assimilation cannot serve as a guide to developing a relationship between Natives and newcomers in the future because it has never worked, it has caused great destruction when it has been tried, and Native leaders are vehemently opposed to it. If persisted in, the assimilative approach will continue to demonstrate one of the basic truths of Native-newcomer history: attempts to impose and coerce provoke resistance that kills any chance of success.

Aside from the two-row wampum and assimilation approaches there is another way of conceptualizing the relationship between Natives and newcomers. This one insists that Aboriginal peoples, most particularly First Nations, are a special kind of Canadian citizen, and their communities enjoy additional rights that ordinary Canadians do not because of First Nations' prior occupancy and historic claims. This view, known as Citizens Plus, was articulated first in the mid-1960s by a government-appointed body, the Hawthorn Commission, whose task it was to survey the conditions in which First Nations lived in Canada. The Hawthorn report argued that "Indians should be regarded as 'Citizens Plus'; in addition to the normal rights and duties of citizenship, Indians possess certain additional rights as charter members of the Canadian community."[4] At the time, the concept was seized upon by First Nations political leaders, and it was used effectively by the Indian Association of Alberta in particular to criticize the White Paper of 1969. Today proponents of this formulation of the Native-newcomer relationship argue that it retains the ties of citizenship and shared empathy between First Nations and non-Natives, while recognizing the special status First Nations enjoy and the special needs their communities usually have.[5]

The attraction of Citizens Plus as a guiding principle to refashioning the Native-newcomer relationship is that it recognizes social and political realities, and it is sufficiently open-ended to accommodate the kind of bargaining that must take place if a viable approach is to be found. Citizens Plus is realistic inasmuch as it faces up to the point that former Chief Justice of the Supreme Court of Canada Antonio Lamer made in the *Delgamuukw* case: "We are all here to stay." It accepts that Aboriginal peoples, like other residents of Canada, are citizens, and uses that shared reality as a platform for defining the basis for common citizenship. Common citizenship is important, political scientist Alan Cairns has reminded Canadians, because, unless both Native and non-Native Canadians have a sense of shared commitment and purpose, the non-Native majority will lack the "civic empathy" that is required to support measures to help the disadvantaged minority. In that regard a Citizens Plus approach avoids the pitfall that the history of Native-newcomer relations has made obvious: without interests in common, the two parties draw apart and the relationship deteriorates. Citizens Plus is thereby stronger than the two-row wampum approach, which keeps Natives and newcomers apart as citizens and voters, and is also superior to an assimilative approach insofar as it assumes common cause between the two groups. In addition to encouraging the development of civic empathy between Natives and newcomers, Citizens Plus is not prescriptive; it leaves open the question of how a shared future might be worked out. The flexible nature of Citizens Plus is desirable in a situation where there are so many different interest groups and in which there is so much distrust on the part of the minority towards the majority's goodwill. The open-ended nature of Citizens Plus as an approach to working out a new accommodation between Natives and newcomers in Canada is one of its greatest appeals. Citizens Plus is a platform on which Canadians, Native and non-Native, can build the small, incremental advances that are needed to dispel the climate of suspicion and distrust that bedevils the relationship now.

Simultaneously, and ironically, for some observers the non-prescriptive and flexible nature of Citizens Plus is also a drawback. To some it is vague and does not provide much guidance to the parties in trying to work out a common way forward. Whether Citizens Plus' non-dogmatic nature is a benefit or a drawback is essentially the question "Is the glass half full or half empty?" For those who are interested in seeking a co-operative future together because of the benefits that each party can derive from interaction with the other, it is half full. However, for those, particularly many First Nations political leaders who have developed a forceful philosophy of Aboriginal sovereignty within the broader Canadian state, who are less interested in going forward together than in protecting their own groups from more of the interference and mistreatment that Canadian history demonstrates has been endemic to the relationship, Citizens Plus is a glass that is at best half empty.

The question Canadians face concerns the best potential approach to resolving the problems in the Native-newcomer relationship that have developed during four centuries of interaction. A reading of that history indicates that Native peoples were vibrant and successful societies at contact, that they continued to thrive while adapting as they saw fit so long as mutual advantage ensured that Native-newcomer relations were generally positive, and that the relationship fell apart and damage ensued when the non-Native majority no longer found the indigenous population to be vital to their interests. The same history also reveals that Aboriginal peoples are sufficiently resilient and adaptive, not to mention determined, in their attachment to their identities and cultures, that they have survived a protracted period when the non-Native majority tried to interfere with their ways of life and modify how they see themselves and their world. The question that arises from these experiences is how Natives and newcomers are going to relate to each other in the future. Much as the first few post-Confederation generations of Canadians had to work out what sort of Dominion of Canada they wanted, or what Canada's relationship should be to the United Kingdom and the United States, or what the role of Quebec was in Canada, so in the twenty-first century the dominant issue is the future of the Native-newcomer relationship. For reasons that should be obvious by this point, I believe that an answer to that riddle is most likely to be found in the Citizens Plus approach, an outlook that seeks to establish a shared basis in Canadian citizenship, and to supplement it with arrangements that reflect both Aboriginal peoples' special needs and their claim by prior occupancy to consideration by newcomers.

Notes

1 Canada. Parliament. *Special Joint Committee . . . [on] the Indian Act: Minutes of Proceedings and Evidence*, Session 1947, June 12, 1947, 1707 (Matthew Lazare)

2 Stewart Phillip, President of Union of British Columbia Indian Chiefs, "An Open Letter to the *National Post*," *National Post*, June 22, 2002

3 Matthew Coon Come, "Reserves kept deplorable to force assimilation," Saskatoon *The StarPhoenix*, May 23, 2003

4 H.B. Hawthorn, ed., *A Survey of the Contemporary Indians of Canada*, 2 vols. (Ottawa: Queen's Printer 1966-67), vol. 1, 13

5 The clearest expression of this approach, to which this account is greatly indebted, is Alan C. Cairns, *Citizens Plus: Aboriginal Peoples and the Canadian State* (Vancouver: University of British Columbia Press 2000). Although Cairns concentrates on the application of Hawthorn's concept to governance issues, I believe Citizens Plus has great applicability to the relationship more generally.

Acknowledgements

This volume appears thanks to the encouragement and help of many people. Jan Walter of the former Macfarlane Walter & Ross publishing firm saw the merit in a historically oriented volume on Aboriginal policy questions. One of the last things Jan did before the manuscript passed to McClelland & Stewart was secure a reading of an earlier submission by an experienced and perceptive editor, Rosemary Shipton. As usual, Rosemary had many constructive observations that have helped to shape this version of the work. Both Jan Walter's support and Rosemary Shipton's helpful suggestions have been instrumental in the production of this work. I would like to thank Jenny Bradshaw, Elizabeth Kribs, and Jonathan Webb of McClelland & Stewart for their careful and imaginative work on the manuscript.

I have also benefited from academic sources of assistance and advice. The research for the essays was supported by a Standard Research Grant of the Social Sciences and Humanities Research Council of Canada, a critically important fund for research in History and other human sciences in this country. In my own department at the University of Saskatchewan I have benefited from answers, advice, encouragement, and occasionally constructive derision from my colleagues Keith Carlson, Janice MacKinnon, and Bill Waiser. Janice and Bill both stole time from intensive work on book manuscripts of their own to read the entire first draft of this book. I appreciate all the help these three colleagues provided, collegial support that makes scholarly life in our department the pleasure that it is. Finally, I thank these valued colleagues with the customary observation that none of them bears any responsibility for the errors and other shortcomings that persist.

Finally, and most important, I am enormously grateful to my wife, Mary, who is not just a great friend and companion, but the best editor, proofreader, and critic an author ever had.

Select Bibliography

Ahenakew, Edward. *Voices of the Plains Cree*. Edited by Ruth M. Buck. Toronto: McClelland & Stewart, 1973.

Ahenakew, Freda, and H.C. Wolfart, eds. *The Counselling Speeches of Jim Kâ-Nîpitêhtêw*. Winnipeg: University of Manitoba Press, 1998.

Arnot, Hon. David M. *Statement of Treaty Issues: Treaties As A Bridge To the Future*. Saskatoon: Office of the Treaty Commissioner, 1998.

Axtell, James. *Natives and Newcomers: The Cultural Origins of North America*. New York and Oxford: Oxford University Press, 2001.

Belshaw, J.D. "Mining Technique and Social Division on Vancouver Island, 1848–1900." *British Journal of Canadian Studies* 1 (1986).

Biggar, H.P. *The Voyages of Jacques Cartier*. Ottawa: King's Printer, 1924.

Borrows, John. "Wampum at Niagara: The Royal Proclamation, Canadian Legal History, and Self-Government." In *Aboriginal and Treaty Rights in Canada: Essays on Law, Equity, and Respect for Difference*, edited by Michael Asch. Vancouver: University of British Columbia Press, 1997.

Brandão, J.A. *"Your fyre shall burn no more": Iroquois Policy Towards New France and Its Native Allies to 1701*. Lincoln and London: University of Nebraska Press, 1997.

———, and William A. Starna. "The Treaties of 1701: A Triumph of Iroquois Diplomacy." *Ethnohistory* 43, no. 2 (Spring 1996).

Braroe, Niels. *Indian and White: Self-Image and Interaction in a Canadian Plains Community*. Stanford, CA: Stanford University Press, 1975.

Cairns, Alan C. *Citizens Plus: Aboriginal Peoples and the Canadian State.*
Vancouver: University of British Columbia Press, 2000.

Canada. Indian Affairs and Northern Development. *Aboriginal Self-Government: The Government of Canada's Approach to Implementation of the Inherent Right and the Negotiation of Aboriginal Self-Government.* Ottawa: Public Works and Government Services, 1995.

———— *Outstanding Business: A Native Claims Policy.* Ottawa: Minister of Supply and Services, 1982.

———— *Statement of the Government of Canada on Indian Policy.* Ottawa: Indian Affairs, 1969.

Chute, Janet E. *The Legacy of Shingwaukonse: A Century of Native Leadership.* Toronto: University of Toronto Press, 1998.

Coates, Ken. *The Marshall Decision and Native Rights.* Montreal and Kingston: McGill-Queen's University Press, 2000.

Cole, Douglas, and Ira Chaikin, *An Iron Hand Upon the People: The Law Against the Potlatch on the Northwest Coast.* Vancouver: Douglas & McIntyre, 1990.

Cumming, Peter A., and Neil H. Mickenberg. *Native Rights in Canada.* 2nd ed. Toronto: General Publishing, 1972. 1st ed. 1970.

Daugherty, Wayne. *Maritime Indian Treaties in Historical Perspective.* Ottawa: Indian and Northern Affairs Canada, 1983.

————, and Dennis Madill. *Indian Government Under Indian Act Legislation, 1868–1951.* Ottawa: Indian and Northern Affairs Canada, 1980.

De Brou, Dave, and Bill Waiser, eds. *Documenting Canada: A History of Modern Canada in Documents.* Saskatoon: Fifth House, 1992.

Demos, John. *The Unredeemed Captive: A Family Story From Early America.* New York: Vintage Books, 1995.

Dempsey, Hugh A. *The Amazing Death of Calf Shirt and Other Blackfoot Stories.* Calgary: Fifth House, 1994.

———— "One Hundred Years of Treaty Seven." In *One Century Later: Western Canadian Reserve Indians Since Treaty 7,* edited by Ian A.L. Getty and Donald B. Smith. Vancouver: University of British Columbia Press, 1977.

Dickason, Olive P. *Canada's First Nations: A History of Founding Peoples from Earliest Times.* 3rd ed. Toronto: Oxford University Press, 2002. 1st ed. 1992.

Dunning, R.W. *Social and Economic Change among Northern Ojibwa.* Toronto: University of Toronto Press, 1959.

Dyck, Noel. *What Is the "Indian Problem"? Tutelage and Resistance in Canadian Indian Administration.* St. John's: ISER Books, 1991.

Eastman, M. *Church and State in Early Canada.* Edinburgh: University Press, 1915.

Erasmus, Peter. *Buffalo Days and Nights*. 2nd ed. Edited by Irene Spry. Calgary: Fifth House, 1999. 1st ed. 1976.

Fingard, Judith. "The New England Company and the New Brunswick Indians, 1786–1826: A Comment on the Colonial Perversion of British Benevolence." *Acadiensis* 1, no. 2 (Spring 1972).

Flanagan, Tom. *First Nations? Second Thoughts*. Montreal and Kingston: McGill-Queen's University Press, 2000.

Ford, Clelland S. *Smoke from Their Fires: The Life of a Kwakiutl Chief*. New Haven, CT: Yale University Press, 1941.

Foster, Hamar. "Honouring the Queen's Flag: A Legal and Historical Perspective on the Nisga'a Treaty," *BC Studies* no. 120, (Winter 1998-99).

Francis, Daniel, and Toby Morantz. *Partners in Furs: A History of the Fur Trade in Eastern James Bay, 1600-1870*. Kingston and Montreal: McGill-Queen's University Press, 1985.

Friesen, Gerald. *The Canadian Prairies: A History*. Toronto: University of Toronto Press, 1984.

Friesen, Jean. "Magnificent Gifts: The Treaties of Canada with the Indians of the Northwest, 1869–76." *Transactions of the Royal Society of Canada* series V, vol. I, 1986.

Fumoleau, René. *As Long as This Land Shall Last: A History of Treaty 8 and Treaty 11, 1870–1939*. Toronto: McClelland & Stewart, 1975.

Goddard, John. *The Last Stand of the Lubicon Cree*. Vancouver: Douglas & McIntyre, 1991.

Goodwill, Jean, and Norma Sluman. *John Tootoosis*. 2nd ed. Winnipeg: Pemmican Publications, 1984. 1st ed. 1982.

Graymont, Barbara. *The Iroquois in the American Revolution*. Syracuse: Syracuse University Press, 1972.

Harring, Sidney L. *White Man's Law: Native People in Nineteenth-Century Canadian Jurisprudence*. Toronto: University of Toronto Press, 1998.

Hawthorn, H.B., ed. *A Survey of the Contemporary Indians of Canada*. 2 vols. Ottawa: Queen's Printer, 1966–67.

Hodgins, Bruce, and Jamie Benedickson. *The Temagami Experience: Recreation, Resources, and Aboriginal Rights in the Northern Ontario Wilderness*. Toronto: University of Toronto Press, 1989.

Jaenen, C.J. *Friend and Foe: Aspects of French-Amerindian Cultural Contact in the Seventeenth and Eighteenth Centuries*. New York: Columbia University Press, 1976.

Jenness, Diamond. *The Indians of Canada*. 6th ed. Ottawa: National Museum of Canada 1963. (1st ed. 1932).

Jennings, Francis. *The Ambiguous Iroquois Empire: The Covenant Chain Confederation of Indian Treaties with English Colonies from Its Beginnings to the Lancaster Treaty of 1744.* New York: Norton, 1984.

———— *Empire of Fortune: Crowns, Colonies, and Tribes in the Seven Years' War.* New York: Norton, 1988.

———— *The Invasion of America: Indians, Colonialism, and the Cant of Conquest.* Chapel Hill, NC: University of North Carolina Press, 1975.

————, ed. *The History and Culture of Iroquois Diplomacy: An Interdisciplinary Guide to the Treaties of the Six Nations and Their League.* Syracuse: Syracuse University Press, 1985.

The Jesuit Relations and Allied Documents. Edited by R.G. Thwaites. 72 vols. Cleveland: Burrows Brothers, 1897.

Lafitau, Joseph-François. *Customs of the American Indians, compared with the customs of primitive times.* 2 vols. Trans. and annotated by W.N. Fenton and E.L. Moore. Toronto: Champlain Society, 1974–7. 1st French ed. Paris, 1724.

Leslie, John, and Ron Maguire, eds. *The Historical Development of the Indian Act.* 2nd ed. Ottawa: Indian Affairs and Northern Development, 1983. 1st ed. 1975.

Long, John S. " 'No Basis for Argument': The Signing of Treaty Nine in Northern Ontario, 1905–1906," *Native Studies Review* 5, no. 2 (1989).

Macleod, R.C. *The North-West Mounted Police and Law Enforcement.* Toronto: University of Toronto Press, 1976.

Miller, J.R. *Canada and the Aboriginal Peoples, 1867-1927.* Ottawa: Canadian Historical Association, 1997.

———— "Great White Father Knows Best: Oka and the Land Claims Process." *Native Studies Review* 7, no. 1 (1991).

———— *Shingwauk's Vision: A History of Native Residential Schools.* Toronto: University of Toronto Press, 1996.

———— *Skyscrapers Hide the Heavens: A History of Indian-White Relations in Canada.* 3rd ed. Toronto: University of Toronto Press, 2000. 1st ed. 1989.

————, ed. *Sweet Promises: A Reader on Indian-White Relations in Canada.* Toronto: University of Toronto Press, 1991.

Milloy, John S. *A National Crime: The Canadian Government and the Residential School System, 1879 to 1986.* Winnipeg: University of Manitoba Press, 1999.

Morris, Alexander. *The Treaties of Canada with the Indians.* New ed. Saskatoon: Fifth House, 1991 (1st ed. 1880).

Nicolai, Martin L. "A Different Kind of Courage: The French Military and the Canadian Irregular Soldier During the Seven Years' War." *Canadian Historical Review* 70, no. 1 (March 1989).

O'Callaghan, E.B., ed. *Documents Relative to the Colonial History of the State of New York*. Albany: Weed, Parsons & Co., 1855.

Ochankuhage (Dan Kennedy). *Recollections of an Assiniboine Chief*. Edited by James R. Stevens. Toronto and Montreal: McClelland & Stewart, 1972.

Opekokew, Delia, ed. *The First Nations: Indian Government and the Canadian Confederation*. Saskatoon: Federation of Saskatchewan Indian [Nations], 1980.

Peterson, Jacqueline, and Jennifer S.H. Brown, eds. *The New Peoples: Being and Becoming Métis in North America*. Winnipeg: University of Manitoba Press, 1985.

Pettipas, K. *Severing the Ties That Bind: Government Repression of Indigenous Religious Ceremonies on the Prairies*. Winnipeg: University of Manitoba Press, 1994.

Plaice, Evelyn. *The Native Game: Settler Perceptions of Indian/Settler Relations in Central Labrador*. St. John's: ISER Books, 1990.

Ponting, J.R., and R. Gibbins. *Out of Irrelevance: A Socio-political Introduction to Indian Affairs in Canada*. Toronto: Butterworths, 1980.

Price, Richard, ed. *The Spirit of the Alberta Indian Treaties*. 2nd ed. Edmonton: University of Alberta Press, 1987. 1st ed. 1979.

Ray, Arthur J. *Indians in the Fur Trade: Their Role as Hunters, Trappers and Middlemen in the Lands Southwest of Hudson Bay, 1660-1870*. Toronto: University of Toronto Press, 1974.

———, Jim Miller, and Frank Tough. *Bounty and Benevolence: A History of Saskatchewan Treaties*. Montreal and Kingston: McGill-University Press, 2000.

Rich, E.E., ed. *Copy-Book of Letters Outward &c: Begins 29th May, 1680 Ends 5 July 1687*. London: Hudson's Bay Record Society, 1948.

Royal Commission on Aboriginal Peoples [RCAP]. *Final Report*. 4 vols. Ottawa: RCAP, 1996.

——— *Partners in Confederation. Aboriginal Peoples, Self-Government, and the Constitution*. Ottawa: RCAP, 1993.

Schmidt, David L., and B.A. Balcom. "The Règlement of 1739; A Note on Micmac Law and Literacy." *Acadiensis* 23, no. 1 (Autumn 1993).

Scott, Duncan Campbell. "Indian Affairs, 1763–1841." A. Shortt and A.G. Doughty, eds. *Canada and Its Provinces*. Toronto: Glasgow, Brook and Co., 1914, vol. 4.

Shortt, A., and A.G. Doughty, eds. *Documents Relating to the Constitutional History of Canada, 1759–1791*. Ottawa. King's Printer, 1918.

Smith, Derek G., "The Emergence of 'Eskimo Status': An examination of the Eskimo Disk List System and Its Social Consequences, 1925-1970." Noel

Dyck and James B. Waldram, eds. *Anthropology: Public Policy and Native Peoples in Canada*. Montreal and Kingston: McGill-Queen's University Press, 1993.

Stone, Thomas. "Legal Mobilization and Legal Penetration: The Department of Indian Affairs and the Canadian Party at St. Regis, 1876–1918." *Ethnohistory* 22, no. 4 (Fall 1975).

Strom, Tracy. "When the Mounties Came: Mounted Police and Cree Relations on Two Saskatchewan Reserves." M.A. thesis, University of Saskatchewan, 1999.

Sugden, John. *Tecumseh: A Life*. New York: Henry Holt, 1997.

Tennant, Paul. *Aboriginal Peoples and Politics: The Indian Land Question in British Columbia, 1849-1989*. Vancouver: University of British Columbia Press, 1990.

Titley, E. Brian. *A Narrow Vision: Duncan Campbell Scott and the Administration of Indian Affairs in Canada*. Vancouver: University of British Columbia Press, 1985.

Tobias, John L. "The Treaty Rights Movement in Saskatchewan." F. Laurie Barron and James B. Waldram, eds. *1885 and After: Native Society in Transition*. Regina: Canadian Plains Research Center, 1986.

Treaty 7 Elders and Tribal Council, with Walter Hildebrandt, Dorothy First Rider, and Sarah Carter. *The True Spirit and Original Intent of Treaty 7*. Montreal and Kingston: McGill-Queen's University Press, 1996.

Walters, Mark. "'According to the Old Customs of Our Nation': Aboriginal Self-Government on the Credit River Mississauga Reserve, 1826–1847." *Ottawa Law Review* 30 (1998–99).

White, Richard. *The Middle Ground: Indians, Empires, and Republics in the Great Lakes Region, 1650-1815*. Cambridge: Cambridge University Press, 1991.

Index